T0384456

# TRICKY COACHING

# TRICKY COACHING

## Difficult Cases in Leadership Coaching

Edited by

### Konstantin Korotov
*European School of Management and Technology, Germany*

### Elizabeth Florent-Treacy
*INSEAD Global Leadership Center, France*

### Manfred F. R. Kets de Vries
*INSEAD Global Leadership Center, France*

### Andreas Bernhardt
*European School of Management and Technology, Germany*

First published 2012 by
PALGRAVE MACMILLAN

Palgrave Macmillan in the UK is an imprint of Macmillan Publishers Limited, registered in England, company number 785998, of Houndmills, Basingstoke, Hampshire RG21 6XS.

Palgrave Macmillan in the US is a division of St Martin's Press LLC, 175 Fifth Avenue, New York, NY 10010.

Palgrave Macmillan is the global academic imprint of the above companies and has companies and representatives throughout the world.

Palgrave® and Macmillan® are registered trademarks in the United States, the United Kingdom, Europe and other countries.

ISBN 978–0–230–28022–9

This book is printed on paper suitable for recycling and made from fully managed and sustained forest sources. Logging, pulping and manufacturing processes are expected to conform to the environmental regulations of the country of origin.

A catalogue record for this book is available from the British Library.

A catalog record for this book is available from the Library of Congress.

10   9   8   7   6   5   4   3   2   1
21  20  19  18  17  16  15  14  13  12

# CONTENTS

CONTENTS

CONTENTS

# PREFACE

The market is full of books, videos, weekend courses, and executive programs—all with the good intention of providing some training and guidelines for coaches. Coaching as a profession is still in its infancy, and the plethora of these offerings is the result of an acknowledged need to explore and define the boundaries of coaching. Researchers and practitioners are also working to create models and frameworks to explain why and how coaching is effective. So why did we decide to write another book on executive coaching?

Although the coaching profession is rapidly evolving in the direction of coherence, standard protocols, and rigorous evaluation, we still see a need for further examination and development. As a group of editors coming from a psychodynamic approach to executive coaching, we are particularly concerned that many executive coaches do not have the proper training, or the necessary supervision, to practice effectively. We acknowledge that there is nothing more difficult than examining one's own behavior but, at the same time, we call for greater reflection and analysis on the part of coaches. As coaches, coaching educators, and coaching researchers ourselves, we argue that the coaching profession should continue to be inspired by psychotherapy protocols of case studies and peer supervision, and we also underline the importance of learning from reflection on own coaching practice and the experience of others. In this book, we cover in great detail the why and how of continually seeking greater understanding about the interpersonal and intrapersonal dynamics that come into play in executive coaching.

When scanning the market for executive coaching offerings, we have been alarmed by the ease with which people can simply pay to post their name on a website, and instantly become an executive coach. We have met people who have made worrying transitions, for example, the tennis coach who segued effortlessly into an executive coach, or the aromatherapist who moved into life coaching and, later, excited about the much higher fees in the executive domain, decided that she was ready to make inroads into the C-suites of organizations. In some cases, a general focus of coaching models available on the market reflects the background of the coaches themselves, many of whom were successful HR directors or executives before moving into a coaching role within their organizations, or becoming external executive coaches. At the risk of appearing cynical, we could add that some of the multitude of training programs, models, survey instruments, and techniques available appear to be a kind of self-branding, as coaches develop and promote their own coaching practices around them. This dispersion of frameworks creates confusion, as coaches cluster in sub-orientations—for example, those who feel coaching should be directive, and those who are comfortable with a more client-centered approach; in our experience, we find that coaches, unsurprisingly, defend the territory they know best.

Another concern is our observation that the clients themselves have become more sophisticated and demanding. In our work with thousands of executive coachees, we have come across many who had been coached in the past. Some of them are adept at telling an inexperienced or hurried coach what the coach wants to hear. This kind of pseudo-agreement means that the coaching session ends on a happy note, but does not ensure any real change on the part of the coachee. Still others go through the motions of the coaching process without becoming truly involved, and later report coaching as a complete waste of their time.

The system of rating coaching interventions currently in place in some organizations is also problematic, since even the most experienced executive coaches may be subtly influenced by the need to hold back and not be too direct with a coachee in order to receive a "feel-good" high post-intervention evaluation. In many organizations a high numerical evaluation is a prerequisite for a coach's repeat business. Ironically, some of the most interesting coaching stories we hear involve a coachee who was initially outraged at the directness or depth of the coach's approach, only to admit much later that not only was the coach right, but also that she had earned the coachee's trust and respect. This is particularly the case in the rarified atmosphere at top leadership levels, such as senior executive teams and boards of directors. These are highly intelligent, driven people who are not accustomed to getting honest feedback, but who appreciate the people who have the courage to give it to them. Needless to say, this type of coaching intervention requires tremendous self-knowledge and emotional intelligence on the part of the coach. But how does an executive coach learn and develop the ability to create a holding environment in which clients feel safe, and able to integrate their coach's honest feedback and challenging support?

To put it bluntly, there is still no definitive agreement on what the process and outcome of coaching should be, nor is there any standard for training and evaluation. As a profession, we are still exploring what goes on "inside the black box," that is, the elements and factors we can isolate as being necessary for a successful coaching intervention as measured by coach, client, and organization. Unfortunately, we are still in an era of *caveat emptor*—buyer beware.

There are, of course, thousands of well-trained, highly effective executive coaches working today. Many are affiliated to reputable coaching organizations, and work regularly with a supervisor. However, the truth is that there is still no standardized diploma or international accreditation system that can help someone seeking a coach make a first cut. So how do we know if someone is a "good" executive coach? An individual may appear to have a great reputation for working effectively with top executives—that reputation may be deserved, but it could equally be a result of good self-marketing. There may also be an element of "new car syndrome"—that is, no one wants to admit that their expensive purchase has turned out to be a lemon. Are there other ways within the current, evolving context of the executive coaching profession to identify the most effective and responsible executive coaches? These questions and concerns became the driving motivation for writing this book.

## OPENING UP THE BLACK BOX

We, the editors of this book, are involved in two of the largest and best-known leadership development centers in the world, in terms of the numbers of executives we work with. In December 2009 we decided to bring faculty, HR professionals, and experienced executive coaches together to explore and discuss some of our concerns about coaching. To prepare for this event,[1] we asked participants to submit a short case describing one of their own coaching interventions. They were to write about a coaching situation in which they had been involved and felt it had been difficult or even, in their own mind, unresolved or a failure. All the cases were based on real-life coaching situations, although identifying information related to the clients was disguised to protect their privacy. Participants were also asked to read and comment on each others' stories. During the Colloquium, the coaches were divided into small discussion groups in which they had in-depth debriefs and discussions about their tricky coaching stories.

We soon realized that, whereas the authors of the cases submitted had expected to talk about tricky coachees, instead we were hearing about tricky coaching *relationships*. For example, although many of the coaches who attended the "Tricky Coaching" Colloquium had used contracting appropriately and, in many cases, had carefully established a relevant therapeutic alliance when beginning a coaching relationship, many of the stories we heard were related to a later confusion of contractual boundaries. Some people became deeply emotionally involved and once the contract was completed continued to coach for free; others found themselves drawn into coaching relationships that they felt were outside the scope of the original contract, but felt obliged by external pressure to continue working in this gray zone. Some coaches reported experiencing value clashes that made working with the coachee difficult, while others experienced confusion with regard to their attitude toward a client organization that was doing something wrong, while offering the coach a hefty fee.

It was during this Colloquium—a gathering, it should be emphasized, of experienced and effective executive coaches—that we were all reminded that most coaches (like most human beings) have blind spots, and that many tricky coaching situations arise not from a problem with a coachee, but from minor, and sometimes even preventable, oversights on the part of the coach. In addition, we realized that we were seeing specific themes that seemed to be underlying many of the tricky coaching stories that the coaches themselves wanted to share and work through at the conference. We were intrigued: Here was a group of highly successful, experienced coaches working with top companies and executives, and at the same time, most of us found the experience of sharing our tricky coaching stories very rewarding, even cathartic. In addition, all participants agreed that the act of writing up their case notes and sharing them with others had been very valuable, despite initial reservations about lack of time or writing skills. We realized that we had an opportunity, even a responsibility, to do some critical self-analysis and share our insights with the coaching profession. From this Colloquium, the impetus to write this book was created. We are immensely grateful to the coaches who have contributed their stories for discussion and inclusion in this book.

Our ultimate objective for this book, therefore, is to tap into our group wisdom—our collective and extensive knowledge of the coaching field, and the experience of some of the best coaches we know. Leaving aside the difficult issue of accreditation, we want to propose other ways of understanding and evaluating what an effective executive coach does. In doing so, we aim to help shape the profession in the same way that psychoanalysts and psychotherapists worked together in the early twentieth century to bring rigor and responsibility to a profession that was considered, at that time, to consist mainly of quacks and mind readers.

Toward this goal, we have come to believe that, as a profession, coaches and academics interested in leadership development must step back and examine what is still somewhat of a taboo: Our own motivations and desires for becoming coaches. We must shine light on the dark side, acknowledging that many, if not all, of us are drawn to coaching for reasons that are rational and valid, but should not be left unexplored and unmitigated. To give a specific example, we have worked as supervisors of coaches whose coaching successes—and failures—reflected their reliance on their own values, beliefs, or past experiences. Although in principle there is nothing wrong with this at all, in practice we have seen very experienced coaches derail for this very reason, and take their clients with them, with no real understanding of what happened. If the coaches had had a better understanding of their own drivers, we suggest, perhaps the outcome would have been more positive. Indeed, we should not forget that a careful disengagement from a tricky coaching situation will ultimately be more healthy than continuing an intervention that becomes increasingly murky.

## LET'S NOT REINVENT THE WHEEL: LEARNING FROM THE HELPING PROFESSIONS

When seeking greater understanding of executive coaching, we believe there are lessons to be learned from other helping professions such as medicine, psychotherapy, and teaching. The keystone of responsible practice in these professions is the use of the self as a tool. This places individual practitioners, and their continuing passion for the work, at the center. For example, recognizing the huge demands made on teachers (not to mention students), it has long been an accepted practice for teachers and professors to take long holidays and sabbatical years. Doctors and other health professionals are enjoined to "heal thyself"—not always easy to do, admittedly, but the profession has developed safeguards, including regular peer group meetings, to ensure oversight. Therapists begin their training with years of therapy themselves, and continue to work with supervisors throughout their career.

Executive and leadership development coaching is generally described as occupying a theoretical space at the intersection of counseling, consulting, and teaching. Many of the best coaches have some kind of psychodynamic training, and understand that it is recommended to use "self as a tool" whether they are aware of it or not. They are familiar with the dynamics of interpersonal relationships, teams, and large groups. On the other hand, we have observed coaches who seem to be most comfortable applying consulting-derived protocols and frameworks. These coaches are the "quick-in, quick-win, quick-out" type, focused on measurable performance outcomes for identifiable clients. The coaching profession has undeniably benefited from the practice of consulting, in that it provides models for structuring meetings, mechanisms for negotiating and setting fees, and a tradition of quantitative assessment of results. However, although we believe the consulting model has brought a great deal to the coaching profession, we also feel that some coaches tend to over-rely on frameworks designed for professional service providers for a different purpose.

Along these lines, we cannot overemphasize the fact that although business structures and requirements are the context with which a coach must be familiar, in some ways coaches are more like teachers or counselors than consultants. They are dealing with people's lives, and so they must use their sharpest tool—themselves—responsibly. Every coach's initial training, and ongoing professional development, should include self-reflection and supervision. We can state categorically, as faculty and supervisors in one of the largest coaching organizations in the world in numbers of executive coachees (INSEAD), and in a quickly growing successful executive education center using a lot of coaching (ESMT), that *neglecting to develop self-awareness on the part of the coach, and to examine the self in each coaching intervention, may lead to a tricky coaching impasse.*

That is a succinct piece of advice, but of course it is not easy to put into practice. That is why we have designed this book to be a blend of cautionary tales, shared experiences, scientific observations, and practical application. This book is, to the best of our knowledge, the first of its kind in the currently available coaching literature. We offer first-hand tricky coaching stories in a format conducive to exploration and dialogue. We include commentaries from coaches and reflective questions that will guide readers as they think about their own work. This book is also the first truly international compendium of coaching cases, with stories from Hong Kong, the United States, Germany, France, Russia, Great Britain, the Netherlands, Canada, Mexico, and other countries.

# PREFACE

We invite the reader to look into the "black box" of coaching, namely the specific processes taking place during a coaching session. The cases show that coaching is not as trivial or easy as it may seem, despite the number of people (sometimes from quite divergent professions) who have made a rapid, not to say instant, career transition to executive coach. On the contrary, as we are first to admit, it requires courage and humility to be a responsible coach. Humility pushes us to seek out our own blind spots, and courage allows us to do something about them. We hope that the group of well-respected and effective coaches who tell their tricky coaching stories in this book will be seen as role models for the type of courageous examination that is required for excellence in the coaching profession.

## NOTE

1. The European School of Management and Technology (ESMT) 1st Coaching Colloquium, "Tricky Coaching: Dealing with Difficult Cases in Leadership Coaching," held in Berlin, Germany, December 11–12, 2009.

# ACKNOWLEDGMENTS

There is one group that merits our sincere thanks: The contributors to this book. They are highly experienced professionals who know that the best way to learn is to be asked to teach, and likewise, the best way to grow is to be asked to explore areas for development. They shared their stories openly and honestly, and we think of them as role models for the executive coaching profession.

We also want to express our deep appreciation for the work done by our editor, Sally Simmons, of Cambridge Editorial. Over the years, and even more so with this book, Sally has provided the structure and support that holds our writing team together, and gets the job done. She is not only our colleague, but also our friend.

# ABOUT THE EDITORS

**KONSTANTIN KOROTOV**

Konstantin Korotov is associate professor of Organizational Behavior and Leadership and Director of the Center for Leadership Development Research at the European School of Management and Technology (ESMT) in Berlin, Germany. With over 15 years' work in the field of leadership development, Konstantin combines academic investigation with close monitoring of organizational practices, and the dynamics of the lives and careers of modern executives. His research interests include leadership development approaches and tools, individual identity changes and career transitions, and executive coaching. He is the co-editor, with Manfred F. R. Kets de Vries and Elizabeth Florent-Treacy, of *Coach and Couch: The Psychology of Making Better Leaders* (2008) and *The Coaching Kaleidoscope: Insights from the Inside* (2010) (both published by Palgrave Macmillan), *Leadership Development*, a volume in The International Library of Critical Writings in Business and Management (Edward Elgar, 2011), and *The New Russian Business Leaders* (Edward Elgar, 2005), as well as in dozens of academic and practitioner-oriented articles and book chapters. Konstantin has featured in *Forbes*, *The Wall Street Journal*, *Manager Magazin*, *Deutsche Welle*, *Vedomosti*, *Sekret Firmy*, and multiple professional HR websites.

At ESMT, Konstantin directs open enrolment executive education programs, Leading People and Teams and Lead with Psychological Intelligence, teaches in the EMBA and MBA programs, and contributes to the Developing Leaders and Young Leaders courses. His customized executive education portfolio includes programs for Deutsche Telekom, Deutsche Bank, ThyssenKrupp, Johnson&Johnson, Rosatom, E.ON, RWE, Ernst & Young, McDonald's, Lufthansa, Xerox, etc. Konstantin is the recipient of multiple awards for excellence in teaching executive audiences. The Center for Leadership Development Research at ESMT, directed by Konstantin, aims at advancing our understanding of how managers develop their leadership competencies, how organizations create leadership development cultures, and how leadership contributes to creating effective and sustainable business practices. The Center is a platform for collaboration between academic researchers, educators, HR and learning and development practitioners, and business executives interested in leadership development.

Konstantin consults companies and individual executives worldwide on issues of leadership development, leadership and career transitions, and coaching. He is a frequent speaker at top academic conferences, practitioner conventions, and in-company events in Europe, North and South America, Asia-Pacific, Russia, and CIS.

## ELIZABETH FLORENT-TREACY

Originally from California, Liz has lived and worked in France for over 20 years. As Associate Director, Research at the INSEAD Global Leadership Center (IGLC) in Fontainebleau, France, she leads a team of researchers who take a psychodynamic approach to the exploration of leadership in organizations, executive group coaching, and experiential learning in leadership development executive education programs. In addition, the IGLC research team develops 360-degree leadership survey instruments for use in executive coaching for individuals, teams, and organizations, creating innovative content and methods for IGLC leadership development modules and programs.

Liz presents IGLC research in her role as a guest lecturer in selected INSEAD executive programs, and represents the IGLC research team at top academic and practitioner conferences (including Academy of Management, International Leadership Association, European Mentoring and Coaching Conference) and in IGLC and the European School of Management and Technology (ESMT) conferences on leadership development and executive coaching, for which she has also served as a conference co-convener.

Liz also works as an executive coach in the areas of leadership development and family business, and is trained in group coaching. She has a sub-specialty in coaching academic writing projects. Liz has written 25 case studies on leadership or family business topics, six of which have won top case writing awards (European Case Clearing House and European Foundation for Management Development). She has co-authored or authored 25 articles, working papers, and book chapters. She has co-authored five books on leadership development and family business topics that have been translated into several languages, including *The Coaching Kaleidoscope* (Kets de Vries et al., Palgrave Macmillan, 2010); *Coach and Couch: The Psychology of Making Better Leaders* (Kets de Vries et al., Palgrave Macmillan, 2008); and *Family Business on the Couch* (Kets de Vries, Carlock and Florent-Treacy, Wiley, 2007). She holds degrees in Sociology (BA), Organizational Development (MA), and a Diploma in Clinical Organizational Psychology (INSEAD, magna cum laude). Her thesis identified factors that supported or hindered individual change over time in a multi-module "identity laboratory" leadership development program.

## MANFRED F. R. KETS DE VRIES

Manfred F. R. Kets de Vries brings a different view to the much-studied subjects of leadership and the dynamics of individual and organizational change. Bringing to bear his knowledge and experience of economics (Econ. Drs., University of Amsterdam), management (ITP, MBA, and DBA, Harvard Business School), and psychoanalysis (Canadian Psychoanalytic Society and the International Psychoanalytic Association), Kets de Vries scrutinizes the interface between international management, psychoanalysis, psychotherapy, and dynamic psychiatry. His specific areas of interest are leadership, career dynamics, team building, coaching, executive stress, entrepreneurship, family business, succession planning, cross-cultural management, and the dynamics of corporate transformation and change.

A clinical professor of leadership development, he holds the Raoul de Vitry d'Avaucourt Chair of Leadership Development at INSEAD, France, Singapore, and Abu Dhabi. He is the founder of INSEAD's Global Leadership Center. In addition, he is program director of INSEAD's top management program, The Challenge of Leadership: Creating Reflective Leaders, and Consulting and Coaching for Change (and has five times received INSEAD's distinguished teacher award). He is also the Distinguished Professor of Leadership Development Research at the European School of Management and Technology (ESMT) in Berlin. He has held professorships at McGill University, the Ecole des Hautes Etudes Commerciales, Montreal, and the Harvard Business School, and he has lectured at management institutions around the world.

*The Financial Times, Le Capital, Wirtschaftswoche,* and *The Economist* have rated Manfred F. R. Kets de Vries one of the world's leading leadership theoreticians. Kets de Vries is listed among the world's top 50 leading management thinkers and among the most influential contributors to human resource management. He has been the recipient of the Harry and Miriam Levinson Award from the American Psychological Association and the Freud Memorial Award from the Dutch Psychoanalytic Institute. He has also been given the Lifetime Achievement Award of the International Leadership Association, in recognition of his role as one of the world's founding professionals in the development of leadership as a field and discipline. Presently, Kets de Vries is seen as the leading figure in the clinical study of organizational leadership.

Kets de Vries is the author, co-author, or editor of more than 35 books, including *Unstable at the Top; The Neurotic Organization; Organizational Paradoxes; Leaders, Fools, and Impostors; Life and Death in the Executive Fast Lane; The Leadership Mystique; The Happiness Equation; Lessons on Leadership by Terror; The New Global Leaders; The Leader on the Couch; Coach and Couch; Family Business: Human Dilemmas in the Family Firm; Sex, Money, Happiness, and Death; Reflections on Character and Leadership; Reflections on Leadership and Career Development; Reflections on Groups and Organizations;* and *The Coaching Kaleidoscope.* Further titles are in preparation. His books and articles have been translated into 31 languages.

In addition, Kets de Vries has published over 350 scientific papers as chapters in books and as articles. He has also written approximately 100 case studies, including seven that received the Best Case of the Year award. He is a regular writer for a number of magazines. His work has been featured in such publications as *The New York Times, The Wall Street Journal, The Los Angeles Times, Fortune, BusinessWeek, The Economist, The Financial Times*, and *The International Herald Tribune*. He is a member of 17 editorial boards and has been elected a Fellow of the Academy of Management. He is a founding member of the International Society for the Psychoanalytic Study of Organizations of which he became a lifetime distinguished member.

Kets de Vries is a consultant on organizational design/transformation and strategic human resource management to leading US, Canadian, European, African, and Asian companies. He is the Chairman and principal owner of the Kets de Vries Institute (KDVI), a global leadership development consultancy firm. As an educator and consultant he has worked in more than 40 countries.

The Dutch government has made him an Officer in the Order of Oranje Nassau. He was the first fly fisherman in Outer Mongolia and is a member of New York's Explorers Club. In his spare time he can be found in the rainforests or savannas of Central Africa, the Siberian taiga, the Pamir and Altai Mountains, Arnhemland, or within the Arctic Circle.

## ANDREAS BERNHARDT

Andreas Bernhardt is program director, senior lecturer, and executive coach at the European School of Management and Technology (ESMT), founding member of ESMT's Center for Leadership Development Research, and manages ESMT's pool of executive coaches. With 20 years' practical leadership development and coaching experience, he works as a leadership coach for ESMT, the INSEAD Global Leadership Center in Fontainebleau, France, and beyond, and has designed and delivered executive programs for several international companies. He is a co-designer and convenor of ESMT's yearly Coaching Colloquium, Founding Fellow of the ICPA at McLean/Harvard Medical School, co-organizer of the International Coaching Research Forum in collaboration with the Institute of Coaching at Harvard, a contributor to the World Economic Forum's 2010 Corporate Gender Gap Report, and regularly contributes to top academic and practitioner conferences.

He teaches and coaches in the areas of leadership, organizational behavior, coaching, and change in MBA, executive MBA, open enrollment, and company-specific executive programs. His customized executive education portfolio includes programs for organizations like Allianz, Munich RE, Deutsche Bank, Hogan Lovells, SAP, Deutsche Telekom, E.ON, RWE, Hitachi, Johnson&Johnson, GlaxoSmithKline, Sanofi-Aventis, WestPharma, McDonald's, and the European Union, and participants from more than 30 countries. He regularly combines a variety of teaching, executive coaching, and experiential learning approaches in creating effective leadership development interventions and has authored or co-authored articles and book chapters on leadership development topics.

Andreas consults globally operating companies on issues of executive coaching, leadership development, and leading teams in tough times, and regularly coaches executives on leadership and career issues. Andreas studied clinical and organizational psychology, management and organizational behavior, holds a Master's degree in psychology, and is an alumnus of INSEAD's long-term executive program Consulting and Coaching for Change (CCC).

# ABOUT THE CONTRIBUTORS

## KATHARINA BALAZS

Katharina Balazs works internationally with global clients as a professor of leadership development, leadership consultant, and executive coach, focusing on the design and delivery of top executive programs. With a background in humanities and business administration, Katharina holds an MBA and an M.Sc. from INSEAD, as well as a Ph.D. from HEC Paris. Also, as a graduate from the INSEAD Coaching and Consulting for Change program, she holds the INSEAD Diploma in Clinical Organizational Psychology. Prior to becoming involved in leadership development, Katharina worked as a strategic consultant in Scandinavia and Eastern Europe, specializing in cross-cultural issues in international M&As. In her leadership development activities, Katharina worked with international corporations in various countries (Air Liquide, Arcelor, Areva, Aventis Pasteur, DSM Neoresins+, EDF-GDF, HSBC, ING IM, Kelly Services, Post Denmark, Rexam, Schneider Electric, Smurfit, Societé Générale, Total). She is author and co-author of a number of articles and books on leadership excellence (*Ils Ont Décroché les Etoiles: Quand les Grands Chefs Nous Livrent Leurs Secrets de Management*, Paris: Pearson 2009). Of Hungarian-Austrian origin, Katharina has worked and lived throughout Europe, and has been resident in France since 1993. She speaks English, French, German, Swedish, and Hungarian.

## GRAHAM BARKUS

Graham Barkus is head of organization development at Cathay Pacific Airways in Hong Kong, and also maintains his own practice helping individuals and groups in organizations develop their capacity for adaptive change, innovation, and resilience in complex environments. With an academic background in linguistics and clinical/organizational psychology, Graham is experienced in organizational change and development, human systems management, individual and group coaching, facilitation, and conflict management. He has 20 years' experience in organizational development and learning across Asia and, more recently, Europe and the United States. He is currently developing practical applications integrating social cognitive neuroscience and the clinical approach to organizational behavior, to help organizations successfully tackle adaptive challenges, build resilience, and develop sustainable people practices.

## GUDRUN BECKER

Gudrun Becker is a consultant, coach, and trainer for international organizational development and intercultural management. Her clients are executives and teams from national and international companies in private industry, ministries, and public administration, as well as non-governmental organizations. She worked for more than 20 years as an OD-advisor of complex change processes in the context of international development cooperation, staying for five years in Malawi, Burundi, and Ghana. The main focus of her work is advising public administrations, national and local authorities, and NGOs on improving their organizational and management competence. In addition, she is specialized in assisting German companies extend their business activities (e.g., IT-offshore projects, joint ventures, M&A) to India. Her consulting services comprise change management processes, intercultural team building, executive coaching, and intercultural management.

## PETER BOBACK

For the last 20 years, Peter Boback has been working in global corporations with a focus on leadership and executive development. He has held various leadership development positions in Hewlett-Packard and SAP. Peter works also as an executive coach. Of German nationality, Peter has studied, lived, and worked in Germany, France, and Switzerland. He holds a Master's degree in clinical psychology from the universities of Heidelberg and Paris VIII. Peter has followed training programs in the area of organizational development and change consulting with Trigon in Vienna and systemic consulting with ISB in Wiesloch. He received the Diploma in Clinical Organizational Psychology from the Consulting and Coaching for Change Program at INSEAD in 2006. Peter is a member of the International Society for the Psychoanalytic Study of Organizations (ISPSO). While he continues to work in leadership and organizational development in global corporations, his special interest lies in studying and analyzing the particular cultural, social, and psychological dynamics of "postmodern organizations."

## SHARON CHIRBAN

Sharon Chirban, Ph.D., is instructor in psychology at Harvard Medical School, sport psychologist in the Division of Sports Medicine at Children's Hospital,

Boston, consultant for the Boston Ballet, member of the United States Olympic registry of sport psychologists, and a coach/consultant with Amplifying Performance Consulting. As a trained clinical and sport psychologist, she brings rich expertise to performance coaching with leaders, athletes, and organizations. She has been in independent practice since 1992. She has the fortunate experience of helping promising athletes break through to the elite level in their sport, clinical patients make changes in their problem areas, and executives turn corners in their careers. She maintains a consulting practice in Boston and works with leaders and performers both in the office and on site.

## SABINE DEMBKOWSKI

Dr. Sabine Dembkowski is founder and director of The Coaching Centre in London and Cologne, www.thecoachingcentre.com. Together with her colleagues, she supports members of boards, executives, and high-potentials in *Fortune* 500, Dax 30, and leading professional service firms across Europe. Before she established The Coaching Centre, Sabine was a strategic management consultant with A. T. Kearney and Monitor Company in London. Sabine is co-author (with Fiona Eldridge) of *The Seven Steps of Effective Executive Coaching* published by Thorogood in June 2006.

## YUVAL ENGEL

Yuval Engel is a Ph.D. candidate in the Department of Management and Organization at the Faculty of Economics and Business Administration at VU University, Amsterdam. He is currently conducting research into the careers of firm founders, the implications of their pre-existing knowledge for entrepreneurial outcomes, and the processes they go through as individuals on the path to venture creation and success.

## ELISABET ENGELLAU

Elisabet Engellau is adjunct clinical professor of Management at INSEAD. As program director at the INSEAD Global Leadership Centre, she designs, teaches, and coaches in executive programs, focusing on leadership, high performance teams, and personal and professional development. She has been an affiliate professor at McGill University, Faculty of Management, a teaching fellow at Harvard University, and Concordia University, Montreal, as well as visiting faculty at the Center for Creative Leadership and Stockholm School of Economics. She has produced and directed a number of video films for management education and has been involved in developing feedback instruments for leadership development.

She is the co-author and contributing author to a number of books. As founding partner of the Kets de Vries Institute, she focuses on the dynamics of corporate transformation and change. In her work with individuals and teams in organizations around the world she combines her long-term interest in creativity with a clinical approach to human resource management. She has pursued academic studies at Uppsala University, Harvard University, McGill University, and has undertaken psychoanalytic training in Montreal and Paris.

## ANTONIO GALVAN LUNA

Antonio Galvan Luna is co-founder and senior consultant at GALIKA, a training and consulting company based in Mexico, and a lecturer and researcher at the Monterrey Institute of Technology and Higher Education (ITESM) in Mexico. Upon completion of his Master's degree in Business Economics at the University of Konstanz, in Germany, he obtained practical management experience in large and small companies, in Mexico and abroad, and later built on this to design and lead coaching, training, and consulting interventions with GALIKA (since 2005). Antonio is also the current chair of the Mid-South Region of the Association for Experiential Education, based in Boulder, Colorado, USA. His work as an experiential trainer has allowed him to observe and analyze, first hand, human behavior in companies and organizations. His current research interests include management and leadership in small and medium-sized enterprises in Mexico, cultural differences and management of SMEs, and the effectiveness of training programs.

## BÜLENT GÖGDÜN

Bülent Gögdün is program director at ESMT Customized Solutions. He is responsible for designing and delivering customized executive education programs. Bülent also directs the open enrollment program, Developing Leaders. His work experience as a management consultant and later as a project manager in the non-profit sector triggered a personal search for alternative consulting approaches that support the development of executives and organizations. Today, he strongly believes in coaching as one of the most effective leadership development tools. Since 2007, he has been working as a coach on ESMT's customized and open seminars as well as the full-time and executive MBA programs.

## AGATA HALCZEWSKA-FIGUET

Agata Halczewska-Figuet is head of learning with Crédit Agricole CIB in Paris. Before joining Crédit Agricole CIB she was executive director and executive coach at the INSEAD Global Leadership Center. She focused on leadership development and coaching in many of INSEAD's executive education programs and also coached and consulted for organizations such as HSBC, Manpower, TNK/BP, Pernod Ricard, E&Y, Microsoft, Pfizer, etc. Prior to joining INSEAD, Agata gained extensive international experience in corporations such as Apple Computer, Crown Cork, Bayer, Arcco Chemical, and the Polish Olympic Committee. Her experience is mostly related to human resources management at international level. In her corporate life she focuses on operational international HR, organizational development, change management, talent and leadership development. Agata has an extensive experience of 360-degree feedback and other leadership development instruments. Her strength is the unique combination of her solid, international business experience with a clinical perspective on leadership. She holds a postgraduate qualification in HR management (IGS, Paris) and is also a graduate from INSEAD Coaching and Consulting for Change program, receiving the INSEAD Diploma of Clinical Organizational Psychology. She also runs her own firm, specializing in executive coaching, leadership development, HR processes management, cross-cultural management, and team building.

## BEATE HELLER

Beate Heller is head of executive development at Swisscom, Bern, in Switzerland. She has more than 15 years' experience with executive education and specializes in leadership and talent development in the Swiss finance industry and in international consulting. Beate holds a Ph.D. in French and English literature from Heidelberg University, and a Diploma in Organizational Psychology from INSEAD. She writes articles on talent and leadership development (and its limits) and works as a coach and mentor for executives and high-level female professionals. Beate also works with actors and musicians in Zurich to help them develop hidden potential.

## THOMAS HELLWIG

Thomas Hellwig, adjunct professor at INSEAD, works as an independent consultant, executive coach, and a program director for INSEAD and other leading business schools. He has been associated with the INSEAD Global Leadership Center for more than five years. He is a trained physician with a doctorate in psychotherapy and an MBA from INSEAD. As a medical doctor (cardiology, cancer, pediatrics, and emergency), Thomas leverages his experience from leading high-performing medical teams in stressful situations, having worked for over a decade in some of Europe's leading hospitals. As an executive coach he has been designing and implementing group and individual coaching interventions for senior executives for more than five years. He coordinates health and wellness sections for top management in executive programs. His recent teaching and research focus on change management (team and organizational dynamics), coaching effectiveness, and health and stress management. At INSEAD he has also carried out several research projects with Manfred F. R. Kets de Vries and is a regular presenter at international leadership conferences.

## NIKKI HEYWORTH

Nikki Heyworth is head of business development for Courageous Success, a coaching and consultancy company that turns potential into performance by increasing self-knowledge and authenticity in the work place. Nikki has experience of delivering coaching in many diverse environments. In the last few years her clients have included senior executives from a wide range of companies (engineering, food manufacturing, and biotechnology), professional firms (recruitment, law, insurance), and public sector organisations (National Health Service, UK Cabinet Office). Nikki is a visiting executive coach at the European School of Management and Technology (ESMT) in Berlin where she coaches individuals and teams on bespoke corporate programs. Nikki has a focused, intuitive style of coaching and is passionate about optimizing and realizing the potential of individuals and organisations.

## AMEL KARBOUL

Amel Karboul is founder and managing partner of Change, Leadership & Partners. She is an experienced organization development consultant, executive coach, and a published author, focusing on systemic approaches to learning and change leadership at the organizational, team, and individual level. Amel's corporate and consulting experience includes being a project leader for innovation management and supplier relationships for the Mercedes-Benz brand in South Africa and Germany, and executive for knowledge transfer and leadership development at the DaimlerChrysler Corporate University in USA, Singapore, and Germany from 1996 to 2001. She later became a strategy consultant at The Boston Consulting Group in Germany and prior to assuming her current position, she was managing partner of consulting group Neuwaldegg (Vienna, Austria). She has a Master's degree in mechanical engineering and has done postgraduate studies in economics and psychology. Amel is enrolled in the DCaM (Doctorate for Coaching and Mentoring) at Oxford Brookes University in the UK. Amel conducts programs in Arabic, French, English, and German.

## SVETLANA KHAPOVA

Svetlana Khapova is associate professor of Career Studies and director of doctoral education at VU University, Amsterdam. She is also a visiting professor at the

European School of Management and Technology (ESMT) in Berlin and chair of the careers division of the Academy of Management. Her research interests center on the career behaviors of contemporary employees and their implications for organizations and society at large. Her work has been published in *Human Relations*, *Journal of Organizational Behavior*, *Journal of Occupational and Organizational Psychology*, *Journal of Vocational Behavior*, *Career Development International*, and a number of edited volumes.

## GERHARD LISKA

Gerhard Liska is senior consultant affiliated to USP-D, a consulting company based in Vienna and Düsseldorf. He received his M.Sc. in Human Ecology from the University of Vienna where he is academic supervisor and coach for the Austrian Association for Supervision and Coaching (ÖVS). He has extensive experience in designing and implementing processes and programs related to organizational development and human resources (diagnosis, executive programs, group coaching) in national and multinational contexts. He is particularly interested in all aspects related to leadership and has authored and co-authored several articles in this field. He is a member of the board of ÖVS.

## SILKE MATTHIES

Silke Matthies works as an executive coach and management consultant. Her international clients come from the services, utility, and pharmaceutical industries. In coaching, she facilitates individual change processes with managers who face challenges in communication, conflict resolution, and performance management matters. As a management consultant, Silke participates in international development centers for executives. Before starting her own business in 2006, she gained more than 10 years' professional experience in change management consulting, human resources management, and executive development at Accenture, GlaxoSmithKline, and several other smaller companies. Of German origin, Silke has studied, lived, and worked in Germany, the United States, Canada, Russia, and Hungary. Silke holds a Master's degree in business administration (Diplom-Kauffrau) and a degree in systemic business coaching.

## KATE McCOURT

Kate McCourt is Learning and Development advisor at Bombardier Transportation GmbH, responsible for creating and ensuring the causal link between learning interventions and the resolution of real business issues. Previously, she was Senior Program Manager at the European School of Management and

Technology (ESMT) in Berlin, specialized in the management and delivery of leadership development programs for international senior executives, director of the ESMT program series "Doing Business in Germany," and responsible for the ESMT Annual Forum. In conjunction with her work with the ESMT Center for Leadership Development Research, she was also co-designer and convener of ESMT's annual Coaching Colloquium. Prior to joining ESMT in Berlin, Kate was a trainer, language consultant, and moderator, focused on cross-cultural communication and conflict management strategies for numerous companies and institutions in southwest Germany.

## MURRAY PALEVSKY

Murray Palevsky is a coach at the INSEAD Global Leadership Center (IGLC) and has 25 years of first-hand business experience as a senior executive, entrepreneur, CEO, and founder of a major construction business in Canada. Murray is a graduate of Brandeis University and holds an MBA in Organizational Behavior and Finance from McGill University. He has received psychoanalytic training in Montreal and is a graduate (magna cum laude) of the INSEAD Coaching and Consulting for Change program. Murray has developed a unique, music-focused intervention technique, now being used with clients and in the coaching community at INSEAD, which has been described as an innovative approach to executive and leadership coaching. It is highly recommended as a creative way of dealing with complex developmental challenges and for unleashing the untapped leadership potential of individuals and teams. Murray coaches in North America and Europe. His clients include the Bank of Montreal, Pfizer, University of Texas, The Lahey Clinic, and British American Tobacco. He is a member of the International Coach Federation (ICF). Murray communicates fluently in five languages and has a keen interest in music and art. He is an avid outdoorsman and salmon fisherman. He is married with three teenage children.

## ROLF PFEIFFER

Rolf Pfeiffer is co-founder and managing director of Leadership Choices, a professional services firm devoted to leadership development. He has worked as an executive coach and facilitator since 2003 and has been associated with ESMT as a coach since 2004. In his coaching work (across Europe, the USA, the Middle East, and Africa), he draws upon his consulting and business leadership experience and helps his clients increase their effectiveness in their respective business environments. He is particularly interested in working with executive teams and enjoys helping them make most productive use of their team dynamics. Rolf has significant experience in restructuring and post-merger situations, and his work has taken him to the pharmaceutical/biotech, professional services, telecommunications, financial services, electronics, power, and natural resources industries, working with blue-chip firms and their senior leaders. Rolf is certified to use a wide range of psychometric instruments, is an active member of the International Coach Federation (ICF), and holds the Federation's ACC credential. He is an associate of the Center for Creative Leadership and regularly works in their programs as coach and faculty. Rolf holds dual Masters' degrees in business administration from Technical University Berlin and Ecole Supérieure de Commerce Toulouse (with a major in organizational psychology).

## MARCIA REYNOLDS

Dr. Marcia Reynolds is recognized for her work in defining the challenges and needs of smart, strong, goal-driven women in today's workplace. She speaks globally and coaches top-talent women in making decisions, building strategic relationships, and showing up with strength, grace, and impact. In addition to her book, *Wander Woman: How High-Achieving Women Find Contentment and Direction*, she authored *Outsmart Your Brain* and has been quoted in many publications including *Harvard Management Update, Bilanz, Training Magazine, Forbes. com, CNN.com*, and has appeared on *ABC World News*. Prior to starting her business, Marcia's greatest success story came as a result of designing the employee and organizational development programs for a multi-national semiconductor company facing bankruptcy. Working with the executive staff, the company became the number one stock market success in the United States when it went public in 1993. Marcia was the fifth president of the International Coach Federation (ICF) and was one of the first 25 people in the world to earn the designation of Master Certified Coach. Her doctoral degree is in organizational psychology and she holds two Masters' degrees, one in adult learning and the other in communications.

## SANDY STADELMANN

Sandy Stadelmann is founder and managing partner of the consulting firm Customer Centric Management and its specialized unit Women Business Coaching. A management consultant and executive coach business, her mission is growing identity, growing business. As a coach, she works with senior executives, self-employed professionals, and groups. Her focal areas are strengthening leadership competencies, identity-based leadership development, and attaining goals. She is also keenly interested in fostering multicultural organizations. Topics include balanced businesses, intercultural awareness, and coaching female executives. Before founding her own business in 1999, Sandy was senior consultant at Kienbaum Management Consultants and financial analyst at General Electric Information Services, consulting for major organizations in Europe, the United States, and the Middle East. She studied business administration, marketing, and computer science, and holds a degree in business administration, and is a certified Systemic Business Coach (DVCT) and LIFO trainer. Sandy grew up in the United States, Germany, and Portugal and now lives in Cologne, Germany with her daughter and husband.

## ANNA URNOVA

Anna Urnova is an experienced HR executive with over 15 years' corporate experience in leading multinational companies in Russia and the United Kingdom. In addition to her corporate role, Anna is a practicing executive coach and a known expert on managing organizational and individual change. Anna has an M.Sc. in personnel management from the London School of Economics and Political Sciences (UK) and a Diploma in Clinical Organizational Psychology from INSEAD. Since 2009, Anna has worked as an associate coach at the Center for Creative Leadership (CCL) in Russia.

## ERIK van de LOO

Erik van de Loo is professor of leadership and behavior at Free University of Amsterdam. He is also visiting clinical professor of leadership at INSEAD, where he is program co-director of the Consulting and Coaching for Change (CCC) program. Erik is a partner of Phyleon, Center for Leadership and Change in The Hague, The Netherlands. He is specialized in interrelated change processes at individual, group, and organizational levels. Erik is a licensed clinical psychologist and psychoanalyst. He obtained his Ph.D. in social sciences at Leiden University and holds a Master's in work and organizational health (SIOO). Erik is involved in research applying the clinical approach to leading organizational change, leadership development, creating reflective and transitional spaces, and board dynamics.

## ANNETTE VOSS

Annette Voss is a certified business coach who designs and runs executive programs relating to leadership and coaching at the European School of Management and Technology (ESMT) and lectures on leadership at two universities of applied sciences in Germany. Working within a network of independent trainers and consultants, she accompanies clients during team-building and change processes. Annette received her diploma in business administration at University of Bayreuth. She took part in a management trainee program at a leading commercial bank and joined the HR staff with responsibility for HR marketing.

She has almost 20 years of practical experience in leadership development, working with numerous international companies and executives at a business school near Cologne. In addition to this, Annette gets ongoing business experience through her involvement in a medium-sized family business. Before qualifying as a coach, she completed a qualification for systemic process managers. Annette has done original research on attitude measurement and trends in management development, edited the German *Handbook for Management Development*, and published several articles on executive education, evaluation, accounting, coaching, and project management.

# INTRODUCTION

The following true story is about one of Manfred F. R. Kets de Vries's first coaching assignments. We begin with this story because it captures many of the themes and challenges we will address in this book.

It was approaching 7:30 on a cold November evening in 1977 and I was preparing to leave the office to drive home when the phone rang. I hesitated—it had been a long day and I was keen to get out—but curiosity got the better of me. Who could be phoning me at this time in the evening?

The caller was obviously accustomed to working late. His manner was very matter-of-fact and it was clear that he fully expected to find me still at my desk in my office. But as he spoke I thought I could detect a note of anxiety in his voice. This wasn't a routine call. He introduced himself as Tony Finch, managing director of a commercial laboratory that specialized in testing the safety of products for cosmetics firms. The name rang no bells until he reminded me that he'd attended one of my seminars on stress management some months previously.

This all happened many years ago, when I was a young assistant professor in organizational behavior and strategy at McGill University in Canada. Most of my work at this time was focused on stress research and the seminar that Finch had attended was one of my early forays into the commercial world of leadership development. Feedback from the seminar had been good; the senior executives who had attended generally felt they'd acquired useful knowledge from the activity. But Finch was the first to follow up with a request for further professional help.

His problem concerned a key member of staff who appeared stressed and unmotivated; without some professional help there seemed to be a real danger (at least according to Finch) that he would burn out. This wasn't the first consulting assignment I'd accepted—I'd been consulting for a major apparel firm for a few years—but this was different: It was the first that involved crisis management for a specific individual. I was intrigued. The lab was just 20 minutes from the university campus and easy for me to get to. We agreed that I should provide a one-day intervention later that week.

Two days later I arrived at the lab to be greeted by Tony Finch, who briefed me one-on-one in his office. He told me that his lab took care of product testing of beauty care products. For that purpose, they kept a menagerie of laboratory animals. My coachee, explained Finch, was the lab's veterinarian, a young man named Marc whose job involved caring for these animals and ensuring that they were fit for testing. The problem seemed to be that his work was becoming increasingly slapdash; while the animals were all well-fed and looked after, the essential paperwork that accompanied each individual animal was disorganized and inaccurate, and had, on one occasion, rendered an entire experiment null and void.

At the same time, Marc's behavior was increasingly erratic. Some tasks were completed hastily while others took far longer than necessary. And it had been noticed that Marc would often spend a great deal of time and effort completing relatively minor tasks while neglecting more important activities that demanded greater care and attention. Finch had called Marc into his office the previous week for an informal chat. The two had spoken amiably and Marc had acknowledged the recent decline in his performance at work. Though it wasn't yet a disciplinary issue, Finch had made it clear that things had to improve substantially. Marc had promised to make more of an effort and had readily agreed to Finch's suggestion that they bring in an independent consultant to help him identify the cause of his underperformance and tackle the underlying issues.

Following my initial briefing, I was introduced to Marc. I immediately asked him if he was willing to take me on a tour of the lab. He readily agreed. It was a large facility that actually comprised several laboratories as well as extensive office space. There was an air of calm, well-organized activity throughout the facility and each staff member I met spoke with warmth and enthusiasm about the work they did. Even Marc seemed outwardly to share this *esprit de corps*; had I not been told otherwise I would never have suspected that this engaging young man was struggling to keep his head above water.

Marc had qualified only two years previously as a veterinarian and, on graduation, had been snapped up by the commercial lab, which at that time was on a drive to recruit vets and other specialist research staff. Although the only qualified vet at this large laboratory, Marc managed a small team of three technicians who helped with the day-to-day care of the animals. My first impression was of a man without a care in the world and although I knew that Marc had agreed to work with me I was frankly surprised not to find a hint of suspicion or resentment at my intervention. Indeed, Marc seemed to welcome my presence there and responded well to my questioning.

After the tour was finished, I started by asking about Marc himself, his family background, his education, and how he had come to be in his current job. Further questioning revealed the strain he was experiencing and his fundamental unhappiness with his role in the company. From what I understood, Marc had been around animals all his life; he grew up on a dairy farm in the province of Alberta, and for as long as he could remember had harbored an ambition to qualify as a vet. When at last he achieved this goal, he chose not to follow the usual route of joining an established practice—a career spent neutering pets, inoculating livestock, and testing cattle for tuberculosis didn't appeal. He wanted something a bit more varied; he enjoyed research and he had a vague desire to work in an environment that would use his veterinarian skills to extend the scope of human knowledge.

As a graduate fresh from vet school, Marc was curious about working in a research laboratory. When he responded to the advertisement published by his eventual employer, the company embraced him with open arms. It offered an exciting and dynamic working environment. It was different than the other career opportunities on offer. And it paid extremely well. Now a note of cynicism entered Marc's voice—he had, he said, allowed himself to be "seduced."

During our tour of the facility I had noticed animals in nearly every laboratory. Perspex tanks of rats and mice ranged along the lab walls just as they do in any pet shop. In one lab, half a dozen beagles dozed in wire cages as their human colleagues worked quietly at their computers and microscopes. These dogs could have been pets but for the patches of pink shaven skin on their heads and backs and the plastic tags in their ears. They all seemed healthy enough to me. Only the capuchin monkeys—again, sporting ear tags and clean-shaven patches on their scalps and flanks—bothered me slightly. All too human in their expressions and gestures, they seemed bored and anxious, displaying the obsessive, repetitive behavior of creatures experiencing mental stress.

Animal testing has always been a highly sensitive and emotional issue and I suspected from the outset that animal welfare was at the heart of Marc's problems. But Marc knew that his employer used animals when he took the job—so what had changed in the two years since he started work at the laboratory? Marc then told me something that Finch had omitted to mention: After the experiments had been completed, each animal was destroyed. Marc explained that no animal, post-testing, could be used for further tests as the results might be compromised. And none could be adopted as pets as they were not socialized or domesticated in any real sense. In any case, there would simply not be enough homes available for them.

It was therefore Marc's job to oversee the destruction of these animals on an almost daily basis. It was now clear to me that here was a young man who loved animals, reluctantly playing the role of an evil destruction force. I caught myself realizing that images of Dr Josef Mengele—the "Angel of Death"—at Auschwitz were crossing my mind. The stress and anxiety of the burden felt by Marc was clearly having an effect on his life both at work and at home. He had trouble sleeping, he experienced stomach cramps and headaches, and he had become forgetful. At work he sought out displacement activities (hence the time wasted on menial tasks) and procrastinated when it came to tackling the important jobs. The more Marc described his working environment, the more it seemed to me that he was engaging in some kind of unconscious sabotage of his own department. This wasn't just a minor lapse of concentration; it was an unfolding disaster.

But Marc couldn't just walk away. First of all he needed the salary and did not want to resign his post. There was also something deeper than just the financial bond that prevented him from walking out. When he took the job, he knew what it would involve. Although he felt he'd been sucked in by the promises of a fat salary and rapid career progression, Marc could not lay the blame entirely at his employer's feet. He had actively sought a job in commercial R&D and had avidly accepted the generous package offered by the company. Now he felt that it would be ungrateful and disloyal to let his employer down by walking out of the company just because he felt he couldn't stomach the work. Rather surprisingly, Marc assured me that despite his personal distaste for the duties he had to perform, he still accepted the need for animal testing and supported the work of his employer. The problem—the fault, as he put it—was all his and that is why he had agreed to my intervention. He wanted to conquer his feelings of disgust and continue in his job.

Hearing this filled me with dismay. Everything Marc had said made me want to tell him to get the hell out of there. He was in the wrong job—it was as simple as that. Now I was unexpectedly facing an ethical dilemma of my own. Finch, who was paying my fee, had employed me to help Marc get back on track and continue in his job. Marc, too, had told me unequivocally that he wanted to stay on at the company. But professionally I knew that this was all wrong. Maybe some people are capable of rationalizing such a situation and telling themselves that at least they could provide the most humane treatment for these animals and make the best of a bad job; but not someone with Marc's personality makeup. He was quite obviously misplaced and had started to deal with the problem by artificially compartmentalizing his life and trying to live a divided existence. The stress would inevitably take a huge toll on him.

As far as Finch was concerned, my job was to help Marc defeat his demons and once again become a productive member of the team. I could have done what he asked (Marc was a willing coachee), taken my fee, and walked away from the situation knowing that I had fulfilled my duty. But any benefit would have been short-lived. Marc could never bury the distress that he felt at having to routinely kill animals whose care and welfare had been entrusted to him. The problem would only fester and worsen with time.

So, for the first time in my professional life I resolved to tell my coachee that I could not do what he had asked of me. But first I had to encourage Marc to face up to the reality of his situation. This was more painful than I had expected because it required Marc to acknowledge that he did not have what it took to do this kind of job. His immediate reaction was to reject my suggestion that he resign his post and start his career afresh; he argued that his inability to deal with an ethical conundrum was the real problem and that he had to fix it here and now, not run away and take his problem with him. I found myself in the very uncomfortable position of having to persuade Marc to do something neither he nor his employer wanted.

This was a very tricky coaching case indeed. Who was the client? Finch or Marc? Had the contract changed at some point, from solving Finch's problem, to saving Marc? And what about the courage to have difficult conversations like the coach had with Marc? It can't have been easy to put this new set of cards on the table, and ask Marc to consider them seriously. The story continues:

Nevertheless, my belief that Marc knew deep down that he was not capable of continuing in his current job was ultimately proved right. At the end of a long conversation in which I presented my recommendation, he admitted that he knew as well as anybody that there are many career opportunities for a trained veterinarian that do not involve experimentation or wholesale slaughter, as he put it. Once he had accepted that resigning his post was neither an act of betrayal nor an admission of failure, Marc's relief was palpable.

I then steeled myself for my final interview with Finch. As I had expected, he did not receive my news with much enthusiasm. In fact he was aghast. I knew I had to provide very good reasons for having engineered such an unexpected and unwelcome outcome and accordingly I presented my observations in detail and ensured that I could justify every conclusion I had drawn. Finch expressed irritation that Marc had accepted a job he couldn't do, but his annoyance was tempered by my evidence of Marc's deep sense of commitment and loyalty. However, in the end it came down to a simple proposition: I explained to Finch that if Marc were to stay on he would cost the company a lot of money. His problems would resurface and he would never be a reliable employee; he would make expensive mistakes. And, under increasing stress, Marc's mental state would deteriorate, raising the specter of extended sick leave and possibly even claims for compensation for illness due to workplace stress. It was better for both parties to go their separate ways.

By the time I had finished my assignment, Marc was facing the prospect of a period of unemployment and Finch had the urgent task of recruiting a new company vet. On the face of it, that looked a lot like a massive failure on my part. But I knew I had found the right solution and, more importantly, so did both Marc, my coaching client, and Finch, the client who was paying my bill.

You may or may not agree with the coach's evaluation of this intervention. But this story is important because it leads us into the key theme that runs through this book: *Demystifying coaching*. In tricky coaching stories, there are many layers. In general, coaches are becoming more adept at exploring surface layers, asking themselves questions like: Who is the client? Where does my responsibility or mandate begin and end?

However, there are always undercurrents that influence our own actions and those of the client, and these tend to be hidden or obscure. Take as an example the story of Marc: We might wonder, on a deeper level, what unconscious response this case evoked on the part of the coach. In the story, he tells how he related Marc's role to that of Josef Mengele in the Nazi extermination camp at Auschwitz. As a small child in the Netherlands during World War II, the coach had watched as his young mother deflected the attention of the Gestapo who suspected she was harboring *onderduikers*, people sought by the Germans and hiding to avoid deportation. She was—and she and her parents were later named Righteous Gentiles by the state of Israel. To what extent did these experiences, and their thankfully positive outcome, influence this coaching assignment 40 years later? Was the coach even aware of this as he was helping Marc to, in effect, escape?

Contrast this with another story with a different outcome (this story, like all others in this book, is true but disguised). Although the behavior patterns are similar, a lack of self-awareness caused both the coach, David, and the coachee, June, to derail. This is the coach's story, as we heard it:

> I was originally asked to coach a woman who was on the executive board of a large US company. She was one of several executives who were being considered for CEO, and each of these people had been given the opportunity to work with a leadership development coach. The objective was to prepare the coachees for leadership succession, and then either follow the person into the CEO role as they adjusted to it or, if the candidate was not selected for the top spot, to work with them to find a different career outcome. It was a high stakes coaching job, because it was essentially an "up or out" assignment.

> My coachee, June, was extremely ambitious. She had spent her entire career— boosted by a great education at Stanford, then Wharton—with an intense focus on making it to the top of her industry. She made it clear in our first meeting that she was not going to consider, or discuss with me, any possibility other than being named as CEO. She assured me ("I'm going to let you in on some insider knowledge") that she had already been selected, and the other candidates had better focus on their "out" strategy in their coaching sessions.

> A month later, when it was announced that June had been passed over, her reaction was intense, vindictive rage. We still had several months of coaching together, as agreed by our initial contract, but her post-announcement sessions were all about how stupid and blind her colleagues were.

> June asked to be transferred to another division more closely related to her original specialty in finance. Once there, she soon—perhaps intentionally— generated a mutual sense of distrust with her new colleagues and subordinates. Within weeks, she was fired. The organization agreed to allow her to finish her five remaining coaching sessions with me on an external basis.

6

June was quite upbeat at first, asking my feedback on her plan to start her own company. She said she felt quite free for the first time in years, and did seem calmer and more optimistic than I had ever seen her. A few weeks later, however, she came to see me in a—by now familiar—rage. She had not been able to raise financing, and she blamed her former employer. Once again, she was vindictive. She even made some threats about what she would do if she ever ran into any of her former colleagues.

During our final contracted session I could see that June had clearly begun to suffer from the situation. Normally someone who had always been very well dressed, she now looked terrible. During our conversation she admitted that not only had she run through her severance package, but she was also facing bankruptcy. To my astonishment, she switched abruptly from outrage to despair, breaking down in sobs. She begged me to continue our sessions for a while, as I was providing the only spot of hope in her life. Feeling responsible and not wanting to abandon a coachee in such a state, I agreed.

We continued to meet weekly in a coffee shop downtown. June was no longer talking about starting her own company, but seemed to find a perverse pleasure in telling me about all the men she was sleeping with. She would initiate relationships, and dump them soon after. She seemed to get pleasure out of being a heartbreaker. Once, hesitantly, I commented that it seemed like she was taking revenge on all the men who had disappointed her, including the ones at work. But she would have none of it. She laughed cynically, saying she was thoroughly enjoying her midlife crisis. She apologized at the same time, saying that I was the only man in her life who truly respected and cared for her. I would try to steer the conversation toward her professional prospects but, true to character, June could not be distracted from the objective that was fixed in her mind. Only now, the objective seemed to be self-destruction. I strongly felt that I would have to get her back on some sort of stable ground before terminating our relationship, even though she was no longer making any semblance of paying my fees.

About a month later, at two o'clock in the morning, I was woken by a call from a nearly incoherent June. She had been arrested for selling a small amount of cocaine. From the little I could gather, her story was that she was "just along for the ride with a guy I met. I didn't know what he was up to." I picked her up at the police station and took her to her apartment. When I got home, I had a bad row with my wife. She asked me whether I was performing the "normal services" for a client. I must be crazy. What was going on with me? Lying in bed, unable to sleep, I realized that things had gotten far, far out of hand. Not only would this have to be a wake-up call for June, but it had been a figurative, as well as literal, wake-up call for me as well.

Telling this story later to his supervisor—with whom he had neglected to discuss the case earlier—David started by admitting that he had known for quite a while that this coaching relationship was derailing both parties, but for some reason, which he now hoped to understand, he had been unwilling to terminate the relationship. As an experienced coach, it didn't take long for David to admit that there was a pattern of behavior here that may have had its source in David's own life, making June an unwitting bit player in David's drama.

It now seemed obvious: David had been arrested himself as a university student for playing a small part in selling marijuana on campus. Far from home, he managed to talk his way out of the problem mainly because he was still underage, and dealing with campus police who preferred not to involve parents. Years later, David saw that time as a low point in his life, when he suffered from feeling rudderless and forgotten. He still believed 20 years later that his parents had let him down—they could have helped him out but they were always too self-involved to care about him. They were never there when he needed them.

Telling this story for the first time, David didn't even need his supervisor to point out the parallels to June's case. His supervisor did add, gently, that although David's desire to help June, and even vicariously repair some of his own hurts, was rational and acceptable, David's failure lay in not giving June the right kind of help. David was not a trained psychotherapist, and he should have referred June to someone much earlier on. For David, this discussion "woke me up to what was right."

He met with June twice more, once to explain that their relationship would be ending and to refer her to a psychotherapist, and a last time to reinforce the message that June must now focus on what she was going to do next with her life. When he had completed this final, careful termination meeting, David felt tremendously relieved.

## DEMYSTIFYING COACHING

Coaching, as illustrated by these stories, is complicated. At times, all coaches will get stuck, and the way to deal with getting stuck is to ask for help from others and get a fresh look at the situation. Failure is relative. In some cases, the only real failure is when the coach does not return to the case with a supervisor or colleague to do a coaching debrief, seeking to understand his or her motivations, drivers, and fears, and how these may have influenced the outcome of the assignment. In other cases, what initially appears to be a failure may later turn out to be a great success. We will return to stories like these throughout this book, and with the help of the coaches involved, will tease apart the patterns, themes, challenges, and stumbling blocks that shaped an intervention for better or worse. We want to take a hard look at the mystique of coaching, and reframe it, like other helping professions, as an art more than a science that requires constant self-reflection and reality testing with peers or supervisors.

In the Preface to this book, we made a strong statement: Many tricky coaching scenarios, upon greater analysis, reflect not tricky *coachees*, but tricky coaching *relationships*. We will examine tricky coaching stories in greater depth later in this book, but first, in Part One, we present an overview of the coaching field in the first chapter, followed by insights from the profession of psychotherapy in the following chapter. Our intention is to lay out the issues and challenges coaches face—sometimes as a result of their own behavior and beliefs—before looking closely in Part Two at case studies reflecting the patterns and themes that, in our experience, recur in coaching interventions that are labeled "tricky" by coaches themselves.

In keeping with our leitmotif that coaches must develop a habit of reflection and supervision, we'll begin by examining why people choose to become coaches. There are multiple reasons, and most of them are perfectly valid. However, just as an over-developed strength can become a weakness, coaches who have not explored their own motivation for entering the profession have an inherent blind spot. Nevertheless, by recognizing their own key motivators (e.g., a desire to help people, a need for a balanced lifestyle, a wish to earn a significant income), and potential derailing factors (e.g., too strict adherence to personal values, "blind spots" in one's own behavior, a strange attraction to dangerous relationships, a reluctance to seek supervision from others), coaches are much better equipped to avoid, or deal with, tricky or even dangerous coaching situations.

# PART ONE:  CONTEMPORARY COACHING ISSUES

# 1

# EXECUTIVE COACHES: WHO ARE WE, AND WHY?

There are two particularly interesting features of a career as an executive coach. First, entrance to this professional field is not possible without a substantial amount of previous work and life experience, and second, it is (consequently) a very attractive career transition option for individuals at a midlife and mid-career point. In this chapter, we explore why midlife readjustments and a transition to executive coaching often seem to coincide. We touch on how investments in what have been called the "three ways of knowing" (*knowing-how*, *knowing-why*, and *knowing-whom*) influence career transitions,[1] and what kind of career divestments are required as a person transitions to executive coaching.[2] We describe the process of career transition, highlighting the *intelligent career*, *career entrepreneurship*, and *boundaryless career* frameworks.[3] We look at what kinds of environment (in particular, *identity laboratories*) help mid-career adults to experiment during the transition process. Finally, we also explore some of the underlying reasons why people decide to become coaches.

## TRANSITION TO AN EXECUTIVE COACHING CAREER

Whereas coaching in general may be described as a particular management style, or as a learning and development intervention whereby a manager gets feedback or support from a boss, colleague, HR practitioner, or an external party, *executive coaching* has its own particular definition. Executive coaching is a professional service in which a professional or consultant helps executives to clarify and distil their goals, find ways of meeting them, and overcome obstacles to their realization.[4]

Although for millennia humans have sought advice about their lives from individuals in defined societal roles (shamans, counselors, religious figures, sages), and more recently from medical and paramedical professionals such as psychiatrists, psychoanalysts, and psychotherapists, the world is now moving at such a rapid pace—when we can get all we want (or think we want) at the touch of a mouse—that people no longer recognize the simple need to stop and think, let alone take the time to seek advice. The increased demand for executive coaching, however, undoubtedly reflects a basic human desire for communication and reflection— a need that can now be conveniently met by executive coaching within an already familiar framework similar to that of consulting. Not surprisingly, even though executive coaching is still being formed and shaped as a profession, it has already become a noticeable phenomenon both in terms of visibility and financial turnover.[5]

A second explanation for the rapid expansion of executive coaching is that the job fills a growing demand on the supply side—that is, it is increasingly seen as an attractive career option. It is one of the relatively few professions uniquely adapted to career executives in mid- to late-career phases. Executive coaching is a professional activity that is normally undertaken after the person pursuing it has already experimented with or achieved success in some other profession (e.g., business and management, education, psychology, art, sports, etc.). It allows mid-career professionals to repackage their business knowledge and well-developed competencies, and use them in a new, creative way.

Although there are still virtually no research studies on the career choices and trajectories of executive coaches,[6] it is quite clear that successfully entering the professional field of executive coaching requires a fair amount of accumulated personal life experiences, and it is also clear that executive coaching may well be an attractive career move for executives who are looking for a challenge at midlife that puts a wide range of business context experiences to good use. Practitioner-oriented literature about executive coaching supports the premise that an executive coach "should have enough organizational experience in general to appreciate the realities the client is living with, and be able to bring good 'political' insights to the relationship."[7] At the same time, an executive coach needs a keen self-awareness, and an understanding of the way individuals and groups interact. They also need to know something about personality functioning. Given these basic fundamentals, it is perhaps not surprising that the average age of executive coaches is around 50, and the profession attracts men and women in roughly equally numbers (one of the *only* professions in which this kind of gender balance is to be found).

This chapter summarizes findings from a number of research efforts related to a better understanding of the phenomenon of executive coaching and the careers of executive coaches. As faculty directors for a number of open-enrollment and customer-specific executive education programs, we regularly interview and observe executive coaches, asking questions about why and how they transitioned into the coaching profession. Another ongoing research project looks at coaching as a primary or supplementary professional activity. Our aim in these exploratory research projects is to generate a better understanding of executive coaching as a professional career from the perspectives of the coach and the organization, and to study career actors (a term describing people who take charge of their own careers) who have made a decision— for reasons we are seeking to identify—to move to a new career identity as "executive coach."

## MAKING THE TRANSITION: THE BEST OF TIMES AND THE WORST OF TIMES

It would not be exaggerating to say that continual changes in the sociopolitical environment have resulted in significantly less predictable career trajectories.[8] The era of long-term employment and steady career advancement up a predetermined ladder are long gone. The psychological contract is broken. The traditional "deal" whereby employers could expect long-term loyalty from their employees in exchange for a long-term career no longer exists. Several recent streams of research have looked at the way career actors are making choices, particularly at midlife, and insights from these studies are changing the traditional understanding of career progression as a linear movement toward an apex of achievement at career's end.

Midlife, a key moment in the career cycle, merits special attention.[9] This is a period when people may feel a need to take the time to step back and reframe their lives, and consider where heretofore unexplored desires or professional "experiments" have been leading. This reevaluation is often filled with difficult moments. In career terms, a harsh light is shed on one's work-related progression—and often one finds the result lackluster or insufficient when compared to early dreams or aspirations. On the other hand, this realization often helps people to see more clearly that whereas in their current role they may be stuck, it is still within the realm of possibility to consider career moves that might bring a phase of renewed energy—a possibility that is no longer excluded by a need to follow a rigidly predetermined career path throughout life.

Granted, the very fact that midlife transition and career-related challenges are hot research topics could be seen as a result of the lingering phenomenon of a traditional achievement-oriented society. Our parents' careers are still in some ways a benchmark for us, and it is hard to let go of that idea. Nevertheless, career researchers agree that midlife increasingly coincides with fundamental work-related changes, and therefore mid-career achievement levels or mastery should not necessarily be considered a high-water mark.[10] On the contrary, the key to career success in later life is the ability—at midlife—to constantly experiment, expand one's identity, and develop adaptability through learning.[11]

One stream of recent research explores the concept of so-called illegitimate career moves that people make in order to succeed in the contemporary world of work.[12] Such career behavior is defined as *career entrepreneurship*—bypassing or breaking a legitimate (i.e., socially recognized) sequence of work-related experiences in terms of age, level of education, gender, life stage, cultural or socioeconomic background, job entry, stage of career progression, level of responsibility, etc. The *intelligent career* framework suggests that there is an element of entrepreneurship involved in transitioning to a career outside of the standard path laid out by early professional experiences. This framework suggests that an individual considering an unusual career move will often start by investing in one of three "ways of knowing": *Knowing-why* (e.g., what motivates me to make this career choice?), *knowing-how* (what kind of skills and competencies do I need to develop to succeed?), and *knowing-whom* (whom do I need to meet, establish relationships with, or convince to accept me in the new role?).[13]

For example, people connected to the world of executive coaching as buyers of coaching services (e.g., an HR director) or as coachees (e.g., a CEO new to the role) may at some point start considering coaching as a career option for themselves. Observing coaches (as a consumer of their services) may eventually lead executives in other professions to stage mental experiments about their own potential as a coach. At this point, people will start to invest in the three ways of knowing. The *knowing-whom* investment may provide stimuli to investing in *knowing-how* by acquiring coaching skills (e.g., through attending coaching training, embarking on a psychological counseling program, engagement as a "shadow" coach with an experienced coach, and hiring a coach or psychotherapist as a supervisor for their own professional development). Later, when activating the new career in a new direction, people will balance their investment in other ways of knowing. For example, such observations and discussions with executive coaches may help them realize that they, too, could bring value to self and others by helping people achieve success in their work and life. This proactive approach may help people decide that coaching is the right profession for them (*knowing-why*).

Another characteristic of people who make mid-career transitions is that they take what has been called a *constructive approach* to planning their next moves.[14] Naturally, people who are standing at a crossroads in life will all be looking at somewhat similar paths, but each will see different degrees of promise in each route. The main differentiators influencing their choices are related to a matrix of inherent personality characteristics: (1) an active vs. passive mode of relating to the outside world; and (2) effective vs. ineffective testing of external reality. Career actors who take an active, pragmatic approach to evaluating their career options at midlife can be considered to have a constructive approach to changes in external circumstances. This dynamic but realistic perspective allows them to work through their midlife career reassessment in any of the following ways: By reconciling their initial expectations with their actual achievements to date, and staying happily on the same track; by accepting a differential between their initial expectations and their current level of achievement and then channeling the energy into vicarious success through, for example, helping a new generation; or by making a (radical) career change inside or outside their current organization. Most often, the career transition outcome of this constructive approach will be satisfactory for the individual.

Theories of adult development have contributed considerably to our understanding of the careers and working life of individuals.[15] Although the concepts of career entrepreneurship and intelligent careers have considerably altered the boundaries of career phases (e.g., the former CEO of a global company who opens his own executive coaching partnership to work with boards of directors can hardly be described as a "junior executive," even though he is embarking on a new career), there are still three major phases in careers that are considered to be roughly correlated with age: Fresh energy or engagement with unfamiliar situations; informed direction or pursuance of career pathways; and seasoned engagement or rounding of career experience.[16] (Arguably, these phases may apply more to people who have not deviated from a linear career path—notable exceptions might be serial entrepreneurs, and mothers who refocus more of their energy on their professional life as their children become independent.) Although our understanding of the career phases of fresh energy, informed direction, and seasoned engagement is evolving to allowing increased flexibility about linking career stages with age, an individual's career can still be considered "the evolving sequence of a person's work experiences over time."[17] This fits nicely with the concepts we described above—and acknowledges a new way of thinking about career transitions, based on an individual's ability to actively design, experiment, and transition into a new career at various points in their life.

How does a successful mid-career transition unfold? Once people have recognized the need to reorient their professional life, and have begun to invest in the transition, some level of experimentation begins. Our research shows that, ironically, a traditional business school program for executives, whatever the subject matter may be, can act as a catalyst that sets off a transition. For example, we have found that executives who come to our leadership development programs say that in addition to learning new skills, they are also seeking the time and space to think about their lives. It is not uncommon for them to admit that they seek new challenges within their organization, or even that they are considering leaving their current job to pursue other career objectives. This may well become a topic that individuals explore with their peers in the program, experiment with between modules, and fine-tune in a feedback loop with the critical insights of their peers during subsequent modules.

This observation stimulated a research program on what have been called *identity laboratories*.[18] Recent work on transformational executive education programs suggests that when individuals seek personal change experiences, they may benefit from identity laboratories or special transitional spaces that provide structures and protection for fruitful exploration and experimentation of identity issues, including those related to a professional identity.[19] The concept of identity laboratories as a productive environment for making intelligent career investments brings ideas from leadership development research into the studies of careers and coaching. The notion of an identity laboratory as a special transitional space—protected by temporal, spatial, and psychological demarcations with the outside world and characterized by psychological safety, the presence of guiding figures, and the availability of transitional objects for identity play and experimentation—draws on the psychodynamic tradition, anthropological research, and the recent incorporation of concepts from these literatures in identity, career, and change research. Such an environment, which can exist or be created within business schools, organizations, and many other contexts, may be sought by people who are at a liminal stage in their identity change process, that is, in the process of disengaging from an old identity without having fully left it, and developing a new one without yet fully embracing it. We can't exclude the possibility that individuals may find themselves in such an environment serendipitously, although there is evidence that people may be seeking structured opportunities to engage in exploration of personal change opportunities. Individuals seek opportunities and environments for identity work and, as we have discovered, business schools may be such environments.[20]

This kind of identity laboratory, or transitional space, seems particularly well suited for exploring and testing a transition to executive coaching. This space may help people to identify the ways of knowing what they might want to invest in. For example, after being coached herself in an executive program, and hearing that her peers found her to be a particularly effective listener, one person might start experimenting with coaching others as part of her daily job, as a pro-bono activity. If the experience is rewarding, both internally for the individual and with continued positive feedback from the external world, then she might choose to consolidate this experiment by making it increasingly visible and official.

## EXECUTIVE COACHING: AN ATTRACTIVE CAREER OPTION

Our research and experience in leadership development shows that a transition into executive coaching, negotiated successfully, can allow individuals to enter an energetic new career phase. Many people at midlife find themselves stagnating. For some, there are just not enough spots at the top. Others, having chosen, or been obliged, to follow a non-traditional career path (working mothers, for example), realize that interesting career options in line with their original training are probably now out of reach. Some individuals may well have been very successful, even reaching the top, but now find themselves bored, and hope to spend the rest of their working life doing something that has more meaning. Executive coaching as a career choice provides solutions to many of these issues; rather than excluding people with "failed" linear careers or atypical experiences, as a profession it privileges mid-career newcomers who bring with them broad life experiences, diverse professional backgrounds, and entrepreneurial dynamism. In the following section, we'll outline in more detail some of the reasons people give for becoming executive coaches.

### Influencing organizational life in a boundary-spanning role

Coaching may be seen as a field in which the career actor can experience being an entrepreneur while enjoying certain benefits of corporate connections. Executive coaching encourages and builds upon the ability to work at the boundaries of organizations or groups. Boundary spanning refers to processes or activities taking place at the limit or at the separation line between two or more entities or roles. Executive coaches may be compared to temporary employees who are brought into an organization on a contingency basis when there is a specific need for their skills, knowledge, or other talents. Executive coaches may face challenges similar to those of temporary employees, as they are expected to perform duties inside the company, without being an organizational member.[21] However, many executive coaches see this as an advantage, appreciating freedom from the daily restrictions of being a full-time member of an organization, while engaging in a kind of entrepreneurial venture (e.g., finding opportunities for the use of their competencies across various organizations). On the other hand, it is not uncommon to find executive coaches who, while still in a full-time executive position in an organization, use vacations or unpaid leave to pursue coaching activities. Clearly, executive coaching can allow people to span boundaries in a highly entrepreneurial way.

## Converting acquired competencies in a coherent way

A look at the profiles of executive coaches registered with the International Coach Federation, as well as those who market their services through the Internet, suggests that among this sample group at least, most coaches have a background in business management of some sort. Many new coaches may therefore use their previously acquired *knowing-whom* intelligent career investments to exploit subsequent investments in *knowing-why* and *knowing-how*. On the other hand, because listening and counseling are core competencies for executive coaches, former (or still practicing) psychologists, psychoanalysts, or psychiatrists may also transition quite rapidly into an executive coaching career. Individuals with a psychological orientation may see executive coaching as an invigorating opportunity to work with a completely different clientele who face different challenges (e.g., less psychological pathology and more business effectiveness). In terms of ways of knowing, people with this background can quickly build on their *knowing-how* investment, as their extensive professional and life experience compensates for their lesser degree of management experience. The *knowing-why* investment is also interesting in this case, as most choose their original profession out of a desire to help people work through problems in their life.

## Work–life balance

Interestingly, executive coaching is a career option that seems to be equally attractive to women and men. Recent work on important directions in career research suggests that the midlife career issues of women deserve particular attention.[22] The picture is not as clear as one might imagine. On the one hand, it appears that successful female executives often step off the career ladder not because success on a traditional career path is impossible, but because they believe the costs are too high compared to the potential rewards to be gained from their more intangible personal and family goals in life. On the other hand, we also talked to women who said they transitioned to coaching because they perceived further growth opportunities along the career ladder as fairly restricted or non-existent, or saw the investment required to make the next career step as incompatible with their other life interests. Coaching may be perceived by female career actors as a field where they can excel and prosper with fewer limitations compared to executive life. Similarly, male career actors may also find coaching a potential field where the pursuit of a variety of needs and interests may be more feasible and rewarding.

## Maintaining the good life: Social connections, power, and money

One of the well-known challenges of stepping off the career ladder is losing touch with professional self-identity. In contrast, people who have been at or near the top of a more traditional management career often enjoy transitioning into an executive coaching career in part because they continue to interact with senior executives, with all the intellectual stimulation and perks that it entails. It may be that they can vicariously play a role in shaping strategy, or succession planning, for example, and have access to the corridors of power.

One cannot deny the potential power that coaches have over the decisions made by their clients (and all the risks pertaining to being in such a position). Therefore, it is possible to think that exercising power is a driver for making coaching a career choice. Coupled with the frustration of feeling powerless or on a career plateau in an organizational setting, individuals may start to realize their need for power[23] through engagement in the coaching field.

Executive coaching can also be a good career move in financial terms. Although establishing a reputation as a top executive coach will take some investment, particularly in terms of networking, the rewards can be spectacular. Top executive coaches can earn fees similar to partners in law or consulting firms, and often quite a bit more than mid-career psychotherapists. The fact that coaching is perceived as a valuable service to organizations suggests that coaches expect relatively high fees for their work. At the time we wrote this book, coaches charged anywhere between US$200 and US$3,500 per hour, with a median hourly cost of coaching of US$500 per hour ("the cost of a top psychiatrist in Manhattan").[24] The perception of high fees suggests that an individual stepping away from a corporate job could, in principle, earn comparable (or even larger) amounts of money while enjoying the "perceived" freedom of a desirable lifestyle.

It could be suggested that some people become executive coaches on the basis of a rational calculation of the perceived amount of effort involved versus the return obtained in the form of fees for coaching services. In addition, individuals choosing coaching as a professional occupation may be enticed by the seeming ease with which a novice in the field can start working at a high level of client interactions and responsibility. For example, a newly "graduated" coach (or even someone who is still in training) can relatively easily generate coaching assignments through their previous organizational status and networks.

In fact, there are many other mid-career transition options that offer a chance for career actors to build on competencies or interests, take charge of their work life, and refocus on work–life balance—a midlife refocus on the arts, or non-profit organizations, comes to mind. But few, if any, have the current profile of high-status, low-entry barriers and the potentially very lucrative income of executive coaching.

## Executive coaching: A consolation prize?

Career plateau is a state in which people who have previously made objective career progress find their chances of further advancement limited.[25] Ambitious individuals who are not able to accept this may become frustrated, leading to a decrease in their sense of commitment and job satisfaction.[26] A career step toward coaching may be seen as a kind of remedial action. The realization that they can make no further progress in an organization, combined with their feeling that they have sufficient energy and desire to be noticeable and valuable to other people and companies, may lead people toward the choice of a coaching career. The danger here may be if executive coaches are not self-aware enough to avoid the influence of a desire for vicarious success on their terms. Beware the frustrated puppet master, whose primary, albeit perhaps unconscious, desire is to serve his or her own goals.

## A CALL FOR VIGILANCE

In sum, executive coaching can offer lucrative and pragmatic opportunities for a mid-career transition that allows individuals to step off a career path that no longer suits them, or to consolidate hard-earned personal and professional experience in a coherent and innovative way. For those who make the transition successfully, executive coaching can be very rewarding, both in terms of fees and also by giving a sense of meaning to the executive coach's work life. Executive coaches can play an important role in helping organizations use their managerial talent to the fullest extent. Coaches can help managers be more successful in their jobs and achieve greater satisfaction from what they do, thus arguably contributing to their objective and/or subjective career success. Coaching claims to help both individuals and organizations, through a creative combination of what therapy can bring to an individual, and what consulting can bring to a company.[27]

The advantages of executive coaching are obvious: A potential new career that has low entry barriers, builds on former experience, presents new challenges, is flexible in terms of time and boundaries, and can be financially and emotionally rewarding. However, the full picture is more nuanced. Although it might appear to be the easiest career move a person could ever make, in terms of printing the business cards and getting on with it, long-term success requires careful preparation, experimentation, and evaluation over time.

For many or all the reasons given above, becoming an executive coach often turns out to be a very satisfactory direction to take from the crossroads of midlife, *if* people take a constructive approach to the transition, exploring thoroughly their own abilities and the reality of entering a new profession; *if* they can tolerate a phase of experimentation and exploration; and *if* they understand the underlying personal reasons why they chose to become an executive coach. These important conditions are frequently underestimated, and this is why we call for vigilance, on the part of executive coaches themselves, and the organizations with which they are connected.

Our leitmotif in this book is to encourage coaches to explore their own fundamental motivation for what they do. We point out some of the motivators we have observed—career burnout, a desire for better life balance, financial rewards—not because they are intrinsically wrong, but because they should be thoroughly addressed in a transition phase, ideally in the kind of liminal space described above, before people take the responsibility of calling themselves an *executive coach*. The experienced coach should also continually address self-directed questions, such as: Can I be truly effective in this context, or am I only taking this assignment on for the money? Am I attracted to this intervention because I can vicariously influence the strategic moves of a global company? Do I resolve one of my own unresolved needs through being engaged in this assignment? Again, we emphasize that answering "Yes" to questions like these is not intrinsically wrong, so long as coaches (and their supervisors) are aware of these motivating factors and ensure that they remain strengths (e.g., sources of excitement and energy), rather than potential failure factors.

As part of the progression toward a new career identity, it is not enough just to take care of the investments in a new career. Intelligent career divestments[28] are also necessary. At times career movers do many things right: They enroll in a coaching course, join a professional association of coaches, meet other coaches, and convince themselves that coaching is the right choice for them. However, at the same time, they cling to vestiges of their old identities and previous career investments. Still thinking (and, more importantly, feeling) like a business executive, they find it difficult not to interfere if, in their opinion, the coachee is too slow in making a decision or if the decision is not in line with what the coach (who in reality is wearing a business executive hat rather than coach hat) thinks is the right thing to do. It becomes even more difficult if the coach faces a value conflict with the choices made by the coachee and, still aligned with the executive's role in an organization, tries proactively to push through a solution that is compatible with what the coach (rather than the coachee) finds important. At times the previous know-how investments (made throughout the years of being a successful manager) influence the choice of methods the coach uses: For example, offering possible solutions to the coachee's problems in a consulting mode. We have already mentioned the financial side of coaching motivations: Investments made in one's lifestyle and expected income may force the coach to take financially attractive, but inappropriate, assignments or stick to work that should be abandoned. Asking "What do I need to stop doing in order to be effective as a coach?" and even accepting certain losses are necessary for the successful transition to being a coach.

The next chapter goes into much greater detail about one motivator—the desire to help people. This driver is probably important for most coaches but, like all strengths, when taken to extremes, it can make coaches lose sight of the boundaries of responsible practice, and may be an underlying cause of tricky coaching relationships that do greater harm than good.

## NOTES

1. M. Arthur, P. Claman, and R. DeFillippi (1995). "Intelligent Enterprise, Intelligent Careers." *Academy of Management Executive*, 9(4), 7–20; K. Korotov, S. N. Khapova, and M. B. Arthur (2011). "Career Entrepreneurship." *Organizational Dynamics*, 40(2), 127–35.
2. K. Korotov and S. Khapova (2009). "Intelligent Career Divestments." Paper presented at the Academy of Management Annual Meeting, Chicago, IL, August 7–12.
3. M. Arthur, P. Claman, and R. DeFillippi (1995). "Intelligent Enterprise, Intelligent Careers." *Academy of Management Executive*, 9(4), 7–20; M. Arthur and D. Rousseau (1996). "Introduction: The Boundaryless Career as a New Employment Principle." In M. Arthur and D. Rousseau (Eds), *The Boundaryless Career: A New Employment Principle for a New Organizational Era*. New York: Oxford University Press, pp. 3–20; M. Arthur, S. Khapova, and C. Wilderom (2005). "Career Success in a Boundaryless Career World." *Journal of Organizational Behavior*, 26(2), 177–202.
4. R. R. Kilburg (2002). *Executive Coaching: Developing Managerial Wisdom in a World of Chaos*. Washington, DC: American Psychological Association; K. Korotov (2009). "Liminality and Careers of Executive Coaches." Paper presented at the 25th EGOS Colloquium, Barcelona.
5. D. Coutu and C. Kauffman (2009). "What Can Coaches Do for You?" *Harvard Business Review*, 87(1), 91–7; J. E. Bono, R. K. Purvanova et al. (2009). "A Survey of Executive Coaching Practices." *Personnel Psychology*, 62(2), 361–404.
6. For exceptions, see accounts of executive coaches discussing their career choices and steps in M. F. R. Kets de Vries, K. Korotov, and E. Florent-Treacy (Eds) (2007). *Coach and Couch: The Psychology of Making Better Leaders*. Basingstoke and New York: Palgrave Macmillan; and M. F. R. Kets de Vries, L. Guillen-Ramo, K. Korotov, and E. Florent-Treacy (2010). *The Coaching Kaleidoscope: Insights from the Inside*. Basingstoke and New York: Palgrave Macmillan.
7. A. M. Valerio and R. J. Lee (2005). *Executive Coaching: A Guide for the HR Professional*. San Francisco: Pfeiffer.
8. M. B. Arthur, K. Inkson, and J. K. Pringle (1999). *The New Careers: Individual Action and Economic Change*. Thousand Oaks, CA: Sage.
9. D. J. Levinson, C. N. Darrow, E. B. Klein, M. H. Levinson, and B. McKee (1978). *The Seasons of a Man's Life*. New York: Knopf; L. E. Thomas (1980). "A Typology of Mid-Life Career Changes." *Journal of Vocational Behavior*, 16, 173–82; E. Jacques (1965). "Death and the Mid-Life Crisis." *International Journal of Psychoanalysis*, 46, 502–14; M. F. R. Kets de Vries (1978). "The Mid-Career Conundrum." *Organizational Dynamics*, 7(2), 45–62; M. F. R. Kets de Vries (2010). *Reflections on Leadership and Career Development*. Chichester: Jossey-Bass, a Wiley Imprint.

10. D. T. Hall (2002). *Careers In and Out of Organizations*. Thousand Oaks, CA: Sage; H. Ibarra (2003). *Working Identity: Unconventional Strategies for Reinventing Your Career*. Boston, MA: Harvard Business School Press.
11. D. T. Hall (2002). *Careers In and Out of Organizations*, Thousand Oaks, CA: Sage.
12. K. Korotov, S. N. Khapova, and M. B. Arthur (2011). "Career Entrepreneurship." *Organizational Dynamics*, 40(2), 127–35.
13. M. Arthur, P. Claman, and R. DeFillippi (1995). "Intelligent Enterprise, Intelligent Careers." *Academy of Management Executive*, 9(4), 7–20.
14. M. F. R. Kets de Vries (2010). *Reflections on Leadership and Career Development*. Chichester: Jossey-Bass, a Wiley Imprint.
15. D. E. Super (1953). "A Theory of Vocational Development." *American Psychologist*, 8, 185–90; M. L. Savickas (2002). "Career Construction: A Developmental Theory of Vocational Behavior." In D. A. Brown and Associates (Eds), *Career Choice and Development*. San Francisco: Jossey-Bass, pp. 149–205; L. Baird and K. Kram (1983). "Career Dynamics: Managing the Supervisor/Subordinate Relationship." *Organizational Dynamics*, 11, 46–64; E. Erickson (1959). "Identity and the Life Cycle." *Psychological Issues*, 1, 1–171; D. J. Levinson, C. N. Darrow, E. B. Klein, M. H. Levinson, and B. McKee (1978). *The Seasons of a Man's Life*. New York: Knopf.
16. K. Inkson (2007). *Understanding Careers: The Metaphors of Working Life*. Thousand Oaks, CA: Sage.
17. M. Arthur, T. Hall, and B. Lawrence (Eds) (1989). *Handbook of Career Theory*. Cambridge: Cambridge University Press.
18. K. Korotov (2005). *Identity Laboratories*. INSEAD PhD Dissertation.
19. M. Dubouloy (2004). "The Transitional Space and Self-Recovery: A Psychoanalytical Approach to High-Potential Managers' Training." *Human Relations*, 57(4), 467–96; M. F. R. Kets de Vries, K. Korotov, and E. Florent-Treacy (Eds) (2007). *Coach and Couch: The Psychology of Making Better Leaders*. Basingstoke: Palgrave Macmillan.
20. K. Korotov (2005). *Identity Laboratories*. INSEAD PhD Dissertation; G. Petriglieri and J. L. Petriglieri (2010). "Identity Workspaces: The Case of Business Schools." *Academy of Management Learning & Education*, 9(1), 44–60.
21. C. Bartel and J. Dutton (2001). "Ambiguous Organizational Memberships: Constructing Organizational Identities in Interactions with Others." In M. A. Hogg and D. J. Terry (Eds), *Social Identity Processes in Organizational Contexts*. Philadelphia, PA: Psychology Press.
22. W. Cascio (2007). "Trends, Paradoxes, and Some Direction for Research in Career Studies." In H. Gunz and M. Peiperl (Eds), *Handbook of Career Studies*. Thousand Oaks, CA: Sage, pp. 549–57.
23. D. C. McLelland and D. H. Burnham (1976). "Power Is the Great Motivator." *Harvard Business Review*, 54, 100–10, 159–66.
24. D. Coutu and C. Kauffman (2009). "What Can Coaches Do for You?" *Harvard Business Review*, 87(1), 92.
25. D. C. Feldman and B. A. Weitz (1988). "Career Plateau Reconsidered." *Journal of Management*, 14, 69–80.
26. R. Goffee and R. Scase (1992). "Organizational Change and the Corporate Career: The Restructuring of Managers' Aspirations." *Human Relations*, 45, 363–85.
27. D. Coutu and C. Kauffman (2009). "What Can Coaches Do for You?" *Harvard Business Review*, 87(1), 91–7.
28. K. Korotov and S. Khapova (2009). "Intelligent Career Divestments." Paper presented at the Academy of Management Annual Meeting. Chicago, IL, August 7–12.

# 2

# THE RESCUER SYNDROME

## THE VICISSITUDES OF DOING GOOD

Given the many changes in the world of work, leadership coaching is no longer viewed as merely a tool in the organizational repertoire for dealing with dysfunctional executives. On the contrary, it is fair to say that leadership coaching has become part of the mainstream, as people are much more aware of the high costs of performing below capacity. Ambitious executives now perceive having an executive coach as the right thing to do. Leadership coaches can be particularly effective in cases of change and transition, promotion, stretch assignments, or other new challenges. Whether executives are struggling with a specific career decision, a critical issue at work, or a major life change, coaches can provide the kind of guidance and feedback that is needed to help them attain a more complete grasp of themselves and organizational realities.

As we described in Chapter 1, leadership coaching has become a very attractive career option, not least because it pays well, and often involves working with educated and powerful clients. But when we meet with coaches for the first time and ask why they became a leadership coach, many say that they are driven primarily by a desire to help people. In the light of its popularity, we might even go as far to say that leadership coaching has, to some extent, taken on the role that psychoanalysis (and its various offshoots) occupied in the twentieth century.

However, there are a number of important differentiations between leadership coaching and various forms of dynamically oriented psychotherapies. Coaches (unless clinically trained) limit the scope of their interventions to relatively normal behaviors rather than psychopathology. Because coaching is intended to expedite the way executives deal with their business and personal objectives, coaches tend to be much more action-oriented than psychiatrists, psychoanalysts, and psychotherapists. In coaching, current events in an individual's life are given more prominence than past events. And executive coaches focus more on conscious, rational processes than on the more unconscious (not immediately perceived as rational) ones.

Many people are drawn to the helping professions for genuinely altruistic reasons. Rescuing is a core dynamic found in most interpersonal encounters—notably the relationship between couples. The desire to help people is a very laudable one, and compassion, service, and dedication are real virtues. It is far better to be able to say that someone is in the "helping" than the "not-helping" business. The desire to help, to create a better world for all of us—despite the narcissistic components of this desire—needs to be encouraged.

The human repertoire includes an impulse toward altruism. Empathy is the very basis of all human interaction.[1] Evolutionary psychologists have speculated that we may be hardwired to behave in ways conducive to the sociability of the species. Some neurologists have even speculated about the existence of mirror neurons—cells in the brain that activate similar cells in the person being helped.[2] Thus human behavior is oriented not only toward the survival of the fittest but also the survival of the nicest.

Helping professionals—doctors, nurses, emergency or disaster workers, lawyers, politicians, and so on—have a huge responsibility to look out for their clients' or patients' welfare. However, they are, of course, only human, and experience the same conflicting interests and needs as any other person. Therefore, to be effective in their role, helping professionals must be able either to address their own needs outside the working relationship or to suspend them—the former response is more effective, in the long run, than the latter.

If they are unable or unwilling to examine their own behavior, sometimes a desire to help can go too far, turning helpers into "rescuers" who are unable to differentiate between their own needs and those of their clients. Although this tendency is well recognized in the psychotherapeutic and medical professions, in the still fairly unregulated world of leadership coaching there is a lack of the kind of oversight and protocol that guide other helping professions. Commonly, executive coaches are not specifically trained to be wary of the rescuer syndrome, despite the fact that the boundary between leadership coaching and psychotherapy can be very fuzzy.

Problems arise when people see themselves *only* as helpers. Although the role of helper can be viewed as noble and meaningful, *it should not become someone's sole purpose in life*. For some, the need to help seems to become an addiction. They suffer from "the disease to please."[3] Even more insidious is the possibility that helpers co-opt their clients in an attempt to resolve their own problems. Needless to say, the outcome can be extremely damaging for the client who, without being aware of what's going on, has been handed a whole new set of issues to work through—those of the helper.

Why do some people cross the line from doing great and genuine good, to becoming parodies—rescuers, White Knights, Florence Nightingales, or Mother Teresas?[4] Why are they prone to the "hero complex," compulsively driven to search for people in need?[5] In the process, they may turn into tragic heroes, needing help themselves.

Given the complexity of the helping operational mode, "I want to help people" as a motive for choosing leadership coaching as a career is deceptively simplistic, and may even have dysfunctional consequences. Some individuals may have no real understanding of the underlying reasons that drove them to join the ranks of the helping professionals.[6] Anyone in these professions should reflect seriously, with the help of a supervisor if necessary, on the inner motivations that drive them to pursue this path. Experienced practitioners are very familiar with the vicissitudes of the human condition. The question is: Are they familiar enough with their *own* condition?

Although rescuer syndrome is not an officially recognized disorder, an increasing number of people in the helping professions, executive coaches among them, seem to be affected by it. In this chapter we explore the origins of compulsive and excessive helping behavior, identify this dysfunctional behavior pattern, and discuss strategies for dealing with it. We examine the vicissitudes of rescuer syndrome, particularly in the context of coach–coachee relationships, where we explore the questions of codependency and what it takes to be a constructive rescuer. A better understanding of rescuer syndrome will help us achieve a greater awareness of the intensity of the rescuer within us—and how this behavior can create detours from our original, well-meant objectives.

## TIPPING THE BALANCE: WHEN HELPING GOES TOO FAR

Many of our actions as human beings can be effective *or* dysfunctional, depending on the extremes to which we engage in them. A compulsive desire to please is very different from acting on altruistic motives. This is true in the case of zealous executive coaches who become overly involved in the lives of their clients. When coaches become incessant helpers, this specific modus operandi can incur a cost to themselves and their clients, possibly even fostering an unnecessary, unhealthy, and inappropriate dependency relationship. Ironically, as time goes by, these helpers may begin to feel helpless, powerless, resentful and irritated. Instead of generating exhilarating highs, helping turns into a debilitating energy drain.

Eventually, both coach and client will begin to suffer. Helpers become overloaded and overwhelmed as their interpersonal relationships are increasingly experienced as one-way and unfulfilling, rather than balanced, reciprocal, and happy. Eventually, these rescuers may end up bitter, angry, or apathetic. For their clients, on the other hand, always having someone to rely on is not the best way to develop the skills they need to become self-directive and responsible for their own lives.

These unfortunate collusions between rescuers and the rescued are frequently exacerbated by the rescuers over-identifying so completely with helping others that they fail to realize what they are doing to themselves. They don't perceive that there is a great difference between a desire to help people and a compulsive need to rescue. "Real" helping should be a joint effort; it is never a one-way street. With real helping, great efforts are made to grow and develop the people who are being helped—the ultimate altruistic goal is to make the helper's continuing intervention unnecessary. When the desire to rescue becomes extreme, the people being helped have no choice but to go with the flow, following the helper's directions. Any initiative they take is stifled or undervalued. In such instances, these "saviors" seem to be trying to escape their own issues by immersing themselves in the troubles of others.[7] In other words, their apparently unselfish behavior may be driven by very self-centered motives.

## THE RESCUER SYNDROME

People in the helping professions need to be as "normal" as possible. That is, they should strive to understand and alleviate their own personal difficulties, and any dysfunctional behavior patterns that could muddy their outlook on life, so they can see their clients' disturbances and problems more clearly. If not, helpers may run foul of their own needs by becoming hopelessly mired in transference and counter-transference reactions—acting out the problems of the past in the present.[8] When this happens, people who are ostensibly helping others to deal with their difficulties find themselves having to address issues that are too close to unresolved, conflicting issues in their own lives. Rescuer syndrome manifests itself when helping turns into a compulsion based on one central, but very flawed, conviction: "The only way to get what I need is to do what other people want." Thus helpers don't help others out of choice; on the contrary, they seem impelled to enter into and prolong a kind of rescuer–victim relationship.

Many of us have lifelong practice in reflexively attuning to others' needs. Risk enters when a conscious, caretaking response transmutes into an over-learned, compulsive reaction. It is probably fair to say that people suffering from rescuer syndrome are suffering from an addiction, in the same way that eating, smoking, drug-taking, alcohol, or sex can become addictive. To outsiders, rescuing behavior can resemble some kind of heroic martyrdom. However, there is an upside to it. A closer look at its underlying dynamics may reveal that acting in this way gives rescuers an excuse to avoid dealing with their own problems.

Paradoxically, the more rescuers demonstrate to all and sundry their talent for solving other people's problems, the more problems will be presented to them. Although these requests may make them feel wanted, eventually they become too much of a good thing. Deep down, rescuers are participating in activities that they don't really want to do any longer, but they fear upsetting others by saying "No."

A disproportionate need to be liked—to be seen to be helping—is usually related to a shaky self-image. Rescuers fear that looking after number one will be perceived as unkind, uncaring, and selfish. For them, saying "No" is associated with ending a relationship; "others" will become angry or reject them. Their wish to be liked makes it very hard for rescuers to set limits to others and to maintain appropriate boundaries.

There is also a sense of immediacy in the way rescuers like to help people. Although there are often no instant solutions to the problems that are presented to them, rescuers often feel inadequate if they don't provide concrete, even instant, advice. Unfortunately, in their zeal to be helpful, they may create new difficulties, even going so far as imagining that everyone they encounter has problems. They add to their own misery with feelings of guilt for not accomplishing the unrealistic goals they tend to set for others.

In many situations, all that people who ask for help really want is to be listened to—they do *not* want to be told what to do. Providing immediate solutions may not be the best thing to do. Rescuers have forgotten that the purpose of helping is to help others discover their own course of action.

## THE RESCUER SYNDROME IN LEADERSHIP COACHING

We remember an executive coach telling us how she would call the office of one of her clients to tell them that he was sick, while in fact the client was a binge drinker and had such a bad hangover he was unable to work. This is the kind of help that goes above and beyond normal caretaking behavior. This particular interface between coach and coachee is an example of codependency, where the behavior of the coach is helping to maintain the client's destructive or dependent behavior. When we asked the coach why she did this, she explained that her client had repeatedly told her that he couldn't manage without her and that he always felt much better after she took care of problems for him. The coach said the man was one of her best clients—and it is not difficult to understand why. This example may appear extreme, but in our experience of supervising executive coaches, it is actually all too common.

All relationships have something of a codependent quality. We are all dependent on each other, and many situations of codependency are not dysfunctional. In healthy relationships, there will be a sense of reciprocity. In some cases, however, codependency takes on a more serious, emotionally destructive form,[9] with individuals developing an "addiction" to maintaining one-sided relationships. Genuine caring is fulfilling, while codependent behavior is draining. When codependency occurs, the caring party feels frustrated, unappreciated, and even mentally and physically exhausted. But at the same time, the caregiver is unconsciously seeking validation of the efforts he or she is putting into the relationship.

Ineffective or even harmful codependency is a frequent but underdiagnosed problem in coach–coachee relationships. When it occurs, we may see the rescuer syndrome in full flight: The thoughts, motives, and actions of the coach will begin to revolve around the coachee, to the detriment of the coach's mental well-being. An addictive *relationship entanglement* has formed. The identities of coach and coachee slip toward fusion. They find it difficult to see themselves as separate selves. Some coaches will even continue to work with a coachee after the formal contract ends, without pay.

To complicate matters, coaches with codependent tendencies are drawn to highly needy people. And although—at least initially—the interaction with these people may be gratifying to both parties, this will not last. Rescuing never results in permanent solutions for dependent people. Most people asking to be rescued are usually rather passive. Although they seem receptive, they fail to follow up on good advice, and take very little or no action. They always find excuses for not doing what they are supposed to do, adding to their rescuers' feelings of helplessness and aggravation.

For various (probably unconscious) reasons, some people who ask for help operate under the assumption that the world owns them a living. They are entitled to be helped; it is their birthright. Sadly, the rescuer syndrome can be the biggest obstacle to helping these dependent people resolve their conflicts. Rescuers give these people the opportunity *not* to rise to the occasion and far too often there is stalemate in their interactions.

An additional complication is that rescuers appear uncomfortable in equal relationships; ironically, they may even become anxious when the people they have been helping get their act together, and no longer want their help. When this happens, rescuers immediately look around for someone else they can "save."

Most coaches discover that balancing their needs with those of their clients is like walking a tightrope—an extremely delicate balancing act that requires mindfulness and precision. Although we all have behavior patterns that prevent us from being fully effective, people suffering from rescuer syndrome have blind spots that prevent them from being truly effective. Furthermore, some may have so many rescuing projects that they lose their sense of priority and end up paralyzed.

## RESCUER BURNOUT

With too much helping going on, the helper may be faced with diminishing returns. The emotional labor associated with helping drains energy;[10] it results in a progressive loss of idealism and purpose. Coaches who find themselves in this position become cynical, tired, and apathetic. Their positive outlook and work effort are compromised. Worse, they may unconsciously contaminate their coachees with their own sense of failure and burnout.

Rescuers feel that, at all costs, they need to suppress or reframe their own negative qualities, such as anger, selfishness, greed, rivalry, envy, spite, and vindictiveness. The exertion this requires is extremely tiring. While they may display a positive exterior, under the surface there will be a lot of resentment about the show they have to maintain. Their exhaustion is compounded by the negation of their own needs and their unwillingness to take time out to revitalize themselves.

Rescuers' frustration and disillusionment are increased by their feeling that they don't receive the gratitude they deserve. It may cross their mind that the people they are trying to help don't really appreciate what they are offering or, worse, don't seem to want to be helped. Eventually a point is reached where rescuers fear they are no longer doing anyone any good.

Other indicators of rescuer burnout are feelings of guilt and self-hatred associated with less interest in rescuing people. Rescuer withdrawal is symptomatic of this state of mind. There can also be an increase in "projection"—rescuers start blaming the people they are supposed to help for various misdeeds.

Eventually, rescuers (having become increasingly desperate) may reach the point where they terminate rescue missions that are stalling. They may even deny and conceal the problems of their troubled client in an effort to find a way out. While this is going on, anxiety, emotional detachment, or depression are common. Substance abuse is not unusual. The chronic stress to which they are exposed manifests itself in physical problems, including high blood pressure, diabetes, backache, digestive disorders, and a compromised immune system.[11] These physical stresses may even reduce the life expectancy of rescuers.

Apart from these psychological and physiological problems, people suffering from rescuer syndrome may also lose a sense of boundaries. By acting out some of their own fantasies with the people they are supposed to help, they may find themselves in other kinds of trouble. In any form of therapeutic situation—including coaching—there is always the temptation to engage in unethical behavior. Sexual transgression is a major hazard. People in the helping professions should never forget that, as helpers, they wield extraordinary emotional powers.

## THROUGH A GLASS DARKLY

Executive coaches would do well to recognize the inner forces that motivate them to help others. To be truly helpful to their clients, they need to have a high level of awareness of their own emotional needs and behavior patterns. They must acknowledge that their state of mind will affect the relationship they have with their clients, for better or for worse. This doesn't mean, however, that people in the helping professions need to be perfectly well adjusted and free from any form of dysfunctional behavior. If that were the qualification for entering these professions, very few would ever qualify.

To understand why people are prone to rescuer syndrome, we need to access the unconscious areas of our lives and make sense of the nature of the interrelationship between the self and the other, especially the intensity of the bonds between caretakers and infants.[12] Children who are securely attached have received consistently warm, sensitive, and responsive care from their primary caretakers. From such experiences, they develop internal working models of the other, knowing their caretakers will always be there for them when needed. Consequently, they grow up secure and confident with a healthy sense of self-esteem.[13] But for children whose caretakers are unavailable or needy, the outcome can be very different.

## DYSFUNCTIONAL FAMILY SCENARIOS

The typical childhood experience of people who come from dysfunctional families can vary from neediness, addiction, and neglect—where children have no choice but to take on the parenting role (and in the process lose touch with their own needs)—to families that may look loving and stable from the outside, but in which striving for perfection has created a rather claustrophobic, intimidating environment.

In the first scenario, we find families where needy primary caretakers were unable or unwilling to care for the developing child. The parents responded unpredictably to the children's needs (i.e., with rejection, irritability, or hostility). This type of parenting did not provide children with the attention, warmth, and responsiveness they needed. Instead, it was the parents who needed care. Children living in this type of family grow up thinking that their opinions, needs, and feelings are unimportant. They never feel they are significant to their parents or really loved. They become premature caretakers.

People from families like these find it exceedingly difficult to ask for help from others; they see asking for help as a very selfish act. Because of their unsatisfactory early attachments, they try to repair a damaged sense of self in adulthood by taking on the role of rescuer.[14] This is a way of working through painful childhood experiences that have never been resolved. It is little wonder that people with this sort of psychological and emotional hinterland turn taking care of others into a lifelong quest and see it as a way to obtain some kind of recognition. Unsurprisingly, the helping professions become a good fit for these people.

The second scenario is families where love must be earned. Although outward appearances suggest that the interpersonal dynamics in these families are quite harmonious, the reality for the children growing up in them is very different. For them, being loved depends on being "good," pleasing their parents, and living up to their expectations. The rigid conscious and unconscious rules and beliefs that have been spelled out for them leave little or no room for their individuality. Children in these families don't feel loved for who they are, but for what they do. Their early experience of parental love as conditional turns them into approval addicts as they grow older. As adults, they are still trying to live up to their parents' expectations and their ways of behaving continue to reflect those spoken and unspoken rules. They have an intense desire to put right the perceived wrongs of the past, trying to repair what has been done to them. Their striving to be perfect hides their great and real need to be accepted and recognized. Whatever they do, however, they never feel good enough and continue to feel inadequate, flawed, and inferior.

Children from these specific family constellations learn to believe that the only way they can enter a relationship is through self-denial, suffering, and sacrifice. Exposure to this kind of parenting means they grow up with the feeling that what they want doesn't matter—their own desires and needs are unimportant. Taking on the "savior" role in their families meant attending to the problems and concerns of the other family members.

Choosing to work in a helping profession is a way of dealing with the feelings of anxiety or impotence associated with having to deal with physical or emotional dysfunction or even death within the family.[15] Relieving pain may become a means of redemption. Unfortunately, because of the defective child-rearing practices helpers were exposed to in their early life, they have not developed the healthy sense of self-esteem needed for mature functioning. This may mean that they engage in pseudo-altruism, which characterizes many joy-less and self-denying martyrs with severe masochistic and narcissistic pathology. Their compulsive caretaking and self-sacrifice can be interpreted as a defense against their anger, envy, and need to control other people.[16]

Psychotherapists are a prime example of a helping profession—and many sur-veys indicate that a large number of psychotherapists, when growing up, felt a responsibility to care for physically or emotionally challenged family members. The death of a parent frequently seems to be part of this troubled family scenario.[17] Childhood difficulties, especially in the areas of attachment, care-giving, and illness, created a compulsion to care for others—a defensive reaction to feelings of anxiety, impotence, or isolation.

Helpers from these backgrounds try to remedy the emotional neglect they experienced in childhood by giving to others the care and attention they wanted but lacked. This compulsion has been termed "helping profession syndrome," and is a pattern that contributes to a "severe deficit in the emotional balance of payments."[18] Adopting a rescuer pattern becomes their way of coping with the stresses associated with the physical or emotional issues of family members when growing up. Because of the emotional struggles they experienced, they can be quite effective in healing others. Often, wounded (but self-aware) healers—more so than well-adjusted helpers—can authentically help others, notwithstanding their need to help themselves.

But as with many things, there should be limits, even in the helping world. Too much helping—fueled by troubled childhood experiences—can put these people onto a highly self-destructive course. Studying the childhood scenarios common to these people, we can see that the choice of a career in the helping professions has a Janus aspect. In the first place, the choice means that people continue a pattern of behavior they have learned in childhood. Second, this way of functioning can be a form of defensive projection. In many instances, helpers have an unconscious identification with their client, based on a projection of their own unmet emotional needs. When this happens, the distinction between the helper and the person needing help becomes blurred: The latter becomes a narcissistic extension of the former. Assuming this role may be the result of the kind of role models that were perceived as inspiring and helpful during the res-cuer's formative years.

## GHOSTS FROM CHILDHOOD

As adults, helpers with such a past are still troubled by the ghosts of childhood as these difficult, early life experiences create distorted assumptions of themselves and others. Cast in the role of helper in childhood, and with few emotional resources, they may be left with feelings of guilt for not having helped these ghosts from their past adequately.

Rescuers often operate on the basis of a number of faulty assumptions. For example: "I should always be helpful and try and please others. If not, bad things may happen"; "I should always be happy, and never show any negative feelings toward others"; "My self-worth depends on what other people think of me"; "Unless I do what other people want, I will be rejected." Frequently, this compulsion to help—to please others—is maintained by the many "musts" and "shoulds" that linger from childhood. But these "musts" and "shoulds" become terrible drivers. These helpers become addicted to other people's approval, but to no avail. They never feel pleased with themselves; they never reach their self-imposed standards; and although there is a lot to be said for setting high standards, striving for perfection is another matter altogether. It sets people up for failure. And so people suffering from rescuer syndrome enter a self-perpetuating stress cycle.

Although the scripts that rescuers followed in their early life may have been helpful at the time, they become dysfunctional in the present. If rescuers were to look deeper into their driven behavior, they might discover that they are repeating themes from old, unresolved family dramas. All too frequently, while their heroic actions may take the form of slaying their clients' metaphorical dragons, their real goal (usually beyond conscious awareness) is slaying the dragons from their own past. A deeper analysis of rescuers' inner theater may reveal that their choice of clients, and that the way they treat them, often repeats (symbolically) the same kind of distress that they themselves experienced in childhood. Ironically, it is often the rescuers who are far more troubled than the client. Their scripts have turned into restrictive liturgies, limiting their sense of freedom. They have yet to learn that being "nice" is not a magical formula that provides protection.

Rescuers also have difficulty getting in touch with their own emotions. The needs and moods of others are all that matters. This attunement to others' needs may go so far that they no longer know what they really want or need themselves. Sometimes, they don't even know what to think or feel. No wonder that so many rescuers find it hard to describe themselves or their feelings. Worse, rescuers experience intense stress, feelings of inadequacy, and low self-regard because they persist in looking for "redemption" by helping others; the old script they follow tells them that doing things for other people will guarantee their love and respect. Instead, they may be setting themselves up for use and abuse.

The modus operandi of rescuers is pleasing other people. But by caring and helping others, at their own expense, they risk becoming a caricature of themselves. When rescuing others becomes the main driver, there can be unhealthy consequences for the giver, the receiver, and the relationship as a whole. Trying to meet others' expectations only contributes to self-destructive or unduly self-sacrificial behavior. Rescuers may do more harm than good and prevent people who are looking for help discovering salient issues on their own.

We should point out that it can be perfectly all right to want to feel appreciated for what we do for others. The danger is when people feel *compelled* to seek appreciation and recognition as the *only* way to feel worthwhile. This is a lose–lose situation. Coaches, for example, are on very shaky ground if their self-esteem depends exclusively on their clients. Rescuers are driven to seek constant nourishment—a desperate search that can turn into a mission impossible.

Before they embark on their rescue missions, people suffering from rescuer syndrome would do well to examine their own life situation. They need to find out why they do what they do. They should ask themselves where the need to help people comes from. They need to recognize transferential processes—the acting out of specific scripts that once may have been appropriate but may no longer be valid. Making sense of these scripts can provide insights into their motivation—and may help them to do something different. Ultimately, if rescuers fail to obtain insight about their inner theater, then rather than repairing their sense of self, they will be left with a sense of defeat.

## MANAGING RESCUER SYNDROME

There is a painfully funny joke about someone suffering from rescuer syndrome. One day, he was driving on a mountainous road and hit a patch of ice. As the car slid off the road into a deep ravine, one of his clients' lives flashed before his eyes. People suffering from rescuer syndrome need to find new ways of relating to others. The question becomes: What assistance can be given to move these rescuers beyond their destructive fixer mode?

A good start to tackling rescuer syndrome is to identify the degree of individual contamination. Executive coaches need to find out whether this label could be applied to them.

For this purpose, it will be helpful to reflect on the following questions, and determine their relevance. The questions are a quick way of assessing the degree to which you (the reader) fall into the rescuer trap. *Please work through each question.*

### Assessing the intensity of rescuer syndrome

- Is it hard for you to make time for yourself?
- Is it difficult for you not to respond to anyone in need of help?
- Do you find yourself always willing to help people in need?
- Do you have a tendency to take responsibility for people who are in trouble?
- Do you become enmeshed in the problems of people you believe need to be rescued?
- Are you often unable to stop talking, thinking, and worrying about other people and their problems?
- Do you have a tendency to help everyone around you, whether they ask for help or not?

- Do your coachees sometimes feel like family members?
- Do you continue to work with coachees on an informal basis after the contract ends?
- Do you feel uncomfortable receiving help from other people?
- Does your life often feel out of control because you simply can't say no?
- Do you always worry about what other people think of you?
- Do you feel more worthy as a human being because you have taken on a helping role?
- Do you feel safest and most comfortable when you are giving to others?
- Do you feel guilty when you are unable to solve another person's problems?
- Are you inclined to make decisions for a person in trouble?
- Do you find it difficult to set boundaries when people put demands on you?
- Do you make excuses—explicitly or implicitly—for the person you are helping?
- Do you feel unfulfilled or anxious when there is no crisis to solve?
- Do you sometimes feel anger and/or resentment to be giving all the time?
- Do you sometimes feel taken advantage of?
- Do you feel resentful when others are not grateful enough to you for your efforts at rescuing them or fixing their lives?
- Does constantly helping other people leave you mentally and physically exhausted?
- Did you grow up in a family with a lot of emotional chaos?
- As you were growing up, did you think it was your responsibility to keep the family functioning?

Add up the times you agreed with these questions. If the majority of the answers were "Yes," it is likely that you suffer from rescuer syndrome. If you have a very high score, you may need to take preventive steps to prevent falling into the rescuer trap.

## HEALER, HEAL THYSELF

If executive coaches suffering from rescuer syndrome want to do something about their problem, the best way to start the healing process is to face it squarely. For someone who has spent a lifetime using denial (one of the more primitive defensive mechanisms) to ward off feelings of pain, shame, guilt, or fear of rejection, changing this pattern will not be an easy exercise.[19]

A combination of group and individual therapy (including couples therapy) will provide an outlet to vent feelings, confront resistances, open up and discuss difficult family patterns and how these dynamics affect present-day behavior. Case meetings, supervision (including peer supervision), and working as a team with clients are also useful opportunities for mutual support, and for obtaining greater insights about personal ways of functioning. These interventions will help to create a new sense of empowerment and forward movement in these people's lives. In the process, self-esteem will be enhanced, helping people suffering from rescuer syndrome to recreate and relearn boundary setting and validate personal needs that went unmet during their formative years.

During this journey toward change, a number of issues need to be addressed. Helpers need to learn to be more selfish; they need to be nicer to themselves. They need to actualize their own dreams and aspirations, rather than constantly focusing on those of others. They also need to learn how to have fun—not always an easy proposition. Furthermore, they need to take stock of the kinds of people they are attracted to. They have to learn to become detached from the toxic people in their lives—people who are emotionally and physically draining. They need to reflect on the quality of help they can give. Then they should take a serious look at the reasons why they feel compelled to take on a specific client. If they come to the conclusion that they are once again doing it for the wrong reasons—that they are entering a transferential trap, responding at a deeper level to their own problems, not those of the client—they should not enter into such a relationship.

Rescuers will improve their ability to change their default behaviors if they realize that they have been functioning according to a number of fundamentally flawed assumptions. For example, they confuse the act of rejecting a request for help with rejection of the person. This fear is often exaggerated, however. If sufficient explanation is given, most people will accept the logic of such a decision. Finally, when rescuers realize that they no longer have to heal the whole world as they were encouraged to do in childhood—a time when they were least capable of doing it—they will be not only more effective, but also much happier.

## BEING A CONSTRUCTIVE RESCUER

Constructive rescuers are sensitive to the needs of others—within reason. They realize that their efforts to help should not come at the cost of their own health and happiness.[20] Constructive rescuers make clear to the people who come to them for help that they should recognize and accept the consequences of their own troubled behavior.

As constructive rescuers, executive coaches make it clear to their clients that they own their own life—asking them what they have done to fix their own problems. They make clients understand that they cannot use them as a dump for all their emotional garbage. Helped by the coach, they need to work on their own problems. Constructive rescuers realize that by creating reciprocity in relationships, they will be more helpful than putting others in their debt.

Constructive rescuers act as catalysts in the process of helping people to solve their problems. Their role is to encourage people in need to face their difficulties honestly. Handing the responsibility for the problem back to the people in need, and viewing the problem more objectively—taking account of transferential processes—encourages clients to take ownership of their problems, and work on them to enact change.

Ideally, executive coaches will have the sort of self-knowledge and objectivity that come after having undergone extensive self-examination through various forms of psychotherapy. More than others, they need to develop a high degree of self-awareness, and a deep understanding of the differences between conscious and unconscious processes. They will have the kind of emotional receptivity that creates self-awareness, reflectivity, and non-defensiveness. Using themselves as instruments, constructive rescuers can recognize major themes in the lives of their clients and, simultaneously, attend to their own thoughts, emotions, physiological responses, and behaviors during these sessions. This is what social and emotional intelligence is all about.

Constructive rescuers are reliable, trustworthy, and discreet—within reason. They are respectful of the people they deal with and have a steady regard for other people's autonomy and reality. In their work, they are able to put their own interests and concerns aside in the presence of their clients. They have an unselfish commitment to their clients' well-being. Their overwhelming desire is to help others obtain in-depth insights about the way they function. While facilitating this kind of learning, they have the knack of making other people shine. They enhance the learning process with their skill at asking good questions that make their clients think and feel challenged and supported rather than criticized. They are also prepared to face difficult questions and ready to tell the truth even if it is not what people would like to hear. But they also time their inventions well: Too early and the intervention does not stick; too late and the opportunity has passed. Their openness and frankness, and their ability to recognize and express their own feelings in the interface with their clients, make these exchanges extremely valuable. And they can be even more effective if they know how to use humor well.

Constructive rescuers are exceptional listeners. Their ability to make people feel understood enables them to build an effective working alliance with their clients—the deep, emotional connection that is required between the helping professional and the client to make an intervention work. Establishing this bond necessitates the capacity for empathy, that is, identification with and understanding of another's situation, feelings, and motives. Constructive rescuers have the emotional sensitivity to be glad when others are glad, and sad when they are sad. They are not only capable of insight, understanding, empathy, and compassion, but are also able to act accordingly without losing their sense of boundaries.

Constructive rescuers also have a considerable tolerance for ambiguity. They have what has been called negative capability—a state of intentional open-mindedness—the ability to keep the imagination alive without having the urge for closure. They are able to accept uncertainty without becoming overanxious. They value the cognitive complexity and the ambiguity of the human condition. They can suspend disbelief when they encounter puzzling situations. Naturally, this makes the capacity for patience a *sine qua non*.

From this, we can see that the actions and motives required of helping professionals are not just those of ordinary decent behavior. They imply recognition of the power of both conscious and unconscious processes. This necessitates a deep understanding of self and others. To be a truly helping professional—to be a constructive rescuer—helpers must have sufficient self-knowledge and self-discipline to manifest these qualities under stress, and when faced with the almost overwhelming temptation to behave differently. These people are hyper-aware of how their emotional health affects the quality of their work.

## CONCLUDING COMMENTS

As coaches, all of us—to some degree—are broken and wounded by the world, but we learn to cope. All of us have our own unique constellation of strengths and weaknesses. All of us have a shadow side. All of us may regress, at times. We all need help—including helpers. But it is imperative that helpers help themselves before they start to help others. As all healing starts in the mind, constructive rescuers are willing to look inside themselves to face the source of their pain in order to become more effective. And they systematically discuss their own thoughts and needs with a supervisor or mentor who will help them see what they are unable or unwilling to admit to themselves.

It is not always easy to take an empathic, tolerant, accepting, compassionate, and realistic view of our own humanness. Being an effective helper can be a very challenging proposition. It can be difficult to tolerate not knowing; to be silent with others in a moment of despair or confusion; to be with others in difficult times of grief and bereavement. But effective coaches are prepared to face these issues and accept personal vulnerabilities while doing so. What's more, they understand that the nature of the work, and the stresses and challenges it creates in their personal lives, will cause distress that needs to be addressed proactively. Therefore, constructive rescuers accept that ongoing self-care is needed to prevent burnout and impaired professional competence.

Through self-understanding, helping professionals (including coaches) can raise the quality of their relationships with their clients by becoming aware of their own unique attachments and aversions. By knowing their own limitations, ensuring that they have their own therapeutic support, professional supervision, peer interchange, or other forms of help, they will ensure that they don't fall victim to rescuer syndrome.

## NOTES

1. N. McWilliams (1984). "The Psychology of the Altruist." *Psychoanalytic Psychology*, 1, 193–213.
2. G. Rizzolatti and L. Craighero (2004). "The Mirror-Neuron System." *Annual Review of Neuroscience*, 27, 169–92.
3. H. B. Braiker (2001). *The Disease to Please*. New York: McGraw-Hill.
4. M. C. Lama and M. J. Krieger (2009). *The White Knight Syndrome*. Oakland, CA: New Harbinger Publications.

5. G. E. Vaillant, N. C. Sobowale, and C. McArthur (1972). "Some Psychological Vulnerabilities of Physicians." *New England Journal of Medicine*, 287, 372–5; P. J. Flores (2004). *Addiction as an Attachment Disorder*. Lanham, MD: Jason Aronson.
6. P. Casement (1985). *On Learning from the Patient*. London: Routledge; W. Dryden and L. Spurling (Eds) (1989). *On Becoming a Psychotherapist*. London: Routledge; M. F. R. Kets de Vries, K. Korotov, and E. Florent-Treacy (Eds) (2007). *Coach and Couch: The Psychology of Making Better Leaders*. Basingstoke: Palgrave Macmillan; M. F. R. Kets de Vries, L. Guillen, K. Korotov, and E. Florent-Treacy (Eds) (2010). *The Coaching Kaleidoscope: Insights from the Inside*. Basingstoke: Palgrave Macmillan; S. Bager-Charleson (2010). *Why Therapists Choose to Become Therapists*. London: Karnac.
7. R. Tillet (2003). "The Patient Within—Psychopathology in the Helping Professions." *Advances in Psychiatric Treatment*, 9, 272–9.
8. M. F. R. Kets de Vries (2006). *The Leader on the Couch: A Clinical Approach to Changing People and Organisations*. London: Wiley.
9. P. Mellody (1989). *Facing Codependence: What It Is, Where It Comes from, How It Sabotages Our Lives*. New York: HarperCollins; J. R. Gordon and K. Barrett (1993). "The Codependency Movement: Issues of Context and Differentiation." In J. S. Baer, A. Marlatt, and R. J. McMahon (Eds). *Addictive Behaviors across the Life Span*. Newbury Park, CA: Sage.
10. J. Edelwich and A. Brodsky (1980). *Burn-out: Stages of Disillusionment in the Helping Professions*. New York: Human Sciences Press; E. Lakin Phillips (1983). *Stress, Health and Psychological Problems in the Major Professions*. Washington, DC: University Press of America; R. Hale (1997). "How Our Patients Make Us Ill." *Advances in Psychiatric Treatment*, 3, 254–8; C. Thompson (1998). "The Mental State We Are In: Morale and Psychiatry." *Psychiatric Bulletin*, 22, 405–9; T. M. O'Halloran and J. M. Linton (2000). "Stress on the Job: Self-care Resources for Counselors." *Journal of Mental Health Counseling*, 22, 354–65; Miller, G. (2001). "Finding Happiness for Ourselves and Our Clients." *Journal of Counseling and Development*, 79, 382–5.
11. R. Payne and J. Firth-Cozens (1987). *Stress in Health Professionals*. Chichester: John Wiley & Sons; E. Heim (1991). "Job Stressors and Coping in Health Professions." *Psychotherapy and Psychosomatics*, 55, 90–9; A. Ramirez, J. Graham, and M. A. Richards et al. (1996). "Mental Health of Hospital Consultants: The Effects of Stress and Satisfaction at Work." *Lancet*, 347, 724–8.
12. J. Bowlby (1982). *Attachment and Loss, Vol. 1: Attachment.* (Rev. edn) New York: Basic Books.
13. E. H. Erikson (1956). "The Problem of Ego Identity." *Journal of the American Psychoanalytic Association*, 4, 56–121.
14. J. Bowlby (1982). *Attachment and Loss, Vol. 1: Attachment.* (Rev. edn) New York: Basic Books; M. Ainsworth, M. Blehar, E. Waters, and S. Wall (1978). *Patterns of Attachment*. Hillsdale, NJ: Erlbaum.
15. H. Feifel, S. Hanson, R. Jones et al. (1967). "Physicians Consider Death." *Proceedings of 75th Annual Convention of the American Psychological Association*. Washington, DC: American Psychological Association; R. Pfeiffer (1983). "Early Adult Development in the Medical Student." *Mayo Clinic Proceedings*, 58, 127–34; G. Gabbard (1985). "The Role of Compulsiveness in the Normal Physician." *Journal of the American Psychiatric Association*, 254, 2926–9.
16. B. J. Seelig and L. S. Rosof (2001). "Normal and Pathological Altruism." *Journal of the American Psychoanalytic Association*, 49, 933–58.
17. M. F. O'Connor (2001). "On the Etiology and Effective Management of Professional Distress and Impairment among Psychologists." *Professional Psychology: Research and Practice*, 32, 345–50.
18. D. Malan (1979). *Individual Psychotherapy and the Science of Psychodynamics*. London: Butterworth, p. 139.
19. H. Kohut (1977). *The Restoration of the Self*. New York: International Universities Press; K. D. Neff, K. Kirkpatrick, and S. S. Rude (2007). "Self-Compassion and Its Link to Adaptive Psychological Functioning." *Journal of Research in Personality*, 41, 139–54.
20. J. A. Kottler (1993). *On Being a Therapist*. San Francisco, CA: Jossey-Bass; C. Feltham (Ed.) (1999). *Understanding the Counselling Relationship*. London: Sage.

# 3

# THE COACHING ASSESSMENT: A *SINE QUA NON*

Executive coaching is an art, not a science. As in other professions, however, the art can only happen when form and function are blended with imagination and sensitivity. Take medicine, for example. Although the best doctors are known for their intuition and ability to see connections where others do not, their expertise arises from years and years of training, and reliance on well-defined protocols for diagnosis and treatment. The same kind of rigor should be applied to the art of coaching.

To be effective as a coach, coaching sessions should be structured, pragmatic and goal oriented. But at the same time, coaches' intuition and listening skills must be engaged in exploring the intricacies of their clients' inner and outer worlds. Coaches must also have a clear understanding of the context—what is happening in the client's organization? Equally important, coaches must constantly evaluate and readjust, if necessary, their own role in the relationship. Finally, coaches should systematically write up case notes for each coaching intervention, particularly if it has been a difficult assignment—and should regularly work with a supervisor to evaluate their own strengths and areas for development.

Ironically, although this practice of case history evaluation and peer supervision is standard procedure for practitioners in psychotherapy, and consultants generally write comprehensive assessment reports about their projects, we have found that many coaches do not systematically review their coaching interventions. As yet, it is neither an accepted practice for coaches to carry out a careful assessment checklist before launching into a coaching intervention, nor to write up an evaluation or case history at the end of a coaching session. We suggest that the coaching profession could benefit from a more rigorous application of this kind of continual reporting and review, and in particular, we argue that the discipline that this activity requires can go a long way toward preventing tricky coaching situations. Many things can go wrong in a coaching relationship, and some of them are quite subtle. Therefore, all coaching interventions, tricky or brilliant, should be carefully prepared pre-session, and evaluated post-session. This has proved to be one of the most effective methods to learn and progress as an effective, responsible coach.

A thorough assessment in the early sessions can help prevent one of the most frequent causes of coaching derailment: The client is not fully engaged or willing to be coached. Although this seems obvious, in practice many coaching relationships fail because the coach or client has reasons to go through the motions—lucrative fees, for the coach, or a promised promotion, for the client—but the real motivation for change is not there. To be sure that both parties are engaging in an exercise that they can both commit to, during or after a preliminary meeting, the coach should consider several key themes. First of all: How motivated is the client? What is the client's true objective? How realistic are the client's expectations for the outcome of the coaching sessions? Second: Has the coach taken the time to fully understand the organizational context? Is he or she clear about what others in the organization expect from this particular coaching intervention? Is the coach certain that there is not a hidden agenda that could be harmful to the coaching relationship, or to the client? Third, coaches must be honest about their own motivation and capacities. What are the key factors that made me accept this assignment? What are the potential failure factors that I should look out for? Is it possible for me to feel empathy for the client? Does the client appear to have a degree of psychological or personal problems that goes beyond what I am trained to deal with?

In this chapter, we propose a template, designed to help coaches think through the potential issues that should be considered as they prepare and carry out a coaching intervention, and provide a written record that can be shared with a supervisor, or referred to later if a similar case arises.


## COACHING TEMPLATE: ASSESSMENT AND EVALUATION THEMES

### Section 1: Personal information

The first task is to compile a comprehensive picture of the client. Not only will the coach learn details that might provide clues to behavior in later sessions, but in addition, the client will usually find that a conversation about demographic details is often a non-intrusive and natural way to begin a coaching relationship. The coach will want to ask about (and later write up) the following details:

- Name, age, date of birth, marital status, number of children, ethnic status, religion, education, occupation, social class, and other observations.

The coach may also ask about the client's personal history. The coach may not want to ask these questions directly, but should inform himself or herself about these details as they become relevant to the coaching intervention. He or she may touch on the following themes:

- Childhood: Personality traits, behavior problems, social/family relationships, school experience.
- Marriage (partnership): Age, times married, current relationship, children.

- Education: Highest attained, academic success.
- Occupational history: Current job, previous jobs, relationships, career aspirations.
- Social history: Interpersonal relationships, group activities.
- Present social situation: Living arrangements, income, social environment, risk behavior, stability.

## Section 2: Information about the organization

The coach will have discussed the organization and the goal of the coaching interventions with the client as well as other related organizational members when setting up the initial contract, but it is good practice to cover this again with the client in the first sessions—noting in particular any differences in perspective between the people involved. The coach will also look for differences in "official" roles and responsibilities, and what the client perceives these to be in reality. The coach should ask about

- People in the organization whom *the client* believes should be interviewed by the coach.
- The nature of the organization, the industry, and challenges for the future.
- Organizational role analysis: How the client sees his or her role currently, and how it may evolve in the future.
- Organizational culture: Looking below the surface, what can be learned about the culture; is there a culture of blame, short-term results, with employees seen as disposable commodities?
- Organizational traditions, symbols, and artifacts: What kinds of rituals are important in the organization? What about the office layout? Is the building open and welcoming?
- What is happening to the organization's socio-economic environment?
- What can be said about the organization's leadership?

## Section 3: Chief issues, coaching objectives for the client

As with the questions about organizational objectives, it is good practice for the coach to discuss the client's concerns and objectives in the first sessions. It is not unlikely that as the client discusses his or her issues, new concerns and different goals may emerge. In addition (as we saw in the case of Marc, the veterinarian, in the Introduction to this book) the client may have motivators or desires that lie below the surface, and delicate, repetitive detective work will be required on the part of the coach to make sense of them.

Here the coach will need to carefully assess not only whether or not the client's goals are realizable, but also if there are any hidden potential secondary

43

gains that might hinder the client's ability to take action. Most high-level executives who work with a coach already know what their strengths and weaknesses are—in fact they are struggling to close the gap between what they know they should do, and their motivation to do something about it. A perfect analogy is the individual who knows he should stop smoking, but just can't do it. He knows all the health arguments, and is convinced he should stop—until he lights up the next one. Upon greater analysis, however, it is possible to uncover the secondary gains that the individual is reluctant to give up: He enjoys taking a break every few hours to meet his colleagues outside the building; he likes the aura of danger and excitement that seems to go with smoking; he is genuinely afraid that if he were to give up smoking, he would lose his creative edge, or start eating too many sweets and get fat, and so on. In this analogy, the client's real commitment is to protect what he sees as the greater advantages of continuing to smoke, compared to the relative advantages of quitting. Anyone who tries to convince him (or help him) to stop smoking, is going to get the socially desirable (or brush-off) response of, "Yes, of course you're right, I'm really going to stop this time," followed by yet another failed attempt.

When discussing goals and objectives with the coachee, here are some points to be considered:

- What kind of political processes impact the way the client functions?
- How astute is the client about these political, informal processes?
- What does the client see as the problem?
- How well does the client understand the problem? Furthermore, is the client focusing on the real problem?
- How will the client know when the problem is solved?
- What is the gap between the existing and desired state?
- Concerning the client's problem, are there boundaries that need to be taken into consideration (i.e., different parties who have a stake in solving the problem: HR, CEO, a superior, the organization as a whole)?

## Section 4: Action planning

Until the coach feels that she or he has fully discussed the perceived secondary gains that might hinder the client's ability to change, moving to the next action stage is precipitous and might even be counter-productive. When the coach and client feel that they have brought the client's motivators and hidden resistances to light, and outlined objectives that meet the client's underlying desires, they can then discuss the following:

- Action to be taken before next appointment: This might be in the form of experiments or specific, measurable, action steps.
- Personal action: What action is the client responsible for?

44

- Organizational action: What needs to be done within the organization to support the desired action?
- Support system: Who will help the client and give feedback on progress (could be people in the client's personal or professional realm).
- Potential derailers: What factors does the client need to be aware of that might discourage or prevent her from taking the desired action?

## Section 5: Psychological impressions

Although a good executive coach will instinctively conduct a kind of psychological assessment of coachees, it is important to take note of these details at each session, and compare change or evolution over time. The coach might consider the following:

- Appearance: Overall impression, posture, clothes, grooming, health.
- General behavior: Mannerisms, gestures.
- Attitude toward coach: Cooperative, hostile, defensive, seductive, evasive, ingratiating.
- State of consciousness: Lethargic, alert, hyper-alert.
- Attention: Concentration, attentiveness.
- Mood: Overall emotional state (sad, happy, depressed, elated, anxious, irritable).
- Thought processes: Flight ideas, evasiveness, obsessions, rituals, delusions.
- Judgment: Ability to make rational decisions.
- Insight: Does the client realize that there are issue(s)/problem(s).
- Motivation: Level of energy, willingness to take action.
- Anxiety symptoms: Physical and emotional.

## Section 6: Coachee's apparent strengths (note those that apply)

- Secure sense of self and sense of self-efficacy.
- Social confidence and effectiveness in building relationships.
- Ability to deal with problems proactively.
- Capacity to reframe experiences in a positive way.
- Motivation to spend time on self-reflection and self-analysis.
- Capacity to handle depression, being reasonably resilient to stress and pressure.
- Persuasiveness in dealing with others.
- Ability to balance assertiveness with respect of opinions and feelings of others.
- Being organized, indicating a considerable degree of conscientiousness.
- Playfulness, open to thinking outside the box while maintaining a sense of reality.
- High level of engagement in all principal activities.

## Section 7: Coachee's apparent weaknesses (note those that apply)

- Conviction of personal worthlessness due to feelings of rejection and self-hate.
- Problems with intimacy: Intense longing to be loved combined with the conviction of being not really lovable.
- Feelings of being alone, of not belonging anywhere.
- Considerable distrust of the motivation of others: Not reaching out to others/not much of a team player.
- Feelings of anger, resentment, guilt, hostility, and depression.
- Impressionistic rather than fact-based decision-making.
- Strong preference for rules and regulations, indicative of restricted openness to change.
- Low achievement orientation.
- Keeping busy at the cost of reflective capacity.
- Pessimistic outlook on life: A preference for worst-case scenarios.

## Section 8: General observations (note these or any others that apply)

- Client is easily distracted.
- Client has difficulty sustaining attention for most tasks in play, school, or work contexts.
- Client has trouble listening while others are talking.
- Client has difficulty following through on tasks or instructions (procrastination).
- Client has problems getting organized.
- Client has difficulties with complexity.
- Client has trouble with time management, e.g., is frequently late, hurried, doing things at the "last minute."
- Client is forgetful; has a tendency to lose things.
- Client makes careless mistakes; has poor attention to detail.
- Client daydreams/fantasizes excessively.
- Client is restless or hyperactive.
- Client has trouble sitting still, e.g., is fidgety.
- Client talks excessively.
- Client is impulsive (doesn't think through his/her comments or actions before they are said or done).
- Client interrupts or intrudes on others (e.g., butts into conversations or games).
- Client is anxious.

## GOING DEEPER

In some cases, the coaching intervention may seem to reach an impasse. There may be lack of progress, or the client might disregard elements of the coaching contract that were previously agreed on. Here the coach may need to step back and consider the possibility that the client is resistant to change for some reason. The client might be struggling with issues related to personality traits, or behavioral blind spots, that he or she cannot conceivably give up. For example, an executive (we'll call him Liviu) with whom one of us worked was convinced that his aggressiveness toward superiors, and protectiveness of his team, was not only necessary and effective for his role, but was a part of his value system that he was not willing to change. On the other hand, the CEO of the company clearly stated (in a 360-degree performance review) that although Liviu was clearly capable of a VP role, his tendency toward angry outbursts, and his seeming exaggerated defense of his subordinates, was garnering him some powerful enemies. All this came out in early sessions, with Liviu stating honestly that he knew this, but was not motivated to change his behavior. In fact, he was thinking about leaving to start his own company.

There was no point in coming up with an action plan to help Liviu address these behavior patterns without a better understanding of where they were coming from. In subsequent sessions, we discussed Liviu's earlier life experiences. It turned out that he had grown up in Romania as one of the four sons of a man who had been highly educated but, like most men of his generation, had suffered a loss of autonomy under the regime of Ceauşescu. As the oldest son, Liviu had felt a continuous, suppressed rage generated by his father's helplessness and dismay at his ruined life, and protectiveness toward his (Liviu's) younger brothers. Although when the coach met him, he was a top executive in an Italian company, his extraordinary story of escaping Communist Romania in 1980, leading his younger brothers to a refugee camp in Italy, gave the coach greater insight into Liviu's reluctance to change behavior patterns that had been essential to his survival in the past. But he was listening carefully when it was pointed out to him that behavior that had once been important for survival might no longer be relevant at this point in his life. For Liviu, the outcome of this exploration was that he agreed to reevaluate (rather than try to abruptly change outright) these particular behaviors, and moderate them if he felt they were inappropriate in a particular situation. He was able to do this quite successfully.

Discussions like this about past history can be quite an eye-opener for the coachee. Another way to help coachees think about their behavior patterns—such as lack of self-confidence or over-confidence, reluctance to take a leadership position, repetitive issues of conflict, and so on—is to work with them to complete a family genogram.[1]

Genograms are great tools for mapping families, giving both coaches and clients an overview of family relationships and patterns. When clients are involved in the genogram drawing process, they may feel more comfortable talking about certain relationships, losses, or histories. The genogram also opens up a natural means for the coach to gather information for the life-planning process. But when introducing genograms to clients it is also important to highlight that some sensitive and painful memories may emerge when exploring the family.

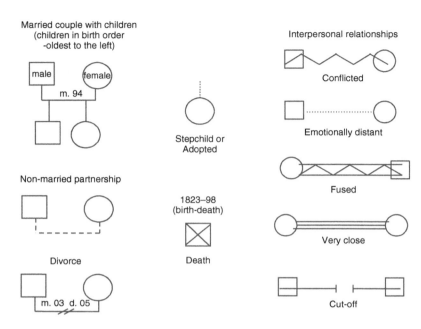

FIGURE 3.1 **Basic symbols used in drawing genograms**

To use a genogram with a coaching client, begin by drawing a family tree, then adding the symbols shown above (see Figure 3.1), where appropriate. The value of the exercise in the coaching context lies in exploring behavioral patterns that coachees may be reproducing unconsciously in their professional relationships. Without having to go into details about transference and counter-transference, the coach may point out to a client that her conflicted relationship with her younger sister is similar to the relationship between her mother and her aunt— and also that it appears to be playing itself out in the client's interactions with younger women in her organization. Once brought to light, these behavioral patterns can be evaluated and, if the client agrees, a plan of action to correct them can be laid out.

## A family story: The Baldinis[2]

The genogram below was sketched out during a coaching session, and gives some clues about succession problems in a family business between two sisters, Julietta and Cordelia. Julietta had joined the family firm after graduating from university, and had thrived as a marketing director. Her younger sister, Cordelia, had a successful career outside the firm. All was well until their parents, Julio and Olivia, announced that they wanted to retire, and that Julietta and Cordelia's husband

Romeo would be the next-generation leaders. The problem was the increasing conflict between the two sisters.

The roots of the conflict between two otherwise happy and successful women were not easy to discern. Her coach asked Julietta to indicate the relationships among the generations of the Baldini family on the family tree, using simple genogram symbols (see Figure 3.2).

As she was completing the genogram, Julietta recalled the period in her life just after her beloved grandmother Maria died, which coincided with the arrival of her own sister Cordelia. Maria had been the primary caretaker for Julietta, while Olivia worked full time in the family business; but when Cordelia was born, Olivia took on caring for the children herself. As an adult, Julietta still remembered feeling lonely and ignored in those days, as she mourned the loss of her grandmother, while her mother's attention was distracted by the new baby.

After drawing the appropriate lines on the genogram, Julietta herself recognized the impact events had had on her and her sister. She admitted that as an adult, she knew that she was not treating her very accomplished sister fairly, but she had never understood why she found the younger woman so irritating. At the same time, she realized that Cordelia might have been jealous of the close relationship that her older sister had with their father Julio. Julietta was beginning to see that outdated relationship patterns were still affecting their lives and the family business. Helped by a coach, Julietta began to rethink her relationship with her sister, reframing it so that she could interact with her sister as an adult

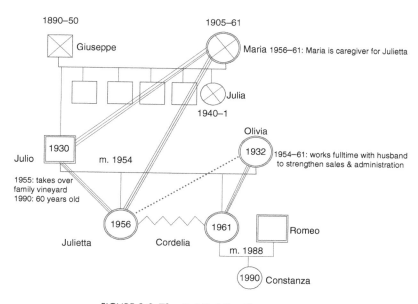

FIGURE 3.2 **The Baldini family genogram**

partner who would be an asset, with her husband Romeo, to the family business they all loved.

## THE COACH: A SELF-ASSESSMENT

Last but not least, we recommend that each coach should draw up a personal checklist or code of conduct as a guide to evaluating their own motivators and performance. It is a good idea to think about themes like these before and after each coaching project. The questions are simple, but if a coach answers them honestly, they can help avoid tricky coaching situations.

- Am I truly the right coach for this person?
- Do I feel overwhelmed by the coachee, or do I feel in control?
- Have I clarified who owns the problem I have been asked to solve?
- Do I understand the coachee's underlying motivation and resistances?
- Am I aware of how this coachee affects me?
- Have I noted and reflected on each session with this coachee?

To put it even more simply; before, during, and after every coaching session, the coach should ask himself or herself: How has this client affected me? What does the client really need? Have I been effective or ineffective in helping the client today, and how can I be more effective tomorrow?

## NOTES

1. M. Bowen (1978). *Family Therapy in Clinical Practice*. New York: Basic Books; M. F. R. Kets de Vries, R. Carlock, and E. Florent-Treacy (2007). *Family Business on the Couch: A Psychological Perspective*. Chichester: John Wiley & Sons.
2. This vignette and genogram first appeared in R. Carlock and L. Van der Heyden (2005). "Trouble in Tuscany: Exploring Business Family Relationships." *INSEAD Case Study 04/2005-5279*. Fontainebleau: INSEAD.

# PART TWO: THE TRICKY COACHING CASES AND COMMENTARIES

# 4

# THEMES IN TRICKY COACHING

Part Two of this book presents the coaching cases selected by the editorial team from the contributions to the first ESMT Coaching Colloquium held in Berlin in December 2009. Submissions to the Colloquium were based on real, challenging coaching assignments faced by leading coaches from all over the globe. Our participants had faced a variety of difficult situations, and as we listened to their stories, we identified several fundamental and recurring themes.

Management of the relationships between the coach, an individual coachee (or a group of coachees), and the client organization were often tricky. For some of the coaches it was challenging to establish a working alliance with a coachee; for others, it was not clear whether they should continue working with a coachee despite the progress being made. For still others there was a change in the contracted theme and scope of services. Some coaches found it difficult to separate the different roles associated with their engagement with the client. Some coaches found themselves over-engaged in their coachee's situation, and some were confused between the various roles, beyond that of coach, they played in the situations described in the cases. Many were puzzled about the outcome, and were curious to know if it was possible to identify themes or patterns in these interventions that might inform coaches in similarly tricky situations. We'll elaborate here on some of the key themes we identified running through the coaching stories.

## A SYSTEMIC APPROACH

Although critically important in coaching, a systemic approach can be described quite succinctly: Know the client, and know the client's business. Surprisingly, we find that many coaches focus too much on one or the other, cutting themselves off from important background information and avenues for exploration.

### Know the client

Although the focus of leadership coaching in organizations is primarily work-related, thinking that we can ignore the dynamics of executives' lives beyond their office buildings is unrealistic. Family dynamics may be a critical aspect of work-related situations, and are omnipresent in any coaching issue within

53

a family business. Personal concerns and real or perceived challenges may have an impact on the coachee's view on the world in general, and work-related issues in particular. Even seemingly positive aspects of a coachee's organizational life—a promotion, an opportunity to do an executive degree program, a long-desired expatriate assignment—may be fraught with ambivalence for a coachee who evaluates them by other criteria. These might range from a partner's concerns about the effect a promotion would have on their life, to deeper psychological concerns, such as doing better than a parent, with all the Oedipal repercussions.

Failure to ignore issues beyond work, and an inability to understand the personal interests and stakes involved in the coachee's behavior or intent, may lead to a tricky situation in which the coachee will not be fully engaged in the exploration of his or her issues and options, or where the commitments made in the light of pure business interests would eventually conflict with personal interests. At times, coaches encourage executives to make changes in their behavior based on suggestions made by colleagues, bosses, or subordinates. How often do coaches help executives get feedback from non-work stakeholders (their children, spouse, and friends)? Coaches sometimes choose to interview coachees' co-workers. What would happen if they did the same with other stakeholders?

We are not suggesting that coaches make an immediate call to their clients' partners or children. Setting up such a discussion may be a necessity in the context of a family business engagement, but in other types of coaching interventions it may be neither necessary nor possible. Still, we believe that exploring the issues at work in a broader light, including the impact of intended change on the coachee's personal life, may be a way of dealing with some tricky coaching situations, such as resistance.

## Know the client's business

A coach should have a full picture of the coachee's organization, including an overview of the industry, and challenges for the future. The coach should analyze the coachee's formal and de facto organizational role, looking for gaps between the job description and what the coachee actually does. In addition, the coach should seek to understand the organizational culture. Is it a culture of blame, a focus on short-term results, with employees seen as disposable commodities? Or is it a place where people see value in their work and enjoy what they do? Are the leaders of the organization innovative and open, or paranoid and controlling?

## THE TRICKY COACHING THEMES

### Fluidity of coaching roles

Despite the claims by coaching practitioners and writers that coaching and consulting are separate phenomena, the reality of the profession is such that boundaries are fluid. Coaches often position themselves as consultants, and consultants may call themselves coaches. In fact, when we interview coaches or look at their credentials, or websites, we notice that quite often they identify themselves as "consultant" and "coach" simultaneously. Some claim that consulting engagements can be supplemented by coaching, or that coaching methodologies can be used in consulting work. Adding to the mix are psychotherapists who have received further training in executive coaching; these professionals will naturally use a psychodynamic approach. These overlapping skills may well be complementary; however, the coach should be aware of any fundamental philosophical difference between their own blended approach, and the expectations of the recipients of the service. It is not uncommon to find that the organization paying the bill has different expectations for the coaching intervention than the coachee; if they are not addressed, such philosophical variations in approach can devolve into misunderstandings or worse. Although a background of varied experiences can be tremendously valuable for the coach, and enriching for the client, responsible coaches will be aware of their own natural inclination to slip back into their former identity of senior executive, psychotherapist, or consultant.

Consultants are usually hired for their expertise, with the understanding that they will find a solution to a problem that has been identified and accepted by the client. Coaching, however, is primarily about helping coachees define their goals, find the focus of their work, identify the options, and make choices. We definitively do not share the point of view of purists in executive coaching who claim that a good coach never gives advice. At times coachees may simply not have the requisite knowledge, experience, or connections to act immediately upon insights that arise from a coaching intervention. In this case the coach may help the coachee by offering examples, sharing stories, suggesting sources of information, or even providing specific recommendations. The coachee, however, has the right to accept or reject the advice; coaches should be very careful not to push for their own view, however convinced they may be that they are right.

Many of today's coaches originated in executive ranks in business or in consulting companies, and have accumulated a lot of knowledge, experience, and workable solutions. As you will see in some of the cases that follow, a consultant who is able to switch into coaching mode can be extremely helpful to a client. We are more wary, however, of a coaching assignment that moves too far into consulting territory, simply because we have seen too many examples where a consulting, advice-giving stance can hinder coachees' ability to explore and identify their own solutions. A coach with a successful consulting background should be wary of turning a coaching session into a consultation. Similarly, former executives who have transitioned into a coaching role should watch out for their own potential tendency to slip back into the mindset of a senior executive dealing with a subordinate facing problems. They may even start demanding certain behaviors from the coachee, which can be disguised as "homework" or post-session practice assignments. Finally, coaches with psychodynamic training may focus too closely on the individual and his or her family system, without giving enough attention to the organizational context in which the coachee needs to evolve. Our point is that coaching relationships differ from psycho-therapeutic interventions, consulting relationships, and executive–subordinate relationships in organizations. Combining consulting and coaching approaches, and/or an over-reliance on psychotherapy, may lead to misunderstanding of the role expectations on the part of the coachee, frustration on the part of the coach, and a lack of desired or effective outcomes.

### Respecting the coaching contract

Although the failure to draw up a proper contract is often seen as one of the deadly sins of coaching, it is still not unusual to see difficulties emerging in a coaching relationship because of inattention, misunderstanding, or lack of full disclosure on the part of the coachee in the early stages of the engagement. The coaching contract, both in its official form (the objectives of the engagement, rules, compensation, reporting outcomes, and so on) and, more importantly, in its psychological form (safety, confidentiality, stable perimeters for time and place of meetings, and so on), defines the expectations of coach and coachee, and also of the organization, which is often the coach's client (represented by human resources or learning and development executives, as well as the coachee's direct boss, subordinates, colleagues, etc.).

The psychological contract defines the boundaries of the coaching relation-ship, and the degree of penetrability of those boundaries. For example, the coach may find it useful to interview various stakeholders before, during, or after the coaching engagement is completed. At times the coach may participate in the day-to-day life of the executive, observing her or him in action, possibly engaging in "live coaching," working with the "here and now" experiences of the coachee concerned. For example, the coach may attend a meeting run by the coachee and, if agreed in advance, invite those involved to go to a meta-level and observe what is going on in the process of the meeting. Obviously, the psychological boundaries and implications of this approach should be clarified in the contract; any kind of intervention that involves other people, beyond the coachee, will have an impact on the whole system in which the latter operates. Other figures in the system, pur-suing their own agenda, may try to use the situation and the coach in order to pass messages, accentuate certain things, and even jeopardize the well-being (profes-sional or personal) of the coachee. Proper contracting will protect the coachee, and also permit the coach to work openly with others in the organizational system.

### Managing boundaries, saying "No"

At times coaches may find themselves becoming very involved in the stories or realities of their coachees. The introductory chapters in this book have provided several examples of how coaches' past experiences or current needs might lead them into a tricky situation. This is obviously a loaded theme: Finding the moment when coaches should warn themselves and their clients that the relationship is going beyond the boundaries that keep the engagement productive and healthy for both parties. The problem is that at times the client does indeed need help, and may have no one else to turn to or trust. The rescuer in the coach (as described in Chapter 3) kicks in, and the coach becomes over-involved in the issues faced by the client. The desire to "rescue" the coachee can be so powerful that coaches may be driven to ignore their own feeling of discomfort that the intervention has moved out-of-bounds.

Another aspect of failure to manage boundaries is related to coaches expanding the intervention into areas where they are not sufficiently competent or confident. At times, moving beyond one's competencies is related to the possibility of increased earnings: The opportunity to continue levying high fees may be a strong inducement to stretch the boundaries. At other times, it may not be greed, but rather a perceived opportunity for the coach to resolve some other needs—such as the need for feeling important to someone else—that may come into play, even if the continuation of the coaching engagement makes no financial sense.

### Coach, or hired assassin?

About ten years ago we came across a newspaper article about coaching, which at the time was really gaining momentum throughout the world. It gave an example of a coach charging a hefty fee for an assignment in which he had to deliver a message to a senior executive in a global organization about his poor personal hygiene, which was causing significant problems to his colleagues and subordinates. Apparently, despite a consensus that something needed to be done, nobody in the organization dared to deal with the issue, because of the explosive character of the executive concerned and their personal discomfort about confronting someone about such a sensitive issue. Finally, an advanced HR manager decided to use a coach for this purpose. Apparently, the coach walked into the executive's office at the time of the scheduled coaching session and said point-blank to him: "You stink!" Allegedly, the client organization was very satisfied with the job done by the coach.

Although this type of assignment may sound interesting to some coaches, due to the efficiency of their time involvement, being a hired assassin is never a satisfying task. The smelly coachee story is funny, but touches on a real problem: All too often the organization uses coaching as a way to deal with an executive it cannot confront directly. Moreover, coaching may be used as a disguised way of suggesting deficiencies to the coachee, or even hinting that the latter should be looking for job opportunities elsewhere. Coachees, in their turn, might also (consciously or unconsciously) try to use the coach to influence specific individuals or the organization at large. Most often, it's a battle that the coach can't win. In fact, the underlying objective in the case of the hired assassin is to do just what the term applies: Get someone else to do the dirty work, and take the blame.

The coach may realize that he or she is being used by the organization or the coachee for reasons different from those used to justify the need for the coaching engagement. Of course the job is sweetened by the regular paychecks for coaching services, and it is entirely possible for a coach to make a real difference for a coachee who might be truly suffering. But in this type of coaching intervention, the coach should be honest about the potential rewards and risks.

## The influence of values

Another tricky coaching situation we've observed has to do with the conflict among various values held by the organization, the coachee, and the coach. Leadership coaching interventions seldom involve very young and inexperienced people. Usually those who make the decision to involve a coach (buyers of coaching services), the coachee, and the provider are experienced and, in most cases, objectively successful individuals. From their point of view their success is inherently linked to their beliefs and values. However, those values or beliefs, which have been productive up to a certain point, may now be insidiously hampering their growth in a new position. A somewhat clichéd but illustrative example is the shop floor team leader who is promoted to a management position, and continues to climb the executive ranks. Where should his loyalties lie? How should profits be used: Salary increases for workers, or dividends for shareholders? And what would his father, a loyal union man all his life, have to say about this?

Although coaches are usually advised to accept clients "as they come," coaches may be drawn to clients who seem to have values similar to their own. Some coaches choose not to take an assignment if there is a value conflict (for example, we know individuals who would never coach an employee of a tobacco or weapons-manufacturing company), and this has the merit of being an honest and clear position. Very often, however, the real differences in values are revealed in the course of the coaching engagement. The coach may find that some of the coachee's statements or expressed beliefs conflict with values the coach holds fundamentally unquestionable. One striking example is when coaches become aware of some kind of sexualization of the workplace, with harassment or gender politics at play. Most people have strong, and often polarizing, beliefs in this area, and it can be difficult for coaches to separate the challenges of the coaching assignment from their own desire to influence the situation.

It is not easy to identify and discuss opposing differences in values in a manner that does not make one party feel undervalued or humiliated. People—coaches and coachees alike—resist being forced to accept others' differing beliefs. However, coachees can be encouraged to revisit values if they can see that those values originate in a past that is no longer relevant in their current organizational context. Courage and a high dose of emotional intelligence are required on the part of the coach—but skillfully handled, this type of conversation can become a learning experience on how to address value conflicts for the coachee. A coaching engagement is often the right environment to explore strongly held beliefs, and evaluate the influence of those beliefs within the context of the organization. Quite aside from the role the coach might play in helping executives explore their own beliefs and values, this can be a helpful exercise for coaches to look at the sources and effectiveness of what they hold dear to their own heart.

## The safe environment

We have touched on the theme of psychological safety, but we would like to elaborate on this important theme a bit more. The principles of psychological safety are critically important for the success of a coaching engagement. When people receiving coaching services feel threatened, ridiculed, or humiliated, they have the natural instinct (not to mention the right) to protect themselves. Defensiveness on the part of coachees can be counter-productive if it is not brought up and discussed in the coaching session. We often hear coaches say that coachees' defensiveness makes it difficult for them to achieve what they think the coachees need. Worse, we frequently hear them complain that organizations that use individual coaching, team or group coaching, or leadership education interventions fail to provide a safe environment, thus diminishing the potential effect of coaching. But to what extent do coaches reflect on their own role in building trust with their coachees? Interestingly, whereas coaches will often report a coachee's explanation for a failed coaching intervention, we very seldom hear a coach reflect on whether or not he or she was able to create a psychologically safe environment. In our previous books,[1] we have covered in great detail the questions of psychological safety and its role in coaching and executive development. The emphasis we would like to make here is on the responsibility of the coach to create such an environment—particularly in an organizational context in which protecting the safe space is not easy.

The task of creating a safe environment goes far beyond the actual session that takes place between coach and coachee, or coaching group. It involves defining the purpose and place of the coaching intervention in a bigger scheme of HR or leadership development programs; careful contracting; dealing with the stakeholders who are not directly involved in coaching; selecting intervention tools (such as psychometric or feedback instruments); evaluating relationships between the coaching sessions and other inputs received by coachees (e.g., performance feedback discussions when coaching is done in organizations, or teaching content and materials when coaching is done in the context of executive education); and the timing and physical space of the intervention.

## Owning change

It would be unrealistic to think that coaches are perfect individuals who are always capable of applying to themselves the ideas or methods that they offer to their clients. Coaches' conscious and subconscious reactions to situations or other human beings may be more or less productive for achieving a collaborative working alliance. The same can be said for their willingness to engage in exploration and experimentation, and their desire for personal success. As coaches are enmeshed in the net of their clients' issues, as well as their own emotions, hopes, concerns, and anxieties, it may be difficult for them to keep a constant eye on the self as a critical tool in the process of leadership coaching.

When coaches misinterpret or ignore the role (positive or negative) their own behavior plays, the coaching situation may become really tricky. The discipline of reflecting on the role of self, for example through supervision and peer-supervision sessions, is critical. Recognizing one's own challenges and limitations requires courage. Coaching also requires a certain degree of humility, in that coaches should be honest with themselves about their capacity to be of use in a specific context, and also in acknowledging the extent to which the coachees themselves deserve the credit for successful interventions. If we truly believe that the bulk of work in making changes and moving forward is to be done by the coachee, the same principle should be applied to the way we allocate credit for the outcome: Most of it should be seen not as the coach's achievement, but rather as the result of the hard work of the executive concerned.

## From "quite good" to "even better"

Another subtle but important theme running through the cases is the coaches' willingness to look at their own interventions critically, asking, in effect, "How can I improve next time?" The way we perceive and deal with our own coaching interventions is one of the most accurate predictors of our progression in growth and maturity as coaches. This means not only thinking honestly about mistakes, but also not being too harsh on ourselves. If we take the time to deconstruct the experience—what we did wrong, what we did right—we become accustomed to assessing the ambiguities and paradoxes that arise in all coaching interventions. Here again the coaching profession should be informed by the therapy protocol: The only real failure is failing to reflect on what the therapist did this time, and what they could do better in the next session. If we as coaches develop the habit of debriefing coaching interventions with trusted colleagues or supervisors, then coaching interventions that were good enough will evolve into interventions that are even better. None of the tricky coaching cases you will read here were catastrophes, and some might not seem very difficult to an outside observer. But even when it appears that the problem is essentially that the coachee is stuck or the intervention is stalled, the case authors themselves mention the usefulness of writing up their case notes and discussing them with peers.

## A meta-theme: The psychodynamic lens

The leitmotif that runs through all coaching interventions, whether successful or tricky, is the coach's awareness (or lack of awareness) of what lies beneath the surface. Any coaching intervention takes place at two levels: The visible (actions, decisions) and the hidden (interpersonal and systemic forces that influence beliefs and behaviors). To be fully prepared to deal with underlying streams of influence, a coach should have some familiarity with psychodynamic concepts.

Coaching as a leadership development intervention has great potential at both individual and organizational levels. But far too often leadership coaches and executive education providers only see the obvious, and miss the hidden dynamics that affect interpersonal and team dynamics. As a result, change initiatives may be oriented toward the quick fix. But real, lasting change will not occur if the out-of-awareness dynamics that underlie surface behavior are ignored. Because we want to go beyond the quick fix, much of our work in organizations is grounded in a psychodynamic orientation. The goal of this approach is to help people to revisit past experiences and expand their freedom of choice to explore new challenges in life. It is essential for healthy functioning that we do not remain strangers to ourselves.

This approach can be described metaphorically as a way of exploring an individual's inner theater. Behind the curtain, we all have a rich tragedy-comedy playing out on our inner stage, with key actors representing the people we have loved, hated, feared, and admired in our lives. Here we find memories and desires that are connected with emotions, some positive, some negative. To have a better understanding of ourselves and others, we need to identify the recurring themes and patterns that come up in connection with these key figures, and explore any repetitive attempts to avoid distressing thoughts and feelings. These transference or counter-transference reactions may be repetitions of relationships that were important in the past, but are now acted out inappropriately in the present.

Transference can be viewed as a "false connection," an unconscious redirection of feelings from one person to another. In other words, perceptions and expectations that evoke a figure with whom one had experiences in the past, may be projected onto someone else in the here and now. For example, a team leader may admit that she has an "inexplicable" dislike for a new, younger woman who has joined the team from another department, despite the young woman's obvious professional talent. On reflection, the team leader might discover that the young woman reminds her of her own sister, with whom she has always had a conflictual relationship—for which the new member of the team obviously cannot be blamed.

Counter-transference is a similar process, but seen from the perspective of the coach. Like transference, it occurs when the coach begins to project his or her own unresolved conflicts onto the client. In the past, counter-transference was seen as an impediment to treatment, as such feelings can be damaging if not properly recognized and managed. Nowadays, however, counter-transference is seen as an important source of data for the coach to use in helping the client.

To summarize, our early key relationships affect not only the way we love, choose friends, or express ourselves as adults, but are also reflected in our inter-actions with bosses, colleagues, and subordinates. They affect the way we make decisions, our leadership style, and many other aspects of our work, as well as non-work related parts of our life. We all bring our own inner theater, with all its tragedies and comedies, to the workplace.

We often say that working in organizations can be like trying to navigate through a field of icebergs: Much of the danger lies hidden below the surface. This concept also helps people visualize the overt and covert interpersonal dynamics that can affect team performance. We remind people that even in organizations:

- All human behavior, no matter how irrational it may seem, has a rational explanation.
- Our unconscious plays a powerful role in determining our actions.
- Motivational needs systems create the triangle of mental life: Cognition, emotion, and behavior.
- We all have blind spots and defensive reactions that make it difficult for us to explore our own inner theater.
- Our emotions shape and influence our identity and behavior.
- The past is the lens through which we can understand the present and shape the future.

This approach of examining a coachee's challenge or tricky coaching situation, and the coach's response, with a psychodynamic "lens" can be valuable when thinking about key themes in tricky coaching situations. This is not to say that all coaches must be psychotherapists—but we believe that in addition to basic business knowledge and common sense, a coach should be able to go beneath the surface to interpret his or her own behavior, the possible unconscious motivation of the coachee, and the group and systemic dynamics at play. In addition, we insist that a grounding in psychodynamic concepts prepares coaches to "do no harm," by allowing them to set the boundaries and scope of each intervention. In other words, coaches should be able to recognize patholo-gies or situations that are outside of their area of training or expertise, and not hesitate to refer the coachee to other professionals for evaluation, even if this means terminating the coaching contract. As the proverb says, "a little knowledge can be a dangerous thing," and a smattering of psychodynamic techniques used improperly is no exception. To summarize, we believe that responsible coaches will have a level of psychodynamic awareness and train-ing that allows them to go far enough and deep enough with in a coaching session: Dealing with the rational reasons for ostensibly irrational behavior; evaluating past experiences and reframing future possibilities; watching for transference and counter-transference; thinking systemically—but neither too far, nor too deep.

## REFLECTING ON THE THEMES WHEN READING THE CASES

We recommend that the reader reflects on these themes as he or she works through the cases presented in the following chapters. It will soon be clear that the cases often reflect more than one theme, and that the themes we have listed here are neither exhaustive nor mutually exclusive. In fact, to an extent, they may all be present at the same time, and singling out one principal causality (which aspect of the coach's performance triggered which theme) may not be easy. However, without attempting to do this, we may lose the learning opportunities the case authors present to the reader. The uniqueness of the opportunity for all those entering the profession, securing their position in it, or moving it forward is that the multilayered case studies presented by these leading coaches—and we would like to underline their remarkable courage and humility once again—will allow others to learn vicariously and reflect on their own practice.

We recommend that the reader starts by reading a case carefully, and before looking into the commentaries or the case author's post-case note, takes a couple of moments to reflect on the following:

- What themes appear in the case? If you were a coaching supervisor working with the coach, what themes would you find important to explore with the coach in a supervisory session?
- Is important information incomplete or missing? How does this affect the way you evaluate the case?
- What kind of emotions or feelings are you experiencing now that you have read the case?
- How would you feel if you were the protagonist (the coach) in this case?
- How would you feel if you were the coachee in this case?
- What makes this case tricky? Could the trickiness have been prevented? Could the coach have prepared the intervention in a different way?

After you have worked through these questions, read the commentaries written by other coaches, then reflect on the following:

- Has your first impression of the situation changed after reading the commentary?
- What, in your opinion, is the most valuable part of the commentary for the coach in the case?
- What is the most valuable part of the commentary for you?
- With which parts of the commentary do you agree and disagree?
- If you were asked to provide the commentary to this case, what would you say?

We suggest that you finish by reading the post-case note provided by the author (presented after the main case narrative and commentaries). We suggest the following reflection points:

- How do you feel about the outcome or end point presented here?
- What, in your opinion, could the protagonist (the coach) learn from the experience reflected in the case and the commentaries provided?
- What have you learned for your own practice as a coach or executive?

You will notice some difference in the degree to which the case authors go into detail about the overall situation in which the patient is embedded, motivations of various parties involved, issues of family history (at times very remote ones) that can shed light on the current situation, and the coach's own feelings and reactions to what is presented to her or him.

Some of the cases do not offer much information about the past of the coachee or the issue he or she is facing. When working through a particular case, you may feel that additional information could have helped your understanding of what is going on. Ask yourself if the coach was asking the right questions, and reflect on the questions you would have asked.

Chapters 22–24 include three cases without commentaries. This is the opportunity for you to make your own attempt at figuring out what is going on, how the people mentioned in the case are affected, and what you learn about yourself as you explore this case study.

Our suggested questions for reflection are just one way of using this book for learning about coaching or reflecting on your own practice. The cases might also be discussed in a small group workshop or in a coaching course classroom. Participants may discuss their reflections on the cases and commentaries, write their own comments, or role-play a supervision session with the coach. Engaging in discussions with others may be a great opportunity to learn not only from the cases and comments presented in this book, but also from diving deeper into the experiences of other coaches and learning and development professionals who have similar stories to tell.

**NOTES**

1. M. F. R. Kets de Vries, K. Korotov, and E. Florent-Treacy (2007). *Coach and Couch: The Psychology of Making Better Leaders*. Basingstoke and New York: Palgrave Macmillan; M. F. R. Kets de Vries, L. Guillén, K. Korotov, and E. Florent-Treacy (2010). *The Coaching Kaleidoscope: Insights from the Inside*. Basingstoke and New York: Palgrave Macmillan.

# NO JOB FOR A HERO

## *GRAHAM BARKUS*

*Case summary*

Graham Barkus discusses the dilemma of a coach facing a client whose well-established defense routines prevent him from making a substantial and much-needed change. The situation is exacerbated by the challenging personal circumstances of the individual involved, as well as the management team's reluctance to take ownership of the coachee's developmental challenges. Management seems to outsource the issue to the coach.

*Context*: The case takes place in the technology department of a multinational financial services organization in Singapore.

## BACKGROUND

Some clients believe—wrongly—that a coach is some kind of troubleshooter who will parachute into their organization and solve all their problems for them. Others mistakenly think that a coach will act as their enforcer and collude with them to impose their will on colleagues and staff. In the case I am about to describe, I encountered both types of client within the same organization.

The main client was the technology department of a large multinational financial services business based in Singapore. The department employed about 350 people and was led by a team of 13 senior managers, one of whom—my coachee—had special responsibility for developing new business models. The company was in the second year of a major five-year program of corporate reorganization, and my coachee (I shall call him Lee) had been given the task of managing the change process for his management colleagues.

Lee had interpreted his role as one of a leader and saw himself as the individual responsible for driving the group development process and directing his colleagues along the correct path. In practice, the way he approached his task had the opposite effect and contributed significantly to dysfunction within the group. Although it was clear to his superiors that Lee was actually compounding existing problems rather than finding solutions to them, Lee appeared to be completely unaware of it.

In fact, he was convinced that he had the answers to all the problems he was being asked to solve. When I began coaching him, he assumed that my role was to support him in persuading those around him to follow his lead rather than to help him analyze his role and make changes to his own behavior.

This was tricky enough. But while Lee's bosses readily acknowledged that the person they had appointed to run the change process was making things worse, they did nothing to address the problem themselves. Indeed, they valued Lee's sincerity and conscientiousness so highly that they seemed unable to criticize him and give him effective feedback. Compounding the problem was Lee's personal situation. He was an expatriate whose extended family overseas was heavily dependent on his income; in particular, his young son, who had been badly injured in a road traffic accident and was now severely handicapped, required specialist medical assistance. I later learned that in the immediate aftermath of his son's accident, Lee felt that the medical care being given was inadequate but had given way to the trauma team when they insisted they were doing the right thing. Now, convinced that he had been right all along, Lee blamed himself for not having intervened more forcefully.

The fact that Lee was such a likeable and well-intentioned person, who appeared passionately committed to both the change process and his own professional development, prevented his bosses from tackling him head-on. In fact, they didn't appear to see it as their problem—in their eyes, it was mine and they had chosen to outsource their dilemma to me in the hope that I would provide some organizational development magic to resolve the situation.

Lee's role in the development of new business models meant looking for ways to improve processes and systems, identifying opportunities for efficiency and productivity gains, and a loosely defined notion of change management. Under Lee's management, much of the technical activity of the department had, over the previous five years, been outsourced in the interests of cost effectiveness and the role of the senior management team had become less technical and more to do with managing the outsourced suppliers.

The department was now undergoing a significant restructuring (of which the outsourcing initiative was a part) in an attempt to tackle problems and create efficiencies through more systemic methods of working. A key element of this was to replace the old culture, in which senior managers focused on their own area of specialization, with a new culture in which cooperation and collaboration with colleagues was paramount. Under the old regime, most decision-making was more about the will of one individual overriding the others.

## MY ROLE AS COACH

I was brought in as an organizational development specialist to help the team discover and understand how their working culture and interpersonal dynamics were getting in the way of executing their strategy and securing the desired efficiency gains. My approach was to set up workshops, individual and group coaching, and case-in-point teaching sessions with the management team to help them bring about changes in the way they worked among themselves and with suppliers. While the brief sounded good, there was little in the way of real ownership of the problems affecting their interpersonal dynamics by any one of the executive team members. While they each acknowledged the team dysfunction, they tended to see it as a group thing that they as individuals could not address. Only somebody from outside the organization could solve it for them.

## THE CHALLENGE

My interviews with the team revealed that they all shared three basic views of their organizational challenges: First, "soft" skills or interpersonal effectiveness were irrelevant and a waste of time; second, they all believed that the problem lay with their colleagues and not with themselves; and third, they believed the problems were the fault of top group executives who, while pretending to be setting a clear agenda, could not in fact agree on corporate strategy. Lee was the only exception. He claimed to be fascinated by people and development issues; he read extensively on interpersonal effectiveness issues and had undertaken executive education in a number of psychological disciplines. And he frequently expressed frustration at the inability of his colleagues to see what, to him, seemed blindingly obvious—that it was the way they worked as a team that was getting in the way of improvement. Lee told me that he had personally identified significant opportunities for business and efficiency gains but felt blocked by his colleagues' lack of vision: "They just don't get it, they think I'm just a maverick," he told me.

Lee's frustration was compounded by a fear for his own future in the company. Whether this threat was real or imagined, it was a significant issue for Lee because of his personal circumstances. Not only did he have to keep providing for his family, but he also held himself absolutely accountable for his son's condition. The belief that his failure to insist more forcefully on better treatment had resulted in his son's severe handicap had a massive impact on Lee's attitude to his work, as he explained to me: "I learned the most important lesson of life: Never rely on others to make decisions—if you know what needs to be done, insist on it being done and avoid the tragic consequences of inaction." It is not difficult to see how this played out in Lee's working environment. Despite all his reading and enthusiasm for positive psychology and group dynamics, he was unable to apply any but the most rudimentary techniques of what he thought of as interpersonal effectiveness. In particular, what he saw as advocacy and encouragement was seen by his colleagues as exhortation, coercion, and the imposition of his own worldview. When his attempts to persuade his colleagues failed, Lee became disengaged and fell into a mood of self-loathing and paranoia exacerbated by the fear of losing his job and the means to support his family. Consequently, his instinct was actively to solicit my partnership in changing the behavior of his colleagues and showing them the error of their ways—although he remained blind to his own contribution to the problem.

## MY APPROACH

My approach was to use both individual and group coaching sessions complemented by individual profiles generated through a leadership behaviors 360-degree survey instrument, the Global Executive Leadership Inventory (GELI),[1] that each member of the executive team had completed.

The main elements of the coaching process included:

- Supporting the senior team in their efforts to frame the case for change and address the "adaptive challenge" (as opposed to the "technical" challenge, which simply requires doing what is currently done only harder, faster, or smarter). Adaptive challenges require learning, experimentation, and the discovery of new problem-solving techniques.
- Group workshops to describe and define the best leadership culture for their future organization.
- Feedback from those directly managed by the executive group to enable us to identify the biggest gaps between the desired leadership culture and current practice.
- Workshops for the executive group and project teams involving some members of the executive group to highlight areas where the desired leadership culture was not being applied.
- GELI feedback.
- Individual coaching.

The GELI feedback for Lee included some useful insights into how other people perceived his actions. We explored the gap between what he intended to achieve and the actual impact of his behavior; most of our coaching sessions ended with Lee focused and optimistic about small incremental changes he'd committed to in order to modify his operating style. Unfortunately this inspiration seemed to last about as long as it took for Lee to leave the meeting and return to his office. He would return to our next meeting feeling helpless and unable to cope with the actions of others, which he felt not only prevented him from trying to modify his own behavior, but also increased the pressure on him to deliver. He was caught in a cycle of paranoia, self-loathing, and consequent inaction. Curiously, his professed interest in areas such as positive psychology and interpersonal effectiveness actually made the situation worse. He would assimilate the theoretical concepts he'd read about and instead of using them as tools to help him manage changes in his own behavior he would internalize them as "knowledge" that he now possessed and needed to advocate to others. Thus each new piece of insight he gained was transformed into a crusade to "help" others see why they ought to change their own behavior.

## BREAKING THE IMPASSE

The main challenge I faced with this assignment was to find a way of breaking through Lee's well-established defense routines to help him reflect on his own behavior while remaining mindful of his personal anxieties and insecurities. At the same time I had to re-establish the executive team's ownership of the problem and convince them that only they had the solution. To do this, Lee's bosses needed to take an active role in addressing Lee's shortcomings and providing him with critical, but supportive, feedback. And one final challenge for me was to ensure that I remained objective and focused and did not become blinded to possible solutions by my own response to Lee's predicament.

## NO JOB FOR A HERO: COMMENTARY 1

*Sandy Stadelmann*

I will start with my understanding of the situation faced by the coach. The author was brought in as an organizational development practitioner on a brief to help the client deal with interpersonal dynamics that were getting in the way of business outcomes. The tricky part of the case relates to Lee, one individual participant in a group coaching process within a large department of a multinational organization going through a change process. Senior executives find themselves unable to give Lee effective feedback about the impact he is having on his peers and the change process itself due to their empathy with his positive intent in the organization and personal situation. The coachee is described as a person who actively takes it upon himself to lead the change process and who relies on a strong, action-oriented dogma based on experience in his personal life: "Never rely on others to make decisions—if you know what needs to be done, insist on it being done and avoid the tragic consequences of inaction." Lee is apparently unaware that his behavior contributes in a significant way to dysfunctions within the group. He has a generalized and disrespectful opinion of his peers that places him outside of the group: "They just don't get it, they think I am just a maverick." Lee seems to regard this as one reason why his good ideas aren't implemented. Lee also fears losing his job and feels pressure to deliver. He wants Graham, the coach, to help him persuade the others to follow his lead. Lee seems to be intellectually fascinated by psychological literature and the importance of soft skills.

To deal with the difficulties described, Graham may want to consider the two following questions:

1. How can the coach find a way to break through well-established defense routines to enable Lee to reflect on his own behavior and impact, while being mindful of his personal inner theater and its deep and painful roots?

The coachee knows something has to happen, since he perceives that pressure on him is growing. His "operating temperature" for coaching seems sufficient but needs to be steered away from *changing others* toward *working on himself and/or the aspects he can influence.*

In a first step, the coachee could be confronted with the fact that although one cannot change others, one can identify ways to interact more effectively with them. The coachee is open to soft skills knowledge. It could therefore be helpful to introduce him to a personality style instrument such as LIFO.[2] This personality-style survey incorporates a strong humanistic philosophy and supports perspective shift, as well as a systemic view. The basic thesis of LIFO is that knowing yourself and understanding and respecting the styles of others is a key to self-reflective and effective interaction with others. The survey would:

- Give Lee an opportunity to better understand different styles and their strengths.
- Help Lee to understand his own strengths and the effect they have on others.
- Help Lee to better understand his peers and stakeholders.
- Help Lee to learn how to adapt and control his behavior to make interactions with others richer.
- Help Lee to learn how to adapt his argumentation to reach his goals successfully.

In addition to this first step it could be helpful to analyze how his dogma fits with the fields to which he is applying it and perhaps work out a more appropriate dogma for the business context he is in.

Furthermore, it could be helpful to take a closer look at the goal he is trying to reach (what exactly is his task/refinement of his task and his role?) and reflect mutually on which activities and behavior would be most appropriate to reach these goals.

2. How can the coach find a way to support the senior executives play the role they need to play in terms of giving Lee performance feedback, while they continue to be paralyzed by the fear of confrontation and the risk they perceive of opening up deep wounds related to Lee's personal life?

The way of giving feedback very much relates to the national cultures involved. Whereas giving feedback directly from executive to subordinate is expected in "individualistic" cultures, it is not appropriate in "collective" cultures. Within an individualistic culture, the coach could draw attention to the importance of feedback for learning and the effects of failing to give feedback. It could be helpful for the senior executives to learn how to give constructive, respectful feedback and how to take stress out of stressful conversations. Additionally, they should reflect on what they value in the way Lee performs his role, what they expect from the subordinate on a personal and a business level, and how they measure his success. After this the performance feedback could be given.

## NO JOB FOR A HERO: COMMENTARY 2

*Svetlana Khapova*

This case involves the emotional engagement of both the coachee, Lee, and the coach, Graham. Based on Graham's case presentation, the coachee is incapacitated by emotional challenges. The case gives an impression that the coach is too engaged in the story and does not feel comfortable with it. In order to help the client, the coach needs to disengage emotionally; if this not possible, it would be better not to continue with the assignment.

The way the case is presented puts a heavy weight on the emotional side of the situation; there is very little emphasis given to the objectives that need to be achieved by all parties involved, and the organizational processes that facilitate or hinder progress. It seems too simple to suggest that issues of one individual are contributing to the dysfunctional developments of either the group or the whole organization. Lee demonstrates one particular style of behavior. An organization includes many different people, all with different behavioral styles. The management needs to address the general culture and dynamics in the organization at large and this specific group in particular.

One important point is that it is difficult or even impossible to change an adult. Thus, I don't believe that any critical feedback on Lee's behavior would help. Instead, I suggest redefining the role of the change process leader, and even find a way to split this role in two. Only one part of the role would remain with Lee. For the second role a new person should be appointed.

I recommend that Graham should consider whether or not to continue with this coaching case at the individual level. I also recommend him to address the overall group dynamics, as well as the culture of the group and organization. Splitting the leadership role in the change process, as I suggest, may be explored with the senior executives.

## POST-CASE NOTE

*Graham Barkus*

When I presented this case at the ESMT Colloquium in December 2009, I was interested that delegates suggested my objectivity might have been compromised with this client. The observation that I could be taking on something of a personal crusade rather than focusing objectively on what my role is or should be was salutary. I knew the executive team preferred to see the problem as mine rather than theirs, but I hadn't realized how close I had come to fulfilling their expectations. Two critical elements became patently clear after the small group process in the Colloquium. First, there were two clients here: Lee himself and the executive team, which included his bosses. Although they were connected and although both clients needed help to play their respective leadership roles, they required separate interventions. I needed both to be clear about that and to choose where my focus should be.

Second, I had yielded to a subconscious desire to become the troubleshooter the executive team thought they were hiring. Playing the hero was blinding me to where the real work was and I was falling into what adaptive change theory describes as "work avoidance." I was busying myself doing what I knew how to do and what I felt comfortable doing but I wasn't asking myself what the real work was and what role I should be playing. More importantly I didn't ask myself whether some of the work needed others to lead rather than me.

Reflecting on this feedback it was clear I had started to become wedded to the idea that I was the person who would find the solution, even though I knew that the executive team needed to take ownership of the problem and not ascribe it to me. Perhaps even some of the characteristics I was observing in Lee—in particular his belief that he knew the answers to the problem—were, at least in part, projections of myself onto him.

Given my role as coach and a specialist in organizational development, it was clear that my primary client was the organization. Lee and his bosses in the executive team were only the representatives of the client but it was they who had created and were sustaining the impasse. Certainly, Lee did need help and support—but from another source, not from me. My job as a professional coach in an organizational context was to identify the issues, make them discussible, and support the leaders in implementing the solutions they designed. This was no job for a hero.

## NOTES

1. M. F. R. Kets de Vries (2005). *Global Executive Leadership Inventory: Facilitator's Guide.* San Francisco: Jossey-Bass.
2. LIFO—Life Orientations www.lifo.com.au. Accessed September 26, 2011.

# 6

# WHEN CONSULTING CLIENTS NEED COACHING

## *ANTONIO GALVAN LUNA*

*Case summary*

Antonio Galvan Luna presents a consulting assignment in which he suspects that his clients have a greater need of coaching. He discovers that there are parallel agendas within a family-based business that require different treatments. The consultant-turned-coach makes a choice of entry point to gain the client's trust and later uses it as a foundation for building up his case with the business owners and managers involved.

*Context*: The case takes place in Latin America.

## BACKGROUND

"Family, religion, friends . . . These are the three demons you must slay if you wish to succeed in business." These are the words of Charles Montgomery Burns, one of the world's wealthiest fictional characters according to *Forbes* magazine's annual ranking of fiction's richest—the "Fictional 15." And although Mr. Burns lives only in the cartoon world of *The Simpsons*, his words sum up one of the most difficult coaching interventions I have ever performed.

In mid-2008 I was introduced to an entrepreneurial business group formed by six siblings who, between them, own one of the biggest networks of automotive service stations in their home country. The main source of income is the sale of fuel but there are also accessory units within the stations, such as convenience stores, car-wash facilities, and repair services. Most of the stations are situated at key locations on the highway network, making them very profitable, thanks to the high volume of tourist and freight traffic that stops to fill up, rest, or buy something to eat.

The group was founded by the father of the present owners, a successful entrepreneur who started many businesses in several industries. As the founder approached retirement age, he decided to give each of his children a service station as their inheritance. Each of the siblings kept and ran their respective stations and each individually started expanding their business by opening new

73

stations and launching new ventures, ranging from the manufacture of batteries and lubricants to construction.

Thus several new business groups grew up, each operating as a small conglomerate. It is important to note that each of these groups, with their corresponding stations and other business activities, remained independent of each other and in the sole ownership and management of each of the siblings. Consequently the image, management style, legal constitution, and services offered varied from station to station and from group to group. The invisible barriers separating these independent, yet related, groups were accentuated by the wide age-range of the siblings.

The main activity of these businesses—the sale of fuel—was subject to operating under certain peculiar conditions. First of all, the production and distribution of fuel and other oil products was controlled by a state-owned monopoly that licensed service stations to private investors under a franchise scheme. Consequently, most of the service stations in the country were owned by business groups or small conglomerates, creating an oligopoly in which a small number of operators effectively controlled prices and other market factors. Therefore, a few years ago, the siblings decided to take advantage of the number of stations they owned (32), brand them all under a new image, and so generate recognition and loyalty among their customers. They set about creating a new brand and produced a logo that was displayed in all of the stations. All their convenience stores were also branded under a standard name and image and the partners drafted a procedures and identity manual.

In order to comply with the new image and service requirements, the siblings established a weekly meeting during which important issues relating to the new group were addressed. A central coordinator, paid proportionally according to the number of stations owned by each of the members, was hired to deal with common issues like publicity and promotions, and to ensure that all the stations conformed to the new standards.

In the beginning everything looked promising for the new group. The stations and stores quickly adopted the new image and soon a big advertising campaign—complete with jingles, posters, and a friendly mascot—was launched to promote the brand. The group remained strong in the following years and continued to grow, adding a wide array of complementary products and services. Then new threats began to emerge. Another local group set up in competition, then an American chain of convenience stores entered the country and started opening shops at busy locations on the highway network.

## THE CHALLENGE

In response to these developments the group's central coordinator suggested that the siblings hire a business consultant to help them create a solid structure that could deal with the foreign threats while facilitating the gradual expansion of the group. The siblings agreed and I was engaged as their consultant. At this stage, executive coaching was not on the agenda.

The first contact I had with the siblings all together was during one of their weekly meetings where I was given 15 minutes in which to deliver a brief presentation about my work. Right away I knew this was going to be a tricky assignment: The first meeting with a client is usually a busy exchange of information but this time it was totally different. Only about half of the siblings seemed to be listening to me but even they didn't ask a single question; the other half were leafing through their paperwork, checking their Blackberries or talking to each other. Furthermore their father—the founder of the group—was also there and was clearly uncomfortable with my presence. So I was rather surprised when, at the end of my presentation, they all politely welcomed me to the group and expressed their willingness to collaborate with the project.

Having gleaned what I could about the origin and operation of the group and all its business units, my second task was to familiarize myself with the group's command structure. I started attending the two-hour weekly meetings, visiting all the business units, and interviewing a great many of their staff. I soon discovered that, aside from the name and image, there was nothing uniform within the group or any of its business units. Although the weekly meetings resembled something like a board meeting, and even though the coordinator brought up very relevant issues during these meetings, no real commitments were achieved because no one wanted to compromise their managerial and capital freedom. There was no defined expansion plan, because each sibling looked at his or her opportunities individually. While some members saw marketing campaigns or employees' uniforms, for example, as urgent and necessary investments, others didn't. The older siblings favored a more traditional approach to human resources, managing their staff as employees with a fixed salary, while the younger favored operating with associates who received a percentage of the profits. Some wanted to keep total control of all their business units, and saw the coordinator as a threat to their authority, while others wanted him to have more responsibility. When it came to the products and services offered, some favored standardization of, for example, the food sold at the convenience stores, adopting an American prepared-foods style, while others wanted to keep a restaurant-style service, preparing on demand and varying the menu according to the location.

It was not the difference in opinions or styles that really caught my attention, however; it was the fact that these differences were never mentioned or discussed during the meetings. Quite the opposite: During the meetings everything was agreement and commitment. For example, during one meeting they all agreed on "Clean and free toilets" as a distinctive feature of the group's gas stations; yet during my visits I found that some stations were charging for the use of the toilets. When I asked the managers about this, they replied that they were following direct orders from the owners. Another initiative—a loyalty card that accumulated points that could be exchanged for groceries and fuel—was agreed by all but only adopted by a few stations.

One day something happened to change my whole perception of the situation. During one of the meetings I asked the group to tell me what was the real purpose of operating as a group. They answered unanimously and to my great surprise: Promoting the family's integration and unity.

It was at this point that I saw what the real challenge of this project was: The unity they so wanted to promote didn't actually exist. It was clear that the siblings wanted to increase profits and expand as a group and they knew that the group was in an excellent position to achieve this. I could see that the group had market recognition and a sound infrastructure; all they needed to do was standardize systems across the group and introduce better business practices and more agile operations. This would create a solid base on which to build the business model and ensure growth. But getting the members of the family to agree on a common course of action to which all of them would have to commit was the real challenge.

## MY ROLE AS COACH

It soon became clear that the group had failed to make the essential operational changes not through any ingrained resistance to change but simply because they lacked the ability to let these changes happen. Therefore I decided to use coaching methods with the key members of the group—all the siblings and the group coordinator. In order to discover why the operational changes were not happening, I made individual appointments with each of the siblings so that I could get to know them and hear their thoughts away from the scrutiny of the weekly meeting. As I had suspected, it soon emerged that many operational changes had previously been discussed but never carried out.

Crucially, I also learned that while most of the siblings agreed to these changes, many feared that by following them they would lose control over their businesses. Some did adopt certain changes but only within their own groups, thus widening the operating discrepancies even further. And all the while they each held back, anxious to avoid any confrontation that might threaten family unity.

I also found that most of the siblings had a small-business mindset even though their businesses were far from small. Each of them was personally involved in most of the operations; each made most of the important decisions and solved most of the problems. Consequently the siblings were under constant stress and always short of time, while the central coordinator they had hired had no real authority whatsoever. This made it almost impossible for him to implement successfully any initiative that was lucky enough to be approved by consensus.

Almost six months had passed from the beginning of my intervention with the group, and although I already had a lot of information and had identified the main issues within the group, I still felt unsure of how to proceed. On the one hand, as their coach I was required to find ways of encouraging the business owners to establish real goals and effect changes to their behavior without disrupting the family unity. On the other, once they had accepted me, the siblings all began to view me as a friend rather than a business partner. Their trust in me was high and so were their expectations; I felt that they were prepared to give anything in order to help the group. Consequently, although they knew that the solutions they required were not to their liking, they still wanted me to be there to help them.

## MY APPROACH AND THE RESULTS

After some thought, I decided to focus on the one thing common to all the group members: Their lack of time. I related Michael Gerber's remark that if a business cannot run without the owner, then the owner does not have a business, he has a job. During each session I tried to get them to think about the results that had not been achieved and the important things—business and personal—that were not getting done because of lack of time. This approach worked really well with some of the siblings, particularly on the personal level.

For example, one of them told me that he had always wanted to attend a two-week religious retreat in Spain but he was afraid that his businesses would collapse if he took that much time off. I told him that it was the mark of a leader that he can let others take control and responsibility of their functions and (rather to my surprise) he decided to attend the retreat. This, and other similar episodes, increased the siblings' trust in me and eventually I was given the go-ahead to conduct training sessions with the workers in charge of the stations and convenience stores of each of the six groups.

Although these training sessions would not lead to any structural changes, I believed that if I could make the workers in these six independent businesses understand the benefits of collaborating and working as a group, this would help the business owners enormously when it came to making the necessary difficult decisions.

My second course of action was to coach the group coordinator throughout the intervention to help him establish his authority and implement the ideas he had for the group. In my sessions with him he wrote down specific actions that he thought were necessary to better coordinate all the stations and stores uniformly, while I focused on the abilities and skills he needed to put them forward. I then trained him in negotiation and leadership technique, and on some more technical issues, such as making effective presentations.

Last, but not least, I ran group strategic planning meetings with the siblings. The one-to-one sessions I conducted with each of them individually provided me with enough knowledge of the businesses to lead the planning meetings myself. This allowed me, as a third party, to broach the topics and suggestions on which most of the siblings concurred but were themselves reluctant to bring up for discussion. In this way I facilitated an open debate among them, encouraging a regulated but frank discussion of several potentially divisive issues.

During these sessions, I also presented the results of the work I had been conducting with their coordinator, resulting in several of the coordinator's initiatives being taken up and actually put into practice. Among these was a centralized information system in which each group had to upload critical information such as volume of sales, best-selling products, costs, and so on. This system was itself the result of the workers at the operational level understanding the benefits of collaboration between groups and the ability of the coordinator to capitalize on that consensus. I took care to emphasize to the siblings the fact that the resulting benefits, which included stronger buying power and highly effective group-wide promotions and campaigns, had been achieved by letting other people make decisions and without direct instructions from them.

## WHEN CONSULTING CLIENTS NEED COACHING: COMMENTARY 1

*Bülent Gögdün*

I think that the coach has done a great job in analyzing the situation and identifying the real issues behind the scene. The next step could be to confront the siblings with the results of the assessment and let them think about and discuss possible solutions. They are stuck as a group and not able to make any decisions, let alone take action. Two contradictory forces—the desire to put strengths together to enhance business prospects and the desire to protect independence and autonomy—paralyze them. They seem to avoid confrontation and don't address critical issues even though everybody is aware of them. The fear of open conflict that could destroy the family bond leads to hidden conflicts that cannot be resolved. This hinders the establishment of an effective working relationship that would require controversial discussions and contradictory positions.

My recommendation would be to articulate this situation openly as I believe that this would be a big relief, enabling the siblings to talk about what is in their minds and hearts and about the relationships among them. I suggest a subsequent joint search for solutions that will enable a more effective collaboration. Either the coach presents a couple of alternatives or the group develops several options. Finding "the lowest common denominator" could be one possibility. In other words, the group could identify some basic measures they all agree on and start with them. The strategy of small steps could help the group develop carefully the skills required for effective collaboration. Running a pilot project that allows the sibling to test how things could work out, and also gives them the opportunity to step out anytime, is also an option. For instance, agreeing purchasing activities with regards to selected products could be an interesting project that would enable some quick wins. Last but not least, the siblings could also think about the option not to act as "one group." They still could meet regularly, however, to exchange ideas and experiences and to take joint decisions.

I also believe that the desire for change could be increased by:

- Clearly illustrating the dangers and possible losses of not acting together.
- Offering a compelling vision (e.g., we could be the most profitable gas station group in the country; we could double our revenues by coming together, etc.).
- Showing them that change can be tackled in a step-by-step approach with checks and balances so that nobody has to suffer serious disadvantages.

## WHEN CONSULTING CLIENTS NEED COACHING: COMMENTARY 2

*Gerhard Liska*

I would like to comment on two aspects of the case as it is presented here: Understanding the situation better, and creating action.

First, both the client and the coach will be helped by understanding the situation better. Keeping the family together seems to be a key issue for the siblings. Thus better understanding the family system might contribute to finding a solution. The problem is that a family business usually shows a blending of different systems with different evolutionary logic. On the one hand there is the emotionally driven family system; on the other, the more rationally driven business logic.

1. What role does the father of the business owners play? Is he still influencing the siblings and if so, how?

   Better understanding the father's role might indeed reveal new insights into the situation. The situation for the entrepreneur who passes on his life's work is always delicate. It might be difficult for him to understand that his children might have a different approach than his own. For this reason he might be continuing to influence the siblings from behind the scenes, for example, by sharing his ideas and viewpoints with them (with the hidden expectation that his ideas will be taken as the best solution).

2. How does or did the father contribute to maintaining the belief-system of "keeping the unity of the family by avoiding conflicting discussions"?

3. There is a belief, related to a specific gender model, that the man is the head of the family, responsible for the income and representing the family in society, and the woman is responsible for the upbringing of the children and keeping the home. This might relate to a communication and discussion style within the family where open discussion might not take place. Instead, the head of the family will make a decision (perhaps having consulted some others but at the end remaining the decision-maker). It could be that the siblings never had the chance to learn how to make a decision by sharing different viewpoints and agreeing on a compromise. Moreover, there is no longer any decision-making authority in their current situation as they are all, more or less, in the same (hierarchical) position. This could leave them in a dead-end

position where, on the one hand, they might feel the need for change, but on the other, without any best-practice model or conception of how to perform their roles adequately.

4. Is the father still a role model for the siblings?

One hypothesis is that the father presents the role model of a leader who successfully built up his own enterprise. His children would thus also value his specific approach to management and leadership. A second hypothesis is that he also represents the role model of a father who keeps the family united, securing an equal part of his wealth for each of his children by passing his life's work on to them.

It might indeed be difficult for the siblings to join together or follow a different approach to management, as this would violate their father's approach and his status as a role model. It might also violate their picture of him as a father. This is where the family system comes in.

5. What is the motivation of the siblings?

They might have been put into the position of leaders/entrepreneurs without really being convinced that this is the one and only life-task for them. Instead they might have felt obliged out of family loyalty to step into this position. Valuing the unity of the family highly could then be a form of self-protection, helping them to avoid confronting this fact on a personal level.

Based on these hypotheses, I would advise the coach to address the following areas of action:

1. Analyze the influence the family system and/or the father have on the behavior of the siblings.
2. Take the father's position into consideration when planning the next action steps. I would involve the father personally. This could mean, for example, discussing alternative ways of running a business or the different businesses together with the father. These alternatives could include external (foreign to the family) business executives or managers, going public, or establishing a foundation.
3. Bring the siblings, the coordinator, and the father together to reflect on and discuss the role models of a manager and leader.
4. Create or paint a picture of a possible future, with specific focus on communication flows and structure, which would enable the group of siblings to work together more closely. For a first step this imaginative approach should focus on communication and structure.
5. Address the question of if and how the unity of the family can be kept and still allow room for open and possibly controversial discussion.

**POST-CASE NOTE**

*Antonio Galvan Luna*

At the time of the 1st ESMT Coaching Colloquium I was still working on this project. Taking part in the Colloquium helped me enormously with this client, not least because it allowed me to see how frequently this kind of situation occurs in businesses all over the world. This was particularly useful as one of the most frequent arguments I encountered during this assignment was " . . . but our business is different from everybody else's."

When I revealed to the siblings what I had discovered at the Colloquium, they all expressed surprise but accepted my findings. The news seemed to create a greater degree of openness within the group and encouraged the siblings to question their attitudes toward change. Understanding that many other businesspeople around the world face similar situations seemed to create a more receptive attitude and a greater willingness to question their own behavior. On a personal level, the Colloquium provided me with an opportunity to express my concerns about how I should proceed with this case. It was difficult for me, as an "expert" coach, to admit openly that I was struggling to find a solution to the situation with which I was dealing. In this case, a problem shared really was a problem halved.

# 7

# IS HE LISTENING TO ME?

## *AMEL KARBOUL*

*Case summary*

Amel Karboul works with an executive charged with managing a global workforce in a software company. The coachee requests help with intercultural competencies, managing international leadership teams, and dealing with a strategic transformation in the organization. The coach discovers that her client's lack of experience can't be substituted for by coaching, that current success makes it difficult for him and his team to prepare for change, and that constant pressure prevents the coachee from taking time to stop and reflect. While some of the coach's approaches work, with others she reaches an impasse. The coach also struggles with her dual role as coach and consultant.

*Context*: The case takes place in a multinational company headquartered in Europe.

## BACKGROUND

Dr. Martin, head of R&D in a software company, was highly esteemed by his employers and indeed was one of the best software engineers in his field. He led a team of six who reported directly to him and was ultimately responsible for more than 3,000 R&D staff spread over five locations worldwide. When I started working with him, he had been in his post for about one year and was now facing two major challenges.

First, while highly respected as a software engineer, Dr. Martin had very little overseas experience. Based in Europe, he had never lived abroad and was not used to managing an international team. His six-strong leadership team comprised five men and one woman; two were located in the United States, one in China, and the remainder in Europe. Four of them had a background in software development, one was from finance/HR, and another from sales and marketing.

A 360-degree consultation exercise initiated by Dr. Martin to gauge the functioning of his new department revealed that some of the leadership team and the employees they managed had begun to feel dissatisfied with Dr. Martin's lack of "intercultural competence." Some employees outside Europe felt they were less valued by Dr. Martin than those closer to him geographically.

The second challenge was that the company was undergoing a major strategic transformation and moving away from selling products to selling services. This strategy demanded a change of mindset within the R&D division, which had hitherto operated very much as an autonomous entity. In future, R&D would have to engage with the customer at a much earlier stage in the development process and would have to work more closely with other departments, especially sales and marketing. Dr. Martin had a vague feeling that this strategic transformation would mean a significant change in his relationship with the six core members of the R&D leadership team—though how this change would manifest itself he had no idea.

## MY ROLE AS COACH

I was introduced to Dr. Martin by an old university friend of his whom I had coached some years previously. After our initial two-hour meeting, Dr. Martin declared that he wanted to work with me; it was to be his first experience of executive coaching and he had an open mind when it came to the approach taken and the processes involved. Dr. Martin was looking for a coach who was familiar with international work, who had experience in developing leadership teams and who was used to coaching senior executives through major shifts in corporate strategy. I would be working with him over the course of one year. The good news for me was that I would be free to propose whatever I thought was appropriate and would not be bound by the company's long-standing approach, which comprised two hours' face-to-face coaching every four to six weeks.

My role as coach fell into three distinct phases. The first was analysis, during which I interviewed the coachee and the members of his leadership team individually. Following these interviews I sat in as an observer on two leadership team meetings and one big pre-scheduled employee meeting. This gave me a broad overview of Dr. Martin's role and, following evaluation of my observations, I presented them to the coachee at a meeting during which we agreed specific goals for him to achieve over the coming year.

The second phase was the actual coaching process which, as well as several one-to-one sessions with the coachee, involved shadowing him during leadership team gatherings and facilitating feedback sessions between him and his direct reports—both one-to-one and as a group.

The third phase required me to act not only as a coach but also occasionally as a consultant. I had previous experience of supporting clients during their companies' transformation from product to service provider and I used this experience and knowledge to challenge Dr. Martin from time to time.

## THE CHALLENGE

As a coach, I faced three specific challenges in my assignment with Dr. Martin.

1. Coaching is no substitute for life experience.

   Dr. Martin's lack of international experience and of intercultural competence was a major stumbling block. He was open-minded and keen to learn but his natural response tended to be intellectual rather than empathetic. Between us we were seeking ways in which Dr. Martin could appreciate and respond to different cultural traditions and connect personally with his staff around the world. As a white male in his late 40s, Dr. Martin enjoyed a relatively privileged position in society and, unlike many of his 3,000 staff worldwide, had never experienced negative discrimination. Several of Dr. Martin's employees had specifically raised this point during the 360-degree feedback exercise.

2. Why change if we are successful?

   My coachee's knowledge of his product was profound and his internal network very strong. He was a successful senior executive in an internationally successful organization. At the same time, the company was in the throes of a strategic transformation, the impetus for which came from the top; the sense of urgency among employees further down the corporate structure, however, was low. Most members of staff did not see why they should deviate from the strategy that had brought success in the past. My coachee, while entirely committed to making this transformation, was himself struggling to change his well-disciplined and hitherto successful behavior and mindset.

3. No time to refuel the car—we're busy driving.

   The R&D division's entire setup was geared to product releases. In the days and weeks leading up to each new product launch—of which there were three a year—the whole team would be engulfed in a frenzy of activity and it was difficult then to get them to pause for reflection and future planning. As a coach, I found it very difficult to fix dates for coaching activities over a timescale longer than three months.

## MY APPROACH

Dr. Martin and I began by working together to plan a one-year learning journey for him and his leadership team. The main elements of our plan were to try a new routine for leadership team meetings; to introduce group coaching for the leadership team; to shadow and observe Dr. Martin's interaction with the team and provide him with feedback on my observations; to conduct one-to-one coaching sessions with Dr. Martin and to get him to keep a "decision diary."

## Meeting routine

The leadership team's established routine for exchanging information was a fortnightly video conference lasting four hours. Through my initial interviews I discovered that most of the team found it difficult to interact on strategic or behavioral topics during these meetings. The team member based in China found this particularly frustrating and expressed a need to meet colleagues face-to-face more often. A relatively new addition to the team, this individual felt strongly that the video conferences did not allow him to convey to the other team members what was happening in China.

After consultation, the team agreed to supplement their existing fortnightly video conference with five two-day team workshops, one in each location, for a period of one year. I would be with them shadowing, observing, and coaching Dr. Martin during breaks and after the workshops. Allowing for vacations and other scheduled interruptions we held a workshop on average once every eight weeks. This was a significant undertaking for the team but by the end of the year it was clear that this had been the most effective intervention of all.

Discussing the strategy and business transformation in relation to China was far more effective at our workshop there than talking about it during a video conference, or in a European location. The leadership team members, including Dr. Martin, used the opportunity of being there in person to schedule meetings with employees and managers on site. Some of the team visited the lab there for the first time and saw for themselves that China was no longer just a low-cost location in which to outsource boring programming. It had developed into a center of competence for sophisticated software development staffed by motivated and highly educated employees.

Staff turnover in China was very high because these employees were ambitious and disliked being treated as a cheap workforce. The leadership team member from China had spent much of the previous year trying to explain this to the other members but his protestations remained a somewhat abstract concept for most of his colleagues until they visited the site themselves. Dr. Martin, who had visited China some years previously, reported that he was deeply impressed by the tremendous changes that had taken place since his last visit.

As a direct consequence of the China workshop, the team undertook to devote more resources to this location and retain their best people. Similar revelations took place at all four locations outside Western Europe; for example, the leadership team was amazed to enter a full employee meeting in Eastern Europe and find that the average age was 28 (compared to 48 in Western Europe). In this instance it was noted that this younger workforce took on board the strategic shift from products to services far more readily than their Western European counterparts.

Throughout these regional workshops I continued to coach Dr. Martin—during breaks, evenings, and in longer sessions after each workshop—and this allowed him to try new methods directly and get immediate feedback. Dr. Martin was very open about the coaching process, always introducing me as his coach, and over time more members came to me to ask for feedback. Finally, we agreed that I would coach the group in its totality but with the condition that if any member wanted individual coaching, they would have to ask for another coach.

I asked Dr. Martin to keep a diary in which he recorded his decisions. The purpose of this was to allow him to reflect on his thinking at any specific time and see if it was consistent with achieving his main goals of dealing with the issue of cultural diversity and implementing the strategic shift. We held regular coaching sessions in which we would review this diary together and go through decisions he had made on issues of personnel, investment, and so on.

## POSITIVES AND NEGATIVES

My coaching experience with Dr. Martin had many positive features. In particular, the coachee was anxious to learn and eager to increase his self-awareness through group coaching and intense feedback. I found this attitude helped me provide appropriate support and understanding, especially during some of the tougher times. However, there were also factors that I found extremely difficult to deal with.

During the year we worked together, Dr. Martin made many intercultural *faux pas*, most of which were entirely avoidable and resulted (directly or indirectly) from his disregarding my advice. One unfortunate incident happened in the Middle East during one of our five regional workshops. One of the leadership team members, through stress or exhaustion, suffered a breakdown and was temporarily hospitalized. Dr. Martin immediately took a personal interest, taking care of his colleague, and driving with him to hospital. The next day the team was due to leave the country but I urged Dr. Martin to stay a day longer. I felt it was important that Dr. Martin should remain as a sign of support not only for his sick colleague but also for his employees in the lab there. However, neither Dr. Martin nor the sick man himself felt Dr. Martin's continued presence was necessary. Indeed, the hospitalized person insisted he was happy for the rest of the team to depart, confident that he would recover after a couple of days' rest.

Unfortunately, the lab staff felt very differently. When it became clear to everybody that Dr. Martin and the team had left, a small revolution broke out. Almost all the employees felt this was a scandal: How could their boss leave a close colleague in hospital and fly home? There was a strong feeling of betrayal among the lab staff and the sense of outrage was so strong that my coachee was obliged to return immediately in order restore peace and win back the trust of his employees. Dr. Martin had clearly underestimated the symbolic message conveyed by his apparent desertion of a department in crisis.

Three other incidents of a similar nature occurred during our year together and in each case the problem arose after I had given my coachee advice that he decided not to follow. Dr. Martin was fully aware of his own intercultural shortcomings and yet he frequently failed to capitalize on my own intercultural competence. For example, he failed to appreciate the added value of many quite small interventions that I proposed—such as greeting people in their own language, a simple yet extremely beneficial gesture. I felt a great deal of frustration with the fact that although Dr. Martin had hired me explicitly because of my international background, he repeatedly chose not to exploit it. I suspect that my frustration at times influenced my own behavior and that, during debrief sessions following such incidents, my response was somewhat judgmental. As a result, our reflections on these incidents rarely bore any fruit. To this day I wonder what I could have done differently, given the coachee's stubbornness.

Generally speaking, the shadowing, observing, and feedback during group coaching sessions were successful. However some team members (perhaps understandably) tried to exploit my position to get their own messages through to Dr. Martin and influence his decisions. This was often done with great subtlety and I suspect that I was unable to identify and deflect this interference at times.

Of course, throughout this exercise I worked alone and occasionally felt in need of support, especially during the international team workshops. However, Dr. Martin did not want to employ a second coach and it is difficult to see how I might have organized better support within the team.

My personal relationship with my coachee was also a source of difficulty at certain times during our work together. Dr. Martin is by nature very reserved, rational, and physically undemonstrative whereas I am strongly intuitive and can be quite emotional in my response to events. Consequently, I often found it hard to interpret Dr. Martin's minimal body language and follow his take on a given situation. Sometimes, when working with both Dr. Martin and the whole leadership team, I could feel a palpable tension in the room but when I subsequently mentioned this to my coachee he always replied that he had felt nothing. In order to test my own perceptions, I asked the team individually if they too had noticed any tension developing during meetings. Without fail, only two of the six members (and it was always the same two) reported feeling similar tension in the room. The other members of the team felt that I was conjuring up non-existent conflicts from thin air.

Some members of the leadership team wanted more decision-making power but in open discussion and where difficult decisions were required, they invariably drew back and let Dr. Martin make the decisions as usual. This developed into a universally acknowledged pattern. And although everyone talked about changing it, the same behavior always reasserted itself; in difficult situations one party inevitably re-established the status quo. If Dr. Martin remained passive and waited for his team to make the decision, they would eventually push him back into decision-making mode; but if he jumped in with a snap decision, they would complain about disempowerment. Although this pattern soon became transparent, any behavioral change was minimal. All parties were willing to discuss the problem and we talked about how we might break the cycle but there was a deep reluctance to break out, especially in the run-up to a release deadline. I was therefore unable to find any way of dealing with this kind of conscious behavioral pattern.

## IS HE LISTENING TO ME? COMMENTARY

*Nikki Heyworth*
Amel has clearly laid out the three main challenges in this situation. These are:

1. Lack of cross-cultural sensitivity on the part of the coachee.
2. The need for strategic change.
3. Focusing on the important rather than the urgent.

It is good that Dr. Martin has acknowledged that he needs support and is open to change. However, I suggest that he needs to take a reflective look at his role as head of R&D. It sounds as if he has not yet totally made the shift from being a practical engineer to becoming a strategic leader. I have observed that promotion to a senior level can often be the result of functional expertise and success that does not often immediately translate into successful strategic leadership.

Amel comments that it was difficult to set anything up long term due to the frenzy that takes place around release of a new product. I would use this as my starting point to challenge Dr. Martin. The first question I would ask is whether Dr. Martin, as the head of R&D, should be directly involved in the new product launch frenzy. If the coachee is unable to plan coaching sessions that are important for him in the long term, what else could be suffering from his short-term focus?

Amel states that Dr. Martin is supportive of the company's shift from product to solution provider but that he has struggled to change his behavior and mindset as he had been so successful previously. I would ask if the department that has allegedly made a shift from selling products to selling solution has routines that are built solely around product releases. Analyzing why there is frenzy three times a year may be an interesting way to explore whether or not the strategic shift has occurred. I think Dr. Martin himself needs to be very clear why the company is instigating this change of strategy. He currently may be in the "Why change if we are successful?" mode. Until he can shift that belief to "We must change to continue our success," he will not be able to instill a sense of urgency in his team. I would ask him what he needs to do to make that shift. It may be that he needs to spend time with his superiors, those who have initiated the change, to fully understand what has driven it. I would get him to look for evidence that would support the benefit of this shift: Maybe it is something their competitors are doing, or maybe they have done this in one area of the business, or around one product, and it has worked well. Once he has internalized this new belief, he can then think about how to create the mindset shift in his direct reports.

Running alongside this strategic issue is the issue of intercultural competence. I do wonder if some of the cross-cultural issues are actually more a result of lack of strategic leadership, which people are articulating as cultural insensitivity. A question about how, for example, Dr. Martin's European team feels about his leadership might reveal whether there is a cross-cultural issue or a general leadership challenge.

I don't think a middle-aged, male, senior manager who has not lived abroad would be able to internalize diversity and its implications in this situation. I would work with Dr. Martin to revisit the 360-degree feedback results and findings from the initial interviews to look for specific instances where intercultural *faux pas* were made or when the international team members felt undervalued. I would then help him explore these specific examples to understand how he had been perceived and how he could handle each incident differently if it were to arise again. Time constraints are obviously a factor but spending time face-to-face with all his team both one-on-one and as a team would be invaluable in improving his relationships.

I would propose he uses the "strategic shift" problem as a focal point for his leadership team. How do they see it? Have they bought into the necessity for it? Are they aware of the consequences if it is not implemented? I would suggest that based on Amel's previous experience she runs a workshop for the team. This workshop would address the issue of strategic change within R&D. Amel could help Dr. Martin's leadership team explore such questions as the implications of the strategic shift for the team, the appropriateness of the structure to the strategy, the desired end state of the change process, the timeline for change, etc. The question of cultural issues associated with the implementation of the change process could also be put on the agenda. By involving his team in finding the answers to these questions and redefining success in a way that encourages co-creation and collaboration, Dr. Martin could start to make progress, both in driving strategic change and showing the team that they are valued.

## POST-CASE NOTE

*Amel Karboul*

The separation between my dual roles—on the one hand as Dr. Martin's coach and on the other as a consultant assisting in change management—gradually became more and more difficult to maintain. I was increasingly faced with having to decide whether to employ my knowledge of change processes and the transition from product to service provider or to focus solely on Dr. Martin's behavior and his team's effectiveness. Thus I was constantly torn between my duties as a coach and my duties as a consultant.

The usual way of distinguishing a consultant from a coach is that the consultant is an expert who brings solutions and the coach is an expert who helps his clients find their own solutions. However, my consulting practice had evolved over the years. I would describe it as a systemic approach that, rather than attempting to give answers, attempts to enhance the problem-solving capability of the client by asking inspiring, provocative, and challenging questions. Perhaps this is why, in this case, I sometimes found the line between coaching and consulting becoming blurred. It was made even more tricky by the fact that my client did not know the difference between consultant, coach, trainer, etc. As far as he was concerned, they were all the same—all he cared about was that whomever he employed should help him find solutions to his problems. Consequently, discussing the boundaries of my contract with him was very difficult since he did not have the experience to understand these nuances.

Finally there was the question of my status in relation to Dr. Martin's department. His was an "expert" organization, staffed by highly trained people undertaking extremely complex technical work. As an outsider, I did not share any of this specialist knowledge and there was almost certainly a tendency, especially among more junior staff, to question whether I could appreciate their roles and understand the intricacies of their working environment. By the same token, I felt they possibly did not fully appreciate my coaching role. This raises the question of how I could have demonstrated to them that I also have expertise that could "save" them. This is a theme that emerged strongly from the supervision session of the ESMT Colloquium. Some colleagues considered this to be a question of organizational development rather than a coaching intervention. Others wondered whether a motivational dynamic in coaching is the desire to be the "hero" who will change an individual's behavior and in so doing, benefit the whole organization.

# 8

# PICKING UP THE COACHEE'S INSECURITIES

## *PETER BOBACK*

*Case summary*

The client asks Peter Boback to help him resolve a difficult situation—he has been offered an attractive and potentially highly visible and rewarding assignment but despite its attractiveness, he is concerned about the resources available and whether he has the competencies to make the assignment a success. The coachee seems to expect the coach to confirm his pre-established expectations, while the coach is reluctant to reduce his engagement to a confirmatory or advice-giving role.

*Context*: The case takes place within a dynamic, international, high-tech company in Europe.

## BACKGROUND

Very early one morning I received a call from Geoff, a former colleague with whom I had worked during the 1990s and subsequently kept in touch. Geoff had endured a sleepless night, and was tormented by problems at work. Feeling trapped in a situation from which he could see no escape, he called to ask if we could meet and talk.

Geoff works in a dynamic high-tech company where he is in charge of the global leadership development portfolio, organizing and running seminars for top managers. He is a leading expert in his field and works as part of a global network embracing other individual contributors and teams—both within his organization and externally. The nature of his work means he has no formal line management responsibility and no people reporting directly to him.

I began by asking Geoff when and how the problems causing him so much anxiety had started. He traced them back to a voice-mail message from Steve, the organizational head, three management tiers above Geoff and directly below board level. Steve, having seen Geoff performing in his role as director of the company's leadership development program, had clearly formed a good opinion of Geoff—so good in fact that he asked him via voice-mail to take responsibility for setting up and running a global meeting in Miami for the organization's top HR executives from around the world.

The message was completely unexpected and hit Geoff out of the blue. He was immediately thrown into a panic that only worsened when he discovered that the assistant to the HR board director had already been informed of this recommendation and was waiting for a call to arrange a meeting with Geoff in order to start the planning.

Geoff told me that this request had put him under a lot of stress: On one hand he felt pleased and proud to be asked to manage this important meeting. It brought him to the attention of senior managers right up to and including board directors. He felt under pressure to do well, build his reputation, and strengthen his position as a senior expert. But at the same time he felt the weight of expectation was intolerable. Moreover, he doubted his ability to carry out this assignment effectively given his other professional and private commitments.

Taking a realistic look at this request Geoff could see that given the tight deadline it would be extremely difficult to reorganize his current workload and free up enough time for the new task. The availability of staff and other resources for the project was unclear and, to cap it all, it seemed that Geoff would be unable to reconcile this additional task with the holiday plans he had made for his family at the beginning of the year.

His initial response to this dilemma was to think positively—"No risk, no fun" was the way he put it—and he told himself that by taking the risk (instead of paralyzing himself by over-analyzing the situation) he could show the engagement and commitment that his superiors expected of somebody prepared to make his way in the company. Galvanized, Geoff threw himself into a frenzy of activity, working tirelessly to recruit colleagues to join him in this exciting venture. With no team of his own behind him, Geoff's overtures were made to colleagues in other departments, virtually all of whom appeared skeptical about the workload and the scope of the project. Most of them also felt that the extra effort they would be required to contribute was unlikely to be rewarded.

Geoff called the assistant to the HR board director as requested and scheduled a briefing meeting. This provided Geoff with more information on the precise nature of the job and allowed him to get a better idea of what he was taking on. The more he learned, the more he began to doubt he was the right person for the job. The programs he had managed successfully in the past mostly required different skills than those needed to set up and manage a large-scale event. But while he became more hesitant, he felt unable to acknowledge his reservations openly; backing away from an assignment that top management had aimed specifically at him would make him look like a poor performer. There was a very real danger that his career prospects would be irrevocably damaged and that he would be forever branded a "nay-sayer."

And yet Geoff still could not help being seduced by the potential rewards for taking on this project. It was undeniable that people who took on a challenge of this sort without raising too many questions—people who knuckled down and performed with commitment and passion—were invariably rewarded with promotion. Indeed they were often rewarded even when such projects had to be aborted for strategic reasons before they had a chance to deliver tangible results. Geoff felt that passion, commitment, and a willingness to take risks were expected and that a tendency to hold back and ask questions would be perceived as inappropriate behavior. He found himself trapped: If he backed away from this new task, his chance for promotion would be gone forever and he'd be consigned to some backwater. But if he took on the challenge without the time, resources, or experience he needed to ensure success, he could find himself with a huge and very visible failure on his hands.

This was the conundrum that Geoff presented to me when we met. And underlying this crisis there emerged a general uneasiness about his position in the company that had been gnawing away at him for some time. Looking back over the previous three years, Geoff conceded that his performance had not been "too bad"—in fact, when pressed, he admitted that his performance had consistently met (and sometimes even exceeded) the expectations documented in the performance appraisal system. But Geoff is a highly self-critical person and still harbored doubts about his ability to "add value."

Given the need for Geoff to make a decision as soon as possible we agreed to meet again the following day. At that meeting, Geoff told me that after a sober assessment of his ability to meet the requirements of the task—and for the sake of his work–life balance—he had decided there was no alternative but to turn the assignment down. But he still did not know how to do it and was very concerned about the negative consequences of doing so. One of my first questions to Geoff was to ask what had been the opinion and advice of his direct line manager. This question came as a surprise to Geoff—it turned out that his line manager had not even been informed of the original request and that Geoff had "forgotten" to involve him. This sounds ridiculous but is more easy to understand when it is explained that Geoff's department was undergoing its third reorganization in nine months and that his line manager was his fourth in as many years—the role being vacated and filled again on average once every nine to 12 months. Under these circumstances, it is not very surprising that Geoff didn't even consider his line manager as a potential source of support during his present crisis.

## THE CHALLENGE

In some respects, the fact that Geoff and I knew each other personally—even practicing some peer coaching together in earlier days—gave me an advantage as his coach in this case. I knew the company and I understood Geoff's working environment. However, I soon discovered that this personal, professional, and even cultural familiarity could also give rise to difficulties.

The first challenge for me as a coach was the pressure of time: We needed a swift resolution to this crisis and the pressure was on immediately. Consequently,

I felt that there was the expectation that I would give immediate and direct advice about whether Geoff should accept this assignment or not. This created considerable tension because the process of reaching a workable solution to the problem demanded time for reflection and deliberation—time that we did not have.

The essential problem—Geoff's inability to decide whether the proposed assignment was a great opportunity or an impossible challenge that was doomed to failure—engendered a parallel ambivalence within me. This was partly because of our closeness and familiarity; I felt "infected" by Geoff's indecision and found it difficult to remain engaged while maintaining an appropriate distance from the problem.

As Geoff's coach, I saw it as my duty to remain impartial and avoid making the decision for him at all costs. My role was to help Geoff learn how to cope with the crisis and restore to him the ability to make his own decisions. But I very soon began to feel that what he really wanted was for me to give him the strength to believe he could take on this new challenge. In retrospect, Geoff's understanding of the role of a coach differed markedly from mine: Although he outwardly acknowledged that the final decision should be his, I believe that subconsciously he actually wanted me to bolster his confidence so as to prepare him for the challenge ahead while downplaying the risks.

This belief is strengthened by the dramatic way in which Geoff presented the issue and his portrayal of the likely detrimental consequences of turning the assignment down. In the short time available to me it was very difficult to work out the extent to which Geoff's assertion that "No" was not an option was based on a realistic assessment of the situation, and how much was down to his own self-doubt. Here again I found it difficult to take a neutral and impartial view and felt myself being infected by Geoff's own internal conflicts. Intellectually, I could see that it ought to be acceptable to reject a clearly unreasonable request from above, but at the same time I could not entirely suppress the feeling that I was myself being over-cautious and risk-averse.

## MEETING THE CHALLENGE

Together, these misgivings affected me in a way that compromised my objectivity, reduced my room to maneuver, and blurred my thinking. I tried to turn my confusion into a positive factor by analyzing my own response in the hope that this might shed light on the internal conflicts with which my coachee was struggling. Eventually, I was able to reconcile my personal response sufficiently to produce a set of basic principles upon which I could base my interventions.

1. If, having assessed your abilities realistically, you still feel you are not the best candidate for this assignment, accept your own judgment and do not deprecate yourself for this decision.

2. It is better to risk refusing this assignment than to take the risk of accepting a "mission impossible." Say "No" with confidence, even if your refusal to accept the challenge appears to run counter to company culture.
3. Put "caring" before "risk taking." Think of the effects of your decision on yourself and on others.
4. Reflect on the workings of a high-performance ideology that systematically makes you feel "not good enough."

By asking Geoff what the opinion of his line manager had been, I introduced a new element to the situation. Geoff, having hitherto not even considered involving his line manager, now decided to consult him and use his authority within the chain of command to legitimize his decision to turn down the assignment. This also meant that Geoff had to break out of the mindset of believing this was something he had to handle in isolation. He started to reconsider the strategy he had developed for coping with frequent changes in management demographics—namely, performing his job in a vacuum without any expectation of direction from above or, as he put it himself, "despite" management.

Our conversations also had consequences on a more psychological level. Geoff made a conscious decision to stop judging himself as a "poor performer" simply for making a realistic assessment of the gap that existed between his skills and those required for the given task. Finally, he resolved to try and learn to concentrate more on his role within the company and less on the perceived cultural expectations within the organization. He decided to learn to feel comfortable enough to say "No"—even when addressing top management.

## PICKING UP THE COACHEE'S INSECURITIES: COMMENTARY

*Murray Palevsky*

Peter starts his case by describing the coachee's sleepless night. I learn from this that Peter is a very concerned and caring coach and the coachee's angst is affecting Peter—perhaps more than it should? I have a suspicion that Peter may feel over-invested in the client's anxiety, making it more difficult for him as a coach in helping Geoff find a solution. Peter acknowledges this as the crux of the trickiness in the case.

The mandate seems clear. Geoff wants Peter to coach him on the merits of accepting or declining the responsibility to run the Miami meeting. To me, there is also a more hidden coaching mandate and that is for Peter to sensitize Geoff to the possibility of non-either/or thinking. His comment—"No risk, no fun"—sounds like he is trying to convince himself and in doing so, drag the coach into his either/or way of thinking.

Geoff is described as being in charge of the company's leadership development strategy but without line responsibility. In addition, he has no direct reports. This leads me to the conclusion that Geoff feels himself to be a kind of insider/outsider, cut off from day-to-day activity in the company and interacting sporadically with different top managers of the firm. He is at times connected and at others disconnected to the managers he works with. This specialist role makes it a challenge and difficult for him to think of himself as a team player. This is further supported by the fact that he doesn't even think of going to his superior for advice or feedback, ostensibly because he "forgot about him," or because his superior has been changed several times in the last four years.

As I read through Peter's tricky coaching case, his client Geoff reminded me of an over-anxious impresario trying to manage the expectations of a fickle and inscrutable audience. This again made me feel Geoff's sense of isolation.

Does Geoff feel that his career and performance are characterized by either successes or failures? Why is he so stark and self-critical? Moreover, how does shirking family responsibility play into all of this? Is it that he feels that in the event of accepting the assignment and failing to meet the expectations of the top HR board member, he can actually console himself with the guilt of having sacrificed his family holiday on the altar of his unfailing commitment to the firm?

In my reading of Geoff's case, what lies at the heart of the trickiness is the drama he sets up. That is what is tricky for him (as a client). For the coach it may not be necessarily the same. The coach wants to help his client and the client sets himself up as being unable to act and pushes on to the coach the dilemma, in the form of Geoff being stuck.

Why so stuck? Is there no potential here for a more balanced kind of job performance without the highs and lows of sublime success and abysmal failure? Geoff fantasizes about whether he is "the perfect fit" for the Miami assignment, as if somehow he has to fit into a glass slipper. Perhaps the coach can bring Geoff to the realization that he can be a "good enough" fit.

A positive element that Peter has identified is that Geoff is aware of the skepticism for this particular project on the part of the colleagues he usually works with. This is a good thing and Peter could use this element as part of a reinforcement strategy aimed at reinforcing Geoff's perception of his skills set. The people he works with are not described as being part of his team, and collaboration seems somewhat foreign to him. Yet Geoff stops short of recognizing the potential for win/win by saying "No" to an assignment that does not have enough potential for success. This underlines Geoff's preference for performance of any kind above judgment, a point that Peter as coach could expand on. A question he might like Geoff to answer is: What is the worst thing that could happen if you say no and substantiate your position?

There seems to be a fantasy on Geoff's part that his "performance" is a show and as such it should be spectacular. Perhaps what he needs to hear from Peter, is that he is a creative designer of programs and an important specialist member of various teams.

Peter can help Geoff see himself more as a developer of executive talent and not so much of an impresario that simply showcases it. Hopefully this will help to dispel Geoff's gnawing doubts about himself and help him recognize that he does bring value to the company.

I believe that Peter has already demystified the trickiness of this case by showing that he is aware of a few important issues.

1. Peter struggles to keep the appropriate distance and remain nonetheless emotionally connected to the client. Although he claims to struggle, he does it quite well.
2. When the client asks Peter to "Help me believe I can make it," Peter resists the temptation to give Geoff bad advice. Vacillating as a coach can be a good thing, leaving decision-making ultimately in the hands of the client.
3. Peter recognizes that although Geoff wants Peter to guide him, this case is not really about making the correct decision or being right, but rather about understanding all the elements and then making his own judgment call.

## POST-CASE NOTE

*Peter Boback*

Geoff seemed to understand that his doubts about being "good enough" were a product of the corporate culture within which he worked. His decision to stop judging himself as a "poor performer" required a psychological shift and, although I regard this is a positive result, I nevertheless wonder how robust and sustainable this "decision" is. I am not entirely convinced that he will not fall into the same trap the next time similar requests or "opportunities" arise.

Similarly, I came away from this exercise feeling that Geoff might not be ready to give up his desire to be recognized as a smart, top-performing individual with high potential. Despite his insight and his ability to self-analyze, his behavior suggested to me that he still found exposure to high performance expectations very attractive and that he actually thrived on the excitement generated by highly visible tasks, even with an element of ambiguity and uncertainty.

# 9

# UPSETTING YOUR CLIENT, UPSETTING YOUR BOSS

*BEATE HELLER*

*Case summary*

Beate Heller is tasked with helping a management team improve its performance. In the process, the coach realizes that the team considers the affair between their boss and one of their fellow team members to be the main source of tension. The coach has discovered something unexpected that she may not have been meant to uncover, and is faced with the question of whether she should confront the client. The coach's own boss takes a different position from that of the coach.

*Context*: The case takes place in France.

## BACKGROUND

One of the trickiest coaching assignments I have ever attempted took place some years ago when I was employed by a global consulting firm. I was sent to France to coach a team of executives that was rapidly becoming paralyzed and dysfunctional due to hidden conflicts, poor communication, and mutual distrust.

At the time I knew nothing of the team or of the company for which they worked. As far as I could tell I was given the assignment mainly because I spoke French and was thought knowledgeable about French culture and employment practices, having previously lived and worked there myself. The team comprised of seven executives, all in their 30s, five of whom were women and two men. Their boss—Pierre—was a larger-than-life figure in his 50s who had worked with this same company throughout his entire career. He was a company fixture, popular and influential, and a *bon viveur* who had a reputation for wining and dining that he was apparently intent on living up to. Pierre was clearly not very interested in coaching and although not exactly hostile to me, showed no great desire to involve himself in the coaching process. He was quite happy to stand back and let his team—as he put it—"play with the coach" if that's what they wanted.

## MY ROLE AS COACH

Although I knew nothing about this team, I was nevertheless intrigued by this assignment as it had been the team itself, rather than Pierre, who had asked for support. It is quite common for senior managers to employ coaches to help them iron out cultural or behavioral problems within the team they manage; and for reasons that are self-evident, it is quite unusual for a dysfunctional team actually to request a coach. Therefore this particular case seemed very attractive as it is a great advantage for a coach to be assigned to a team that is clearly receptive to intervention. My role as coach was also clearly outlined: To be a neutral expert who would evaluate their team dynamics and help them improve their communications, both horizontally within the team and vertically with the management structure.

## THE CHALLENGE

At our first group session, I presented the team with a fairly straightforward introduction to the characteristics and dynamics of high-performance teams and of typical team roles. I then asked them collectively how close to this ideal they saw themselves as a team. Their answers were surprisingly vague and evasive and they were clearly uneasy speaking in front of each other. Indeed, only three of them spoke at all and it was clear to me that I should begin by conducting individual interviews.

What I heard in these one-to-one interviews was consistent across the team, but even when out of earshot of their colleagues, each team member remained very guarded. Their comments sounded rehearsed and were generally negative: "We do not share information," "So-and-so doesn't respond to e-mails," "It's all getting political," "Confidential matters are only discussed with certain people," and so on. Something clearly wasn't right, but I couldn't tell what it was. I was certain that there was something as yet unspoken behind all these vague and distrustful remarks and I resolved to discover the hidden truth.

My attention soon focused on a particular team member, Pierre's personal assistant Denise, who said nothing at all and clearly seemed to be hiding something. She showed no interest in discussing anything with me; every time I attempted to arrange an interview she made some excuse and moved quickly on. And I was not the only one she kept at arm's length; I noticed that she never stopped to chat with any of her colleagues, either. As for their boss Pierre, he remained completely aloof toward me.

Ten days after my first introduction to the team, Françoise, the oldest team member and the person who had first made contact with my organization, requested a meeting with me on neutral ground—what she termed a "safe" location. We arranged to meet in a local café where she told me that Pierre, a married man with four children, was having an affair with Denise and that this affair—which Pierre and Denise apparently believed was still a secret—was the cause of immense unease within the whole team. Françoise told me that none of the team knew what to do and hoped that I—the expert coach—could find a solution to what had become an "unbearable" problem for them.

## MY APPROACH

### Analyzing the situation

What had at first appeared to be an attractive and relatively easy assignment suddenly revealed itself as a highly complex and potentially explosive situation. My first question to Françoise when she told me of the affair was how the "unbearable" situation manifested itself. She explained that, while everybody in the team knew all about Denise and Pierre's affair, they each—individually and as a team—had to pretend to know nothing. This continual subterfuge and pretence hung like a black cloud over the entire team, explained Françoise, and put every member of the team under enormous strain. Nobody could openly acknowledge that Denise and Pierre's secret had been discovered because to do so would put them in direct conflict with Pierre, which could seriously harm their career prospects within the company. They needed a neutral adviser to do this difficult job for them.

Naturally I became extremely nervous about confronting Pierre about his affair, although this was clearly what was expected of me. How could I confront this complete stranger with his sexual infidelity within the context of a sober business environment? How could I possibly expose him to the inevitable feelings of guilt and shame when I was neither a priest to hear his confession, nor his wife to demand fidelity, nor even his boss to question his professional conduct? In fact, who was I? What was my role? The more I looked at the situation, the more it seemed to me that my expected role was to do nothing more than to point out the elephant in the room and then get thrown out of Pierre's office for poking my nose where it was not wanted. That, it seemed to me, would probably benefit nobody (least of all myself) so I decided to test the assumptions of the team by cross-examining Françoise.

I probed and delved to see if there was any room for doubt—after all, people have been known to jump to conclusions and imagine improper relationships when there is a perfectly innocent explanation. So what evidence did Françoise have? Who else shared her suspicions? Her response was unequivocal: The entire team knew and talked about it constantly. Then she showed me a photograph, taken by a colleague on her cell phone outside a cinema, showing Pierre and Denise—believing themselves to be unobserved—clasped in a passionate embrace.

So there was no denying the affair, then. But I was no nearer deciding how to tackle the problem. All I could do was continue interrogating Françoise in the hope that some natural course of action would eventually present itself. How did Françoise feel about this situation? Why did she think this affair was any business of hers? Why worry about other people's private lives? She replied that she (and her colleagues) felt betrayed. They also felt jealous that Denise had probably had privileged access to work-related information that was important to the team but denied to them. And, as Françoise pointed out, there was probably quite a lot of pillow-talk between Pierre and Denise concerning team members, which was why none of the team felt safe speaking openly in front of Denise. Responding to my direct question, Françoise said that Pierre and Denise's private lives could not be isolated from the work environment; it directly affected the team situation.

I then began to ask about the wider context: Did Pierre's boss know about the affair? Could Françoise talk to Pierre's boss? Had anything like this happened before? And was there a company code of ethics that could be applied to the situation? Her replies were all in the negative. The team didn't know if Pierre's boss was aware of the situation nor could they approach him about it. And there was no code of ethics addressing such topics. It wasn't the moral or ethical aspect of the affair that upset Françoise and her colleagues so much—they wouldn't have cared less if their boss was having an affair outside the office. But here he was, conducting a clandestine love affair with one of their own colleagues, and that offended their sense of equal rights.

By now it was clear that the time had come for me to make the decision whether or not to continue working with this team. I could tell them the situation was too hot for me to handle and that they would have to sort it out for themselves. But the likelihood was that they would continue to sit on their hands and do nothing while the problem festered. It would probably only then resolve itself after some catastrophic eruption of resentment, accusation, and counter-accusation. The consequences could be disastrous and several careers could be seriously damaged.

Alternatively, I could request a meeting with Pierre during which I would put before him, in as measured and diplomatic a way as possible, the fact that his affair had been exposed and that it was affecting his team. But then he might simply deny everything, kick me out of his office, and let the situation carry on—only this time there would be mistrust and resentment on all sides. Of course, if he were to deny the affair, I could always produce the incriminating photograph, taken outside the cinema—but would I, could I, do anything so humiliating to a client? I'm not a private detective. Executive coaches teach, mentor, and instruct their clients in a supportive way to help them improve their performance at work—it is not for us to confront them with incriminating evidence of sexual infidelity in order to force a behavioral change.

I also had to consider that if I were to confront Pierre with the truth, he might feel himself betrayed by his own staff. He would discover that his team had been sharing extremely private information about him with an outsider. He might quite justifiably consider this a breach of trust and demand to know why they had not had the courage to bring the matter up with him themselves. He might very well tell me that this was a matter between him and his team and that this was none of my business.

## Deciding a course of action

After my discussion with Françoise, I next wanted to talk to other team members, all of whom confirmed their unease with Denise and Pierre's behavior and wanted to clear the air and be able to work again. I also wanted to speak to Denise—but as ever, she never had time. Nevertheless, I now knew for certain that this was a problem shared by the whole team and not just something that upset Françoise alone.

Before wading in and tackling the problem in my own way, I decided to ask my own boss what he would do. His immediate response was that I should just get right out of it and let these people wash their dirty linen in private. That wasn't what I had wanted to hear, and I couldn't take that advice; I was already too deeply involved and was determined to see this through. I eventually convinced my boss that I needed to finish this task and persuaded him to take part in a role-playing exercise to simulate the interview I was planning to conduct with Pierre. The aim of this interview was to make Pierre listen to, and accept, his team's concerns and work with them to find a solution in a friendly, constructive way.

The dry run with my own boss helped me to think through various scenarios and gave me the confidence to go into this difficult encounter feeling that I was well prepared. But although this is fine in theory, it was not until the interview itself that I would discover how far my theory matched the reality. On the appointed day, Pierre opened his office door and ushered me inside in a manner that immediately marked him out as a dominant male figure—expansive, condescending, and in control. A smoker, he offered me a cigarette, even though he knew I didn't smoke; I could see that despite his studied nonchalance he was actually quite nervous. He tried to lead the conversation from the start, trying to keep the tone light and frivolous. This had the effect (intentional or otherwise) of making me feel nervous, especially in view of the serious subject I was going to have to broach. I knew I could not afford to engage in Pierre's small talk and so remained concentrated and stubbornly focused on my central message.

Side-stepping Pierre's idle chat, I came straight to the point and reminded him that I had spent two weeks with his team because they themselves had raised concerns about poor communication and serious tensions within the team. Pierre's response was characteristically light-hearted and dismissive: Of course he knew—this kind of thing happens from time to time. With a patronizing smile he remarked me that women like to gossip (even though there were also two men in the team) and that he should probably give them more work and make sure their minds were more focused on business than these other things.

This was the point at which I knew I had to get down to business. I told Pierre that his team knew that he had "special feelings" for Denise and that this was making it very difficult for them to talk openly and operate efficiently. I didn't dare put it in any stronger terms than this but just waited for Pierre's response—which was of course to ask me what on earth I was talking about.

I then explained that he and Denise had been spotted outside the cinema and that it was clear that they were having an affair. Before I could finish speaking, Pierre (now visibly agitated and looking very indignant) interrupted to ask if I had come here simply to tell him what a bunch of prudes his team were and tell me in very direct terms that his private life was none of my business.

Although very nervous myself, I had the presence of mind to point out to Pierre that, unfortunately, his private life was now mixed up with his business life and that this had caused a rift within the team and between Pierre and his staff. Rather surprisingly, Pierre insisted that he treated every member of his team exactly the same (despite the rather obvious fact that Denise enjoyed very different treatment). And then, just as I had feared, he turned his anger on me and declared that he always knew that coaches were no good and only ever made things worse. I was impertinent to confront him in such a way, he said, and I was to get out right away and on no circumstance speak another word to his team.

## MEETING THE CHALLENGE

I could deal with being thrown out of Pierre's office—in fact I felt quite elated after the interview because I had at least done what the team expected of me and broken the impasse. I could even deal with the dressing-down I would receive from my own boss for allowing myself to get thrown off the case. But I felt frustrated that the situation was still unresolved. I worried that, rather than clearing the air, my bringing the affair out into the open might actually have made things even worse. Despite Pierre's injunction, I contacted Françoise and told her what had happened.

Her response did nothing to allay my fears. She was understandably upset and told me she was sure that now there were bound to be repercussions. I felt wretched: I had handled a delicate problem clumsily; I'd behaved unprofessionally, and had totally failed in my assignment. Pierre, despite his moral failings was right: I was no good and had only made matters worse. My feelings of despondency continued until, a week later as I sat unbillable in our offices, something unexpected happened. Pierre called me to say that, after some serious thought, he had decided that he and I needed to talk.

He then explained to me the nature of his personal circumstances in a way that made me suspect that this was the first time he'd been able to speak to an impartial third party in confidence. In summary, he told me that he didn't know what to do about this complex situation but knew that something needed to be done. This time, unlike our previous interview, it was Pierre who did most of the talking. I hardly needed to offer any advice or suggest any course of action; Pierre was working through it himself and I was just his sounding-board. I felt, however, that he was coming round to the belief that somehow Denise needed to be removed from his work environment.

**UPSETTING YOUR CLIENT, UPSETTING YOUR BOSS: COMMENTARY**

*Marcia Reynolds*

My initial reaction to this case is to question what Pierre, the manager, wants out of the coaching since he had to approve the budget for coaching even if he didn't make the initial request. Is he hoping the coach will fix a problem that he wants to avoid? In my experience, the manager has to be an active player in the coaching relationship, whether the coachee is an individual or a team, even if he didn't request the coaching in the first place. The manager has to work with the coach to define goals, share his perspective about the history and culture of the organization, and identify any roadblocks to success the coach might have. Without the manager's active support, the coaching arrangement has little chance of success. The team will continue to blame all their problems on their uninterested and secretive leader if he isn't engaged in the process.

Therefore, if the coach were to refuse to go any further with this coaching assignment, I would see this as an act of integrity and not as taking flight. The coach would be refusing to be a part of an unhealthy situation that the manager does not want to take responsibility for. If the coach does not clearly state the required terms of the relationship, which includes active participation by the manager, the coach runs the risk of being caught in the web of dishonesty that is going on in this department.

However, if the coach does choose to work with the team, then the coach should help the team be courageous instead of declaring themselves victims. Feeling betrayed and angry is not an excuse for giving up. The coaching approach I would take would be to help the team identify what they can control in this situation and focus on that. It is always better to feel as if you can master some part of your work rather than to feel that you are helpless. Questions I would ask include:

- Would you be willing to explore the part of your work that you can control?
- What are you capable of accomplishing without your manager's support?
- If you were brave, what request would you like to make of your manager? What would be the worst thing that could happen if you made this request? What else could happen?
- What do you know to be true about this situation? (Much of what the team members believe is not evidence-based but comes out of their own gossip and emotions.) Based on the few facts you know to be true, what is it possible for you to do right now to help you feel strong and able to accomplish your goals?

Although it is distasteful to point this out, I have to raise the possibility that the other women on this team might be jealous of Denise because she is having an affair with their boss. Do they know for certain that Denise bad-mouths them behind their backs? Do they know for certain that Denise is favored by the boss? It is best for the coach to hear their concerns and let them vent their emotions, and then help them move into a position of power instead of blame. The boss may be doing something very wrong. Yet the team members can choose to do good work if they want to. Where they put their focus is up to them. The coach can help them take responsibility if they are willing to have this conversation.

Therefore, if the coach is to be successful in coaching this team, the coach cannot take sides and commiserate with the team. The coach must remain neutral. The achievable goals must be clearly set. Every team member must agree to the goals and the desire to move forward regardless of the love affair that is going on. Then the coach must focus on moving the team forward instead of being stuck in their emotions about the current situation. If the team is up for this movement, then it is possible for the coach to be a great asset for a team caught up in negative emotions.

## POST-CASE NOTE

*Beate Heller*

Sure enough, just days after our phone call I got the news that Denise was gone and that she had ended her relationship with Pierre. That might have been the end of the story, but it didn't stop there. Although the team felt huge relief, their respect for Pierre was clearly damaged irrevocably. He left the company later that same year and set up on his own as a consultant.

This assignment was far from typical for an executive coach, but it provided some useful lessons for me. First, it illustrated very clearly that coaching takes place between sessions and not just during the talks. The client needs time to reflect and decide what needs to be done. It also demonstrated to me, as a coach, that if you are sure of your values and believe that your course of action is for the best, it is worth risking a difficult confrontation with your client and even the disapproval of your own boss.

# 10

# THE DOMINEERING COACHEE

## *BÜLENT GÖGDÜN*

*Case summary*

Bülent Gögdün is running a group coaching process and faces the challenge of a coachee who dominates discussions and, at the same time, avoids dealing with his own issues, as reflected in management assessment and psychological instruments. At the same time, the coachee expects more "active" involvement from the coach. The coach is concerned whether he is doing enough to meet the needs of the coachee and the whole group involved in this group coaching exercise.

*Context*: This case takes place within a multinational convenience goods company's leadership development program.

## BACKGROUND

It's hard enough coaching a dominant and overbearing personality when it's one-on-one; it's even more difficult when you are trying to coach that person as part of a group. This was the situation that I faced during a five-day general management and leadership program for a large convenience goods company. The afternoon of the second day was devoted to coaching sessions in small groups designed to allow participants to discuss current leadership challenges and identify potential solutions through the exchange of ideas. In particular, the participants were encouraged to discuss the results of a management audit and Myers-Briggs Type Indicator Step II (MBTI II) survey that had recently been conducted by another institution. The management audit, based on interviews with all the coachees and their line managers, had produced a detailed evaluation of each individual's current performance as well as recommendations for their future development. The results of each individual audit and MBTI II report had of course been handed out only to the respective coachee and the coach prior to the leadership program.

## MY ROLE AS COACH

The participants' employer was a keen advocate of coaching and regarded the ability to coach as an essential leadership skill. Indeed, the company offered its own managers training courses on coaching, using the GROW model as a standard method.[1] As one of the coaches employed on this program, I explained the model to my group during the introduction to the coaching sessions (not all participants were acquainted with the GROW methodology) and told my coachees that they could expect the afternoon to be a challenging experience.

## THE APPROACH

My group consisted of four managers who, although they all worked for the same company, were all located in different regions and performed different functions. I began the session by asking my four coachees to draw self-portraits to illustrate what was going on in their heads and hearts, in their private and professional lives, what had happened in the past, and what they expected to happen in the future. One by one, they presented their self-portrait to the other three, using the illustrations to outline what they saw as the major leadership challenges. I asked them to start their presentation by giving us their first impression of their MBTI II report. All the while I interjected with questions such as "What makes you feel happy?," "What makes you feel uncomfortable?," "What makes you feel disappointed?," writing down these questions on a flip chart so that they remained visible during the whole session.

Throughout the coaching session, all four participants were active in helping one another explore their work situations in detail and identify possible solutions to the problems they faced. They were all very interested in the GROW model, and repeatedly asked questions referring to it. Their interventions appeared on the whole to be very meaningful and helpful, so I gave them plenty of time and space in which to discuss the issues they brought up with each other. And although I was happy to sit back and let them direct the conversation, I occasionally interjected with my own questions, comments, and suggestions, particularly when I felt that there were issues to explore further or that there was more feedback to give. About halfway through the session (that is, after the second coachee had finished his presentation) I asked the group whether the session was meeting their expectations, to which they replied that it was.

## THE CHALLENGE

As their MBTI II reports indicated, three of the coachees emerged as rather reflective personalities whereas the fourth, Thomas, was a very talkative and extrovert character who tended to dominate the conversation. While the other three seemed to relate to one another and freely exchanged ideas during the discussion, Thomas—even when he shared another's opinions—only offered non-emphatic and inflexible statements. He let the others speak first and then advanced his own ideas, sometimes without reference to anything the others had said. It's not that he wasn't listening—he was listening to me—but he certainly didn't appear to be listening to the other coachees. I quickly realized that Thomas was a dominant individual, who would try to take control and that, as coach, I should do something to protect my domain.

Despite Thomas's overbearing presence, I felt that the group as a whole was doing well and that it was OK to give them plenty of space. The other three coachees were keen to discuss essentially human issues—such as interpersonal relationships within the workplace—in a quite uninhibited way whereas Thomas, who was a manager responsible for IT, tended to introduce somewhat more abstract topics for discussion, for example, what people in other departments considered to be the function of IT services. This was not entirely surprising, as Thomas had stated right at the beginning of the session that his long-term target was to become the company's CIO. When he steered the discussion round to his favorite topic I was happy to let him use the conversation to serve his own agenda.

At the end of the session, I asked the group for feedback. Three of the participants said that it was an easy and smooth session and that they could talk about personal issues in a relaxed and uninhibited environment. They appreciated the honest discussion and one of them declared that the session had exceeded her expectations. Thomas, however, was not so complimentary. He felt I had not given him any real feedback on his MBTI II report and that he would have liked me to have taken a more active role—"coaching rather than facilitating the discussion," as he put it. Thomas also felt that the session had been too relaxed and that I should have taken the four of them outside their comfort zones, a comment with which another coachee agreed. According to Thomas, we had also spent too much time on the self-portraits, an exercise that he clearly thought had very little value, although this was not a view shared by his colleagues.

Most significantly Thomas, besides his general criticisms, remarked that he wished that we could have started our conversation during dinner the previous evening (the delegates and their coaches had gathered socially for a city tour followed by dinner). Indeed, although I had been able to talk with my other three coachees the previous night, Thomas and I hadn't had the opportunity to speak at all.

At the end of the coaching session I agreed to meet Thomas the following day so that we could talk about his report. As he had specifically asked me to be more challenging, I cast a critical eye over his MBTI II report once more and drew up a list of ideas with which to test him. This was quite untypical of my normal procedure, which is to identify and build on the strengths of my coachees rather than to deal with weaknesses. This is because, time and time again, I find myself coaching people who focus obsessively on what they do not do well instead of building on the things they are good at. Normally, I only raise negative issues when I feel that they are critical for the effectiveness, growth, or happiness of my coachees.

Working through Thomas's management audit I noticed a couple of interesting comments to the effect that Thomas had a tendency to talk around subjects without getting to the point; that he would avoid giving direct answers; and that he might sometimes fail to listen to what others had to say. While acknowledging that Thomas was an IT expert, the report recommended that he work on strengthening his self-confidence and at the same time review his possibly over-ambitious career goals.

When Thomas and I met the next morning I presented my observations, based on the results of his audit and MBTI II report, and waited for his feedback. He certainly appeared to be listening but he didn't really respond to what I said, at least not in a constructive way. Ironically, this was precisely the sort of behavior that had been recorded in his audit and MBTI II report. There was no working relationship between us; no meaningful exchange. Thomas having complained that I had failed to challenge him rigorously enough during the group coaching session the previous day, now seemed to be getting nothing of any value out of our one-to-one session. Indeed, it soon became clear that he was not very happy—particularly with the results of the management audit.

## MEETING THE CHALLENGE

This assignment presented me with three distinct challenges:

1. The coachee does not discuss "real" issues but is disappointed when the coach doesn't either.

   At the beginning of every coaching session I ask my coachees about their expectations and what topics they would like to explore. This allows me to map out the direction I take in the session. To ensure we stay focused I often ask them in the second half of the session whether they are happy with the procedure so far and whether there are other topics they want to talk about. When coaching a group of people, I try to avoid raising issues that I think will show one or more of the coachees in a bad light or put them on the spot in front of the group. Unfortunately in this case this approach didn't work. Even the one-to-one coaching session was ineffective, although on reflection this might be because I had already lost the trust of my coachee.

   With the benefit of hindsight, I think I should have intervened more aggressively during the group session instead of letting Thomas sit out and leap in right at the end to make sure he got the last word. His strategy ensured that his opinions were never exposed to analysis by the rest of the group and he was never challenged. I also think that I should have challenged Thomas during the group session myself—for instance, by asking him why he chose to talk in a more general, abstract way about IT instead of the particulars of his management audit.

2. The group is doing a great job. But where is the coach?

There is nothing more satisfying for a coach than to interact with a group that works well together and is fully engaged in the coaching process. There are two ways in which the coach can contribute to such a group. The first is to coach as if part of the group itself—in other words, ask questions, answer others' questions, guide the conversation, and encourage the group to explore various areas without actually taking control and adopting the role of leader. This was essentially the approach I took in this case. The other method is to adopt the role of observer or adjudicator, challenging the group whenever appropriate and getting the group to reflect on the process by interrupting the discussion at critical points and holding a mirror up to show the group how they are interacting with one another. This obliges the coachees to adopt a self-critical attitude and really analyze their thoughts and actions. And that's what I didn't do, but probably should have done, in this case.

3. One person dominates the coaching process—and it is not the coach.

One way of taking back control from a domineering coachee is to encourage the others to express their ideas and opinions freely and frequently so that no vacuum is left for the alpha-coachee to fill. In this group, however, the three other coachees gave their best and yet Thomas was still dominant. Thomas's *modus operandi* was interesting: He allowed the others to speak first and then made his comments, so that he always had the final say. The effect was deceptive: At first it appeared that Thomas (though clearly an extrovert) was being considerate and holding his tongue in order to give the other, more introverted participants space. With the benefit of hindsight I can see that it was simply a ruse to sidestep the discussion and avoid being challenged. The effect was to undermine the others' contributions. I should have tackled this by asking Thomas to speak first every now and then.

Occasionally, a dominant member can be recruited by the coach as a kind of "partner," using their confidence and enthusiasm to open topics for discussion. Unfortunately, this was not possible with Thomas, who failed to engage with me in any meaningful way. We remained wary of each other throughout: I was afraid of Thomas usurping my position as coach; he was distrustful of me and the whole coaching process.

## THE DOMINEERING COACHEE: COMMENTARY 1

*Antonio Galvan Luna*

This case clearly exemplifies the fact that coaches need to be prepared to adapt to a coaching session, especially a group session, and not to expect the session's participants to adapt to the coach. During group sessions it is almost impossible to find homogenous groups, in terms of attitudes and personalities. These differences can make us work with the group dynamics in order to achieve the goals required.

In my opinion, the biggest challenge for the coach in this case was dealing with the specific type of personality that Thomas presented, which, in my experience as a coach, trainer and consultant, is fairly common in organizations of all kinds. Thomas's behavior during the group sessions closely resembles that of several people I've come across during training sessions I've conducted and which have also made these sessions quite challenging. For example, I once met a recent economics graduate who wanted to become a top investment banker at a Swiss bank. This person was participating in a session about building effective work teams for a French manufacturing company in Mexico, where he worked as a purchasing trainee, but his attitudes were very similar to those described in the case: He constantly insinuated that it was a waste of time; instead of talking about challenges in his current position, he talked about his plans; he continually asked questions about recruitment in big companies; and, of course, he evaluated the session with a very low score. I met these personalities so frequently in the companies for which I do interventions that I started making a list of characteristics that I found in people demonstrating this behavior:

- Very ambitious career or personal goals.
- A strong desire to showcase their talents, abilities, successes, or plans.
- A significant tendency to attribute positive outcomes in their lives to their own skills.
- Strong preference of individual activities or tasks over group work.
- Strong preference for mastering technical knowledge over soft skills.
- Bad listeners.
- Highly competitive.
- Always on the lookout for new information or skills that they think will give them an edge for achieving their goals.
- Charismatic, although their confidence is based on many of the previous points.
- See people as resources.
- Need to appear invulnerable to others.

I must clarify that this list is the result of empirical observation, and in no way tries to identify a specific type of personality; nor is it the result of formal research. Also, I am not implying that these characteristics are necessarily negative. But it was interesting to find similarities in attitudes, expectations, and behavior across the people who presented these characteristics. Moreover, it was even more interesting how they posed very similar coaching challenges, especially group sessions.

To my mind, once a personality with these characteristics is identified during a group session, a different approach should immediately be used with both the group and the individual coachee. Although in general I prefer plenary-style sessions with groups, one approach that I have found useful under these circumstances is to let the group work in dyads, pairing the main coach with the problematic person as a team. This way that coachee feels he or she is getting all the attention needed and will find the session more rewarding from the beginning. This individual session can be used by the coach to identify and target the motivators behind the coachee's problematic behavior. For example, while working with another similar coachee, I presented her with the results of a recent study by the Center for Creative Leadership that revealed that 60 per cent of top managers think that inspiring commitment and leading people effectively are the most useful leadership abilities to gain success. I also presented her with some negotiation theories that emphasize listening and empathy, which caught her attention. Then I tried to make her reflect whether or not she had these abilities and what it would take her to obtain them. I also explained that these sessions precisely intended to develop these abilities. This led to a brief discussion in which we confronted ideas and, surprisingly, her evaluation of the session was very positive. In subsequent training sessions, this coachee was more participative and open to cooperating with the group as a whole.

Another approach I have found useful when confronting this kind of personality is to use experiential activities with the group, like role-playing activities in this case, which will challenge the participants with realistic situations. When the coachees experience, rather than just discuss, what it is to take decisions as an executive, for example, they generate their own sense of urgency to learn the necessary skills and abilities to make a good choice.

I have also found other profiles that pose challenges to group sessions, like the founders of family businesses and older managers, and in these cases I have also benefited from working with them using these approaches.

As to the "Where is the coach?" question, I think the coach conducted an excellent session in this case, especially since the GROW model is the standard coaching technique used in the company. The GROW model encourages the coach to act as a facilitator, letting people generate their own learning through intimate discussions, rather than presenting the coach's perspectives or direction.

In conclusion, I think that coaches need to "listen" hard to the group, and adapt to what they hear, so that the experience is a rewarding one for all participants, and that the objectives are met.

## THE DOMINEERING COACHEE: COMMENTARY 2

*Gerhard Liska*

I would like to start by looking at the three distinct challenges Bülent identified in this case.

1. The coachee does not discuss "real" issues but is disappointed when the coach doesn't either.

A good question to start with is, what is the "real issue" for Thomas? The description of the coachee as an IT expert may raise the question of how familiar, ready, and skilled (in terms of empathic listening and the capability to sense and name emotions) he is to feel comfortable enough to deal with an emotional approach in such a group setting. The approach taken for this session seems to me emotionally driven, reflected, for example, in starting with painting a picture, and then addressing emotions and emotional states throughout the session. It could be that Thomas felt rather insecure and under pressure in this situation. Insisting on facts and figures could be his coping reaction. He could also have felt the need to relate to his understanding of what a coach should do. Should this hypothesis be true, a one-to-one coaching discussion would be a more appropriate setting for Thomas.

Another hypothesis is that Thomas probably tested how far he could go without hitting a clear-cut boundary. Obviously he had been allowed to withdraw by raising a "sterile" issue, in other words to stay within his comfort zone. Probably this should have been addressed immediately by inviting him to step outside this comfort zone. This would mean that the issue was not to provide him with feedback on his report (which he received the next morning without any evidence of seeing value in it) but rather to confront him with his reluctance to step out of his comfort zone, should this hypothesis be true.

2. The group is doing a great job. But where is the coach?

The group coaching session Bülent describes is sometimes referred to as supervision in Austria and Germany, though the Anglo-American tradition has a different understanding of what supervision is. Bülent states that the session was to "allow participants to discuss current leadership challenges and identify potential solutions through the exchange of ideas." This points to a setting characterized by a reflective approach, a discussion process including feedback between peers, and the notion of self-directed group work.

In such a setting the role of the coach could indeed be more the role of a facilitator who provides the framework and takes care of the group process. Taking this notion of self-directed group work into consideration, the session seems to have worked out quite well for three of the four participants.

The clarification of the assignment seems to be important here. It makes a difference if the session is announced as a session in which participants will receive feedback from a coach, or a session in which they will receive feedback from their peers.

3. One person dominates the coaching process—and it is not the coach.

This is of course a difficult issue, one particularly related to group coaching. In a self-directed group process, the role of a coach or facilitator could be to focus the attention of the group on addressing or even stopping the obviously disturbing behavior of one person. The question is whether the group *does* perceive such behavior as disturbing or disruptive. If they do, the facilitator (supervisor/coach) could offer the group a framework to deal with the situation. Again, this would foster the notion of self-directed learning and foster understanding of the coach's background role, supporting and facilitating processes within the group.

Thomas's domineering stemmed partly from the fact that he was allowed to act differently than the others, for example, bringing in a "sterile" issue. This automatically singled him out, compared to the others. Whether this can be perceived as domineering in my opinion depends on various influence factors.

One of these is whether a participant claims the lead in the group or "merely" dominates in the sense of accumulating/demanding a lot of time and attention from the others when dealing with his issues or when bringing in his standpoints. Of course handling both aspects of domination effectively requires different approaches. From this case study, it is difficult to say which aspect of domination might have been predominant and therefore more important.

There is another important issue here that it would be worthwhile to explore further: How much time (in terms of spoken intervention) or how much dominance should a coach have in such a coaching session in order to support the process and trigger development in the coaches?

## POST-CASE NOTE

*Bülent Gögdün*
The feedback following this particular assignment revealed that Thomas had given the coaching session a very low score. Thomas was obviously dissatisfied with my coaching technique and when I asked him to elaborate, he explained that he felt I had stayed too much in the background and had not taken a proactive role or provided much input. He was clearly disappointed—and so was I. As a coach, I naturally want my coachees to value my work and get something useful out of my coaching sessions. But on this occasion I was left with the uncomfortable feeling that, for Thomas, this was a great learning opportunity lost.

I, on the other hand, had learned a valuable lesson.

Looking back, I can see that I need to develop a broader and more flexible approach to my coaching technique. In this case, it would have been helpful if I had been able to maintain a supportive and encouraging attitude while at the same time remaining ready to challenge individual coachees (in this case, Thomas) whenever it would create impact. Most coaches have their own style and tend to apply their preferred techniques and procedures to every assignment. But there is a strong case for developing a repertoire of methods and the ability to adopt a range of styles to suit the specific requirements of the job.

## NOTE

1. The GROW (goal, reality, obstacles/options, way forward) model is a structured, problem-solving methodology frequently used in coaching.

# 11

# "JUST LOOK AT YOURSELF! HOW COULD ANYONE BE LED BY YOU?"

## SVETLANA KHAPOVA AND YUVAL ENGEL

*Case summary*

The case is written from the position of a participant in a coaching program who is finding it difficult to digest feedback and feeling insulted as a result of the intervention. The coachee is perplexed about the coach's role in the process, and the lack of conditions of psychological safety in the coaching process.

*Context*: This case is set in an internal leadership development program at a public university in The Netherlands.

## BACKGROUND

As is the case with several leading universities around the world, a Dutch university had recently introduced leadership development programs for its academic and administrative staff. The idea was to identify hidden potential and to invest in the development of possible candidates for leadership positions. Deans and faculty directors were asked to nominate a few candidates for selection by the "leadership program manager" who would select a group of 15 to become part of a new six-month leadership development program.

Among the nominated participants was Sonya, an associate professor of cross-cultural management and newly appointed director of a new research institute that, at the time, existed only on paper. Sonya's task was to get the institute up and running within eight months. She was well aware of the fact that she had hardly any time for participation in the leadership program. But at 32 she was young and, as a newly appointed foreign national—she was Russian—felt honored to have been nominated for the program by the faculty board. So despite her already busy schedule, she accepted the nomination.

## THE APPROACH

The program consisted of six 2-day residential meetings held at monthly intervals and at a location some distance from the university and the delegates' homes. This was to ensure that there was time for learning, discussion, and reflection in a neutral environment. It all looked very promising and Sonya departed for the first session with a feeling of excitement and enthusiasm.

The first day of the first session did not disappoint. Sonya was her typical self: Full of energy and keen to take an active role in the discussions. Her one minor disadvantage was that her Dutch was not good enough to allow her to communicate effectively in the other delegates' native language. However, this was easily overcome as Sonya and her colleagues spoke good English; just as she often did at work, Sonya could follow the conversation in Dutch but gave her replies in English. It was a solution that seemed to work well.

Certainly, the language issue did nothing to dent Sonya's confidence—and she had good reason to be confident, having recently won a promotion. She was doing extremely well in her new role and, in terms of career progression, was significantly ahead of her peers. She was young, attractive, and—wearing new clothes she had bought specially for the coaching session—felt energetic and very positive about herself.

Toward the end of the second day, and after a series of interactive group sessions, it was time to split the group of 15 participants into three smaller peer-coaching groups. Joining Sonya in her group of five delegates was Marina, another expatriate participant. Together, they were the only foreigners on the program but whereas Sonya was young and struggled with the native language, Marina was at least 10 years older and spoke fluent Dutch.

After a brief introduction, the five delegates were each invited to present their individual leadership cases in turn (the case would become a personal development project during the following six months). Each presentation had to be about 10 minutes long and was followed by feedback from the four other delegates. There were no particular peer-coaching rules in place to establish a "safe" coaching environment. Presenters, however, were asked not to participate in the feedback discussion following their presentation but only to take notes.

## THE CHALLENGE

Seeing that her peers all hesitated to step forward and present the first case, Sonya volunteered. Her leadership case was about her new appointment as director of the research institute. But, not having met any challenges with the institute yet, she decided to refer to previous leadership experiences in which she felt she had not succeeded in motivating her staff to perform at their best. The central theme of her case was "How do you make your team perform well?"

No sooner had Sonya finished speaking than Marina launched a withering attack upon her: "Just look at yourself! How can anyone be led by you? Look at how you dress and how you behave!" Whether the other participants—and their coach—were simply shocked into silence, Sonya couldn't tell but nobody said anything. Marina continued: "You attract too much attention. You do not even speak Dutch. To be able to lead Dutch employees you need to act as they do. You are such a typical Russian! You are so ignorant that you did not even take the time to understand the Dutch culture. Here, people do not like those who stick out from the crowd. You really don't understand their culture, do you?"

Sonya was speechless. The fact that the group's coach had asked presenters not to respond to the group discussion was irrelevant—Sonya couldn't believe this was happening to her, a specialist in cross-cultural management. Neither could she quite believe that it could happen to her in the "safe" environment of the coaching session. She sat in silence and simply took the abuse. Nobody, not even the coach, intervened: Everyone watched in stunned silence, observing the two foreigners until eventually, after several awkward moments, the session continued with further presentations.

In the weeks that followed this incident, Sonya questioned herself and tried to analyze her reactions to it, wondering how she could have dealt with it differently. Her confidence was badly shaken and she sought affirmation and support from every source—her colleagues, bosses, friends, partner, and parents. Marina's attack had been so personal, focusing as it did on Sonya's appearance and choice of clothes, that it had gone way beyond any justifiable criticism of Sonya's professional conduct and capabilities.

Desperate to rectify any possible failings in her professional life, Sonya started to read books on leadership in the hope that she'd find out where she had been going so wrong. But the more she read, the more she was convinced that Marina was wrong and that blending into the background and behaving like everybody else was not the way to lead. In her reading, Sonya found everything that she was looking for. There was widespread agreement among experts that leaders often have distinctive identities that they exhibit in their personal style of dress, speech, or behavior. Soon, with the support and reassurance of her friends, family, and colleagues, Sonya began to feel better about herself.

However, Sonya's greatest challenge in the immediate aftermath of Marina's attack was whether or not to continue with the program. Everybody seemed to know about what had happened, although Sonya herself had discussed it with nobody. But even though her confidence had evaporated, Sonya realized that quitting the program would just damage her reputation; she reasoned that, if she had been considered potential leadership material, she had better show that she could handle harsh criticism and not crumple at the first verbal assault from a hostile colleague. She therefore decided to continue with the program and behave as if nothing had happened.

Sonya arrived at the next two-day session with renewed confidence. She had not altered her style of dress nor did she modify her behavior and adopt a more retiring attitude. She was her normal enthusiastic self. During one session she even chose to sit in a vacant seat right next to Marina rather than make a point of crossing to the other side of the room to take the only other available seat. When the time came for Sonya to deliver her final case presentation, she decided to use the opportunity to describe the development of her leadership style, citing some of the leadership experts whose books she had read (including Goffee and Jones's *Why Should Anyone Be Led by YOU?*[1]) and referencing some of the criticisms that Marina had leveled at her.

Sonya spoke confidently and persuasively and her presentation was well received by the rest of the group. And because she had chosen to address the very issues that Marina had so shockingly introduced in that first group coaching session, it was now possible for the whole group to discuss something they had previously avoided, probably for fear of provoking another unpleasant confrontation. While several of the participants expressed sympathy for Sonya, there were some who confessed that they could understand Marina's criticisms. One delegate admitted to finding Sonya's energy and confidence intimidating at first, although this particular delegate also felt convinced by Sonya that a strong personal identity was a desirable quality in a leader.

Among those listening to Sonya's presentation was the leadership program manager. At the end of the group discussion he thanked Sonya before asking her directly: "What do you think is the real issue in your case? Leaving aside your leadership style, why do you think the faculty chose you to set up the institute?" Now the discussion resumed, but in a different direction. The program manager, who not only knew all the ins and outs of the faculty but was himself a professional coach, guided the conversation to suggest that Sonya had been carefully chosen as the best person to set up the new institute. Her distinctive identity and attitude were what the faculty needed to break through inherited cultural values and bring a new outlook and style that would help make the new initiative work.

The session ended on a positive note, leaving Sonya feeling satisfied that she had been vindicated. Rather than feeling ashamed of being different, she felt renewed confidence that what Marina had identified as her limitations had been reinterpreted as valuable assets. The humiliation she had felt after that initial session was now gone and she was ready for a new start.

## "JUST LOOK AT YOURSELF! HOW COULD ANYONE BE LED BY YOU?" COMMENTARY

*Sandy Stadelmann*

### My understanding of the framework—key aspects

1. Sonya is 32, associate professor of cross-cultural management and a newly appointed director of a research institute at a Dutch university. Her current

task is to build up the institute in the next eight months. She was identified as a high-potential and a future candidate for a leadership position. She was selected to be a participant of a prestigious six-month leadership development program. She is described as behaving confidently as a consequence of doing well at work, and as an active contributor to the leadership program. In terms of career progression—she is significantly ahead of time compared to her peers. This framework indicates that Sonya is a capable person with strong professional skills and a strong motivation to achieve. She is regarded as the right choice for building up a new institute and has potential as a leader.

2. Sonya is non-Dutch. She understands Dutch well, but feels more comfortable answering in English. It is not clear how long she has been living or working in the Netherlands.

3. Peer coaching is part of the leadership development program. In groups of five, the participants in a peer-coaching group are invited to present their individual leadership cases in order to work on this. The group is accompanied by an external coach. There are no particular rules of peer coaching, including rules about establishing a safe coaching environment. Moreover, presenters are asked not to engage in the dialog after their presentation, but only to take notes of the feedback.

Sonya volunteers to present the first case: It refers to her previous leadership experiences in which she felt she did not do sufficiently well in terms of motivating her subordinates and team members to do their outmost for the projects. Her leadership case question is: How to make a team high performing?

It is not clear what "sufficiently" relates to, how others (e.g., Sonya's former boss) would have described the situation, or how high Sonya raises the bar for herself. The brief description doesn't suggest that her leadership had been disastrous. It shows that she is aware that there is room for improvement concerning her motivational skills and she is aware of "creating high-performing teams" as a key leadership topic. Motivating people and creating high-performing teams are core competencies for leaders (not managers) and therefore often part of development programs for experienced leaders. She has a strong topic for her peer coaching.

4. After presenting the case, Sonya is immediately and solely addressed by her peer Marina, who is 10 years older, non-Dutch, like Sonya, but a fluent Dutch speaker. Marina breaks every feedback rule when commenting: She does not refer to the facts of the case; she criticizes Sonya personally in terms of her looks, clothing style, and intercultural behaviour rather than describing her perceptions; she generalizes instead of pointing out concrete aspects and room for improvement. Neither the external coach nor the group interferes.

Sonya behaves as a polite and rule-respecting individual: She sticks to the rule of listening. She fully takes in what she hears as true "feedback." She demonstrates critical self-reflection and during the rest of her course she works on the heard aspects instead of continuing on her former and apparently strong leadership case. In the time that follows, she shows strength in not avoiding Marina, yet it seems she does not discuss the incident with either Marina or the other participants. The incident is soon widely known within the program. This is probably due to Marina and/or other peer-group participants talking or gossiping. The peer group turns out to be anything but a safe environment.

## Core findings: Missing rules

1. Did Sonya deal with the situation correctly?

   Sonya applied the (only) rule of the peer group, although she was attacked in a wholesale and personal manner. Her acceptance of the aspects heard, her self-reflection capabilities, and her will to improve led her to deal with new leadership-related topics. In the end, fortunately, this investment gave her more self-confidence and increased leadership identity. However, she gave up dealing with her original topic.

   Sonya could have behaved differently in several ways. She could have broken the "rule of listening," or better, asked for a neutral space in the group—"a meta-dimension to express a feeling of discomfort"—that would allow her to express her wish for professional feedback according to the feedback rules. Once it was clear that there was gossiping in the course, she could have addressed this with the group coach or within her peer group, in order to introduce the rule of "protected areas/confidentiality." She could have remembered her current achievements to brace herself, to decide not to accept the "feedback" (rule of taking feedback) from Marina, and try to move her real case forward.

2. What could have been done differently in the peer-coaching group that would have prevented the incident?

   Here, clearly, the rule of confidentiality, the rules of giving and receiving feedback, and the "meta-dimension" should have been introduced. As the rules were not introduced by the coach, the group could have raised the issue to introduce them with hindsight.

3. How could the external coach prevent or facilitate the situation?

   The coach should have introduced the rule of confidentiality, the rules of giving and receiving feedback and the "meta-dimension." Having failed to do so, the coach could have interfered and introduced them with hindsight.

4. How could the group have helped Sonya to deal with the situation?

   The group could have given Marina feedback on her non-appropriate comments and asked to establish retrospective rules. They could have given appropriate feedback on the case and encouraged Sonya to stick to her original case. They could have given Sonya sparring and feedback on the topics Marina raised, which had shocked and discouraged her. And in the upcoming sessions they could have addressed whether a peer group should be a protective environment.

## POST-CASE NOTE

*Svetlana Khapova and Yuval Engel*

Although everything ended well for Sonya, she was still thinking about the incident months later. Had she dealt with the situation correctly? She had questioned her own abilities, researched the role of leadership, and decided to stick to her guns. But what about Marina? Had she altered her opinions and should Sonya have challenged Marina directly?

Although she was glad to let the matter rest, she was still intrigued to know what had been going through the minds of her fellow-delegates while Marina was haranguing her. Were they embarrassed? Were they scared of turning Marina's aggression on themselves? Had they been right to remain silent? And if they had spoken up, how could the group have reacted positively after such an outburst?

Sonya also wondered about the role of the coach in all this. The coach, after all, had done nothing to intervene when Marina launched her verbal attack. There had been no "safe" coaching environment and Sonya couldn't help feeling that, had she been a less resilient personality, the psychological effects of such humiliation and ridicule could have proved extremely damaging to her career.

## NOTE

1. R. Goffee and G. Jones (2006). *Why Should Anyone Be Led by YOU?* Harvard Business School Press, Cambridge, MA.

# 12

## WHERE'S THE CHALLENGE?

### *ROLF PFEIFFER*

*Case summary*

In Rolf Pfeiffer's case, a manager returns to Europe from an expatriate assignment and finds he needs to work on his relationship with a particular colleague. However, the nature of the relationship changes as the case unfolds, and so does the coach's assignment. The coach tries to engage the coachee to work on strategic issues, but the coachee keeps returning to what has now become rivalry with his colleague. The coach is concerned that instead of being expected to come up with meaningful questions, he may be expected to provide meaningful answers.

*Context*: The case is set in the European headquarters of a matrixed multi-national company.

## BACKGROUND

Steve was returning to Europe after several years working in Southeast Asia. A high-flying technical specialist with a multinational research-led manufacturer, he had been asked to come back to Europe and take up a challenging new role as technical director of a new manufacturing unit. This was, by anybody's standards, a big deal. Steve's employer was a world leader with annual revenues in excess of US$5 billion and customers in more than 150 countries around the world. The new factory would employ the latest manufacturing technology and, besides being the corporation's biggest investment for years, was the single largest investment of its kind in the industry worldwide. Steve knew that this was the kind of appointment that had the personal attention of the CEO and the rest of the board. It would be the making—or the breaking—of him.

Steve took up his new post confident that he understood his role and knew what needed to be done. But just a few months later he realized that if he were to follow the direction he considered necessary to make this new venture a success, he would soon run into conflict with the director who had overall responsibility for the project. This was potentially disastrous, since the project director was an old friend and colleague with whom Steve had worked, on and off, for more than 10 years. Nevertheless, within eight months of starting his new job, Steve felt so frustrated by the project director's style of leadership that he started looking around for a new job. At the same time, Steve asked the company's learning and development (L&D) department for an executive coach to help him in his current role.

## MY ROLE AS COACH

The L&D department briefed me to help Steve cope with the demands of his new job and find a way of working harmoniously with his colleagues, especially the project director. There were a number of specific issues that Steve needed help with, not all of which related to his interaction with the project director.

One problem was related to the location of the new flagship factory. Originally it was to be on the site of the head office but following a merger with another company the board decided, for political reasons, to build the factory in a neighboring country. This was bad news for Steve, who didn't speak this country's language. The location of the new factory also attracted a lot of opposition from other departments within the company whose contribution to the project was crucial to its success.

Steve's relationship with his boss was also likely to change after the project reached completion. The incumbent regional director at the chosen site was due to retire at approximately the same time as the project's scheduled completion and it was widely assumed that whoever replaced him would be able to speak the local language. This appeared to rule Steve out and leave the door open to the project director, who did speak the language.

Resources were also a problem. By the time I was appointed as Steve's coach, the project was already behind schedule and had used up its entire time and financial buffer a full three years ahead of the scheduled completion date.

Several weeks before I started coaching him, we spoke over the phone and Steve outlined his dilemma. I also received a written briefing from the L&D department explaining my role. However, during our first face-to-face encounter, Steve revealed that the brief had changed: The project director had been moved sideways into a new role and Steve had been appointed project director in his place. This was the role that I was now asked to help him develop as his coach.

## THE CHALLENGE

The challenge for me as a coach was now quite different from what I had been briefed to do. Steve still needed help with his colleague, but for very different reasons; he now had to deal with someone who had become quite hostile toward him as a result of having been replaced. At the same time, the former project director was still in line for the job of regional director on project completion. If so, he would be the person responsible for signing off the successful completion of the project and be in a very powerful position with regard to Steve. Furthermore, Steve was now responsible for handling serious financial problems, many of which resulted from the fact that his predecessor had not kept head office staff properly informed of the status of the project. This exposed Steve to even more personal scrutiny by the CEO since he now had to share all the bad news about the project status. Steve also had the additional task of leading a team of 50 people from a wide range of national and organizational backgrounds in delivering the project. About half of these individuals were expatriates with no clear future after project completion; all of the permanent positions at the site had already been filled by the former project director's appointees.

As coach, I had to address a number of specific challenges. The first was the underlying theme of Steve's rivalry with his old friend and colleague, the former project director. With Steve's appointment as project director, both were now considered to be contenders for succession to the current regional director. This issue became the dominant theme of our coaching sessions and took up as much time as we spent on helping Steve maintain strong performance in his new role.

A leadership feedback report had been prepared by another consultant assessing the main contenders to succeed the regional director following his retirement. This report was written in such a way that it contained no hints as to who was the strongest candidate. Frustratingly, it also gave no hints about what Steve could do to strengthen his position. Everybody knew that the leadership feedback process was supposed to play an important role in deciding senior management appointments. However, my informal conversations with the consultant who had compiled this report revealed that the method used to compile information for these reports often deviated from the process laid out in corporate standards and that the outcome of the feedback process was sometimes completely disregarded.

## MY APPROACH

It so happened that I had a good relationship with the consultant who had compiled the leadership feedback reports and who had actually worked in the L&D department of Steve's organization before becoming a consultant. He was therefore familiar with most of the challenges Steve was facing. This was both helpful and potentially tricky for me, as we both had to respect the boundaries between our respective professional activities. We both had information that was potentially useful to each other, but we had to be careful not to share any sensitive or confidential information that might compromise our ethical standards.

Throughout this assignment, I used collegial supervision to obtain additional perspectives on Steve's case and answer some of the key questions it raised. I also routinely kept thorough coaching notes in order to reflect on my meetings with Steve. These notes were useful in exploring other career opportunities with him.

At the end of the initial coaching assignment, Steve asked me to set up a new set of objectives for a follow-on coaching process. I made it very clear to him that I would only agree to this if we had a distinct set of objectives building upon what we had already achieved. Nevertheless, during the follow-on coaching process, it was increasingly clear that it would be difficult to maintain this as a coaching process and keep it from moving into a mentoring or consulting assignment.

## MEETING THE CHALLENGE

Steve's difficult relationship with his colleague (the former project director) was a major issue in the coaching process. Steve and I explored his impressions of competitor perspectives and actions. I also found that pressing Steve to take a broader perspective on both his motivation and that of his colleague or rival helped a great deal.

On the other hand, I found it difficult to determine the best way to use my insider knowledge of the leadership feedback process to help Steve gauge the likely impact it would have on his professional development. After 18 months of coaching Steve, I began to wonder how best to sustain momentum and ensure that my assignment did not develop from a coaching assignment, in which I was being paid to ask meaningful questions, into a consulting role in which I would be expected to provide meaningful answers.

## WHERE'S THE CHALLENGE?: COMMENTARY

*Gudrun Becker*
The following questions may be useful for considering the possible courses of action the coach can take:

- What was the reason for the replacement of the former project director? What is his new position? How would team members describe his leadership performance?
- What is the reason and purpose of the leadership feedback process? Who is responsible for the organization, execution, and evaluation of the feedback process in the organization? Is the process coordinated by the same department?
- Has anyone else complained about the vagueness of the report written by the external consultant? Is the criticism known to the contracting department? If so, are any action steps being taken? What is the overall role of the freelance and consultant in this organization?

If I were in the coach's position in this case, I would explore a number of hypotheses. It seems that there are two different sets of business interests within the organization, revealed through the personnel decisions. The CEO promotes Steve, the coachee in this case, with the result that the former project director has been replaced some months after the coachee returned from his expatriate assignment. At the same time, it seems that he may be prevented from becoming a potential candidate for the post of the regional director (this is indicated by the report of an external consultant and deviations from the leadership feedback process as it is laid out in corporate standards).

It is also possible that the former project director has a strong network of relationships in the company, in contrast to the coachee, who has recently come back from an overseas assignment. How could this affect Steve's effectiveness and the steps he needs to undertake? This may be worth exploring if Steve fears that half his team members, assigned by his predecessor, could be reluctant to accept his leadership. Another hypothesis for exploration could be the gap between Steve's technical expertise and his executive or leadership competencies. Exploring these issues may help Rolf and Steve come up with a working plan for their subsequent coaching relationships.

## POST-CASE NOTE

*Rolf Pfeiffer*
First, the simple act of writing up this intervention made me step back, reflect, and think thoroughly about the case, my role, and how I could be more effective as a coach. Second, the comments received from my peers provided highly interesting and particularly valuable insights, since their position as observers meant that they did not know the corporate situation, and they were uninfluenced by any additional insights that I had based on other coaching processes within this client organization. Third, the discussion of my case during the ESMT Colloquium offered even more insights, and I had to think on my feet—pretty much as would happen during a coaching session—when responding to those ideas. Most of the people in my group who joined in the discussion provided very interesting, sometimes even very unique, insights—even going so far as to describe their own process of reading the case and wondering where the dilemma was, and then describing their own journey of developing their own opinions and seeing a dilemma pretty much as I saw it.

# 13

# COACHING IN A FAMILY CONUNDRUM

## KATHARINA BALAZS

*Case summary*

Katharina Balazs finds herself in a family-business situation that is charged with past history and current emotions. Financial needs, career prospects, life expectations, and relationships between family members create a multi-layered challenge for the coach, who has a limited number of sessions at her disposal and thinks that years of therapy are probably needed to deal properly with the issues presented. The coach is also challenged by her own confusion about where her loyalties lie: With the coachee or with the party paying the coach's fees.

*Context*: The case takes place in Austria.

## BACKGROUND

Family firms are among the most complex environments in which a coach can work. In addition to all the usual stresses and strains of normal business relationships, you have the deeply ingrained psychological complexities of family life to contend with. In most working environments your clients can at least disentangle their working life from their home life; in a family business, that's often impossible. Uniquely in a business context, childhood experiences and formative early relationships are carried through into the working environment. Coaches can find themselves trying to tackle issues that have remained unresolved for decades.

## THE CLIENT

Dagmar was an ambitious and successful executive who had risen to a senior position in a leading electronics manufacturer. Her career trajectory had been carefully planned: After completing her M.Sc., she had briefly considered joining the family business, a mid-sized manufacturer of security equipment, but had firmly rejected the idea. Dagmar considered the family firm to be a dull choice for somebody with her ambition and sense of adventure. She wanted the freedom to shape her own career and didn't want her father, who had founded the business, nor her older sister, now a senior executive in the firm, constantly looking over her shoulder.

So Dagmar joined a leading European electronics company where she climbed rapidly up the career ladder until she reached the position of finance director. She relished the kudos of her job title (something to which she attached a great deal of importance), enjoyed a generous salary, and got a lot of pleasure from the frequent travel to the different regions for which she was responsible. Life was hectic, busy, and stimulating.

But much as she enjoyed the excitement of life as a top executive, by the time Dagmar reached her mid-30s she was beginning to feel that she was missing out in her private life. She had never married, had no children and was beginning to feel that her life was no longer her own. Yes, she still craved success in her professional life, but the clock was ticking. Like so many female executives of her age, she began to panic. If she didn't start a family soon, the opportunity would pass and be gone forever. Dagmar couldn't help comparing her situation to that of her older sister, Anna, who, despite her relatively uninspiring career in the family business, was at least happily married. Moreover, Anna had recently given birth to a son, an event that had exacerbated Dagmar's feelings of restlessness and anxiety.

With characteristically businesslike resolve, Dagmar set about putting her private life back on track. She signed up to an Internet dating agency and pretty soon found herself a boyfriend, Alex. He was not an obvious match in terms of character and social background, but he was a nice enough person all the same. Alex was not the corporate powerbroker that Dagmar always assumed she'd meet; he was a manager with a regional health authority but was nevertheless successful in his own way. The relationship waxed and waned, however, and Dagmar's single-minded determination to get pregnant became the cause of several major bust-ups. Starting a family had become Dagmar's mission and her repeated failure to conceive was becoming intolerable—in her business life Dagmar had used her knowledge and strategic skills to achieve her goals; she was not accustomed to being thwarted by natural forces beyond her control. Eventually, she could take the strain no more. She resigned her post (though not without taking a nice fat severance payment) and headed off with Alex to the Maldives for her first real holiday in years.

With the pressure of her job no longer there, Dagmar could at last relax and shortly after returning home from holiday she discovered she was pregnant. With the birth of the child—a boy—everything changed. Dagmar sold her apartment, paid off her debts, rented a bigger apartment and settled down to look after her son. Life was suddenly exciting again, but also somewhat precarious. Alex had also left his job to set up his own business, but with little initial success, and soon the couple was living off Dagmar's savings.

Before long, it became clear to Dagmar that they were heading for financial trouble. With her savings dwindling fast, the world in the grip of a global recession, and Alex's business struggling to get off the ground, Dagmar realized she needed to start earning again—and what better way to get back into the job market (in the middle of a recession and with a gaping hole in her CV) than at the family business?

Unfortunately, the family was not so keen on the idea; at least, Anna was not. She and her husband Karl had taken over the business following the death of the founder (the girls' father) five years ago, and under their direction the business (operating in a segment of the security industry) found a new lease of life. Despite the economic downturn the business was now growing strongly, and in fact Anna really needed a competent finance director, somebody with a track record just like Dagmar's. The trouble was that Anna didn't want Dagmar.

The two girls had never been close and their relationship had soured somewhat since the death of their father and Anna's marriage to Karl. In fact, they were as different from each other as day is from night. They had never shared the same interests, their approach to life was completely different, and consequently they had difficulty understanding each other's motivations and behavior.

Dagmar had decided that she was finally going to join the family business and so she set about formulating her strategy as she did with every executive decision she made. She knew that Anna would not accept her easily, so she enlisted the support of her mother, Viktoria, first. This was a wise move given that her mother had control over a third of the business. Thus, with her mother backing her, Dagmar announced her intention to Anna and Karl—presenting them, in effect, with a *fait accompli*. The older sister, understandably, was not amused, and there followed a heated argument that only subsided when Dagmar agreed to join an executive program on leadership development and receive some professional coaching. Only then would Anna make a final decision on whether she could join the business.

## THE CHALLENGE

This, of course, is where I came in. I first met Dagmar at the leadership development seminar I was teaching and to which she had signed up. She made a positive impression on me: She was very intelligent, she had a lot of business experience (although almost no track record in business leadership), and she had a sharp, analytical mind. She was clearly one of those smart "left-brainers," an intellectual bulldozer: Never in doubt, very sure of where she was going and how she would get there, and ruthless in her determination to succeed.

I guess I must have made some impression myself because, following the seminar, Dagmar approached and asked me if I would agree to be her coach. After an initial discussion, during which she outlined her position, I agreed with her request on the condition that I would be able to meet her family—sister, brother-in-law, and mother—individually. She agreed and we started the ball rolling.

Anna, when I met her, seemed to be quite open and willing to talk about the situation. Karl adopted a more distant stance. He was clearly supportive of his wife and seemed to have a rather low opinion of his sister-in-law; but he was determined not to add to the conflict and so gave me his honest opinion and then effectively withdrew from the situation. The mother was even more reticent. Viktoria struck me as an unhappy widow who missed her husband and the good times they had had when he was alive. Now she seemed to invest all her energy and attention in her younger daughter and her new grandson. Once I had conducted my interviews with the *dramatis personae*, the true picture became very clear.

The story was one of classic family conflicts. Dagmar's father had been married twice; his first wife had died tragically young, less than a year after the birth of their first child, Anna. A couple of years later he remarried and when Anna was just four, a second daughter, Dagmar, was born. From the very beginning the new wife, Viktoria, took an almost obsessive-compulsive approach to the infant Anna. Although the little girl had known no other mother, Viktoria had difficulty accepting her as her own. She seemed to feel very little emotional connection with her stepdaughter but she felt very strongly that it was her duty to ensure the girl was brought up correctly. Her relationship with her own daughter was of course quite different. Dagmar was the apple of her eye and thus the object of all her maternal affection.

Meanwhile, Viktoria's mother-in-law appeared to regard her son's second wife as some sort of interloper and a poor substitute for her predecessor. Perhaps sensing Viktoria's lack of affection for Anna, she formed a powerful bond with the little girl; with time this served only to widen the emotional gulf between stepmother and stepdaughter.

It did not help that Anna, a free, creative, and adventurous spirit, was the polar opposite of her highly controlling stepmother and was unable to match her constant requests for spotless clothes, a perfect room, and impeccable behavior. The father was absent most of the time and consequently shone in his daughter's eyes. He was a kind, loving, but unassuming personality who, when on his frequent travels, was happy to have a new wife to take care of everything and give him the time and space to concentrate on his business.

The two sisters grew up in strong complicity to begin with. The rivalry between them did not begin to emerge until Dagmar reached adolescence and developed her own tastes and ideas, which turned out to be very different to those of her older sister. Soon the distance between them (both emotional and physical) began to widen rapidly. By the time Dagmar reached her late teens, Anna had met Karl, married him and moved out of the family home. Shortly after that Dagmar went to study, and subsequently work, abroad.

From then on the two sisters had only occasional contact and the childhood bond between them became progressively weaker. When Anna's son was born, the relationship entered a new phase; Dagmar was suddenly envious of her sister—an unfamiliar sensation for a girl who had always been her mother's favorite. Dagmar's yearning for her own child then surfaced and once she herself had a son, the already infrequent interactions between the sisters became fraught with more and more rivalry. Dagmar's strong competitive spirit, hardened in the masculine environment of the electronics company's management circles, was now turned against her sister, whose success and family life became a source of irritation to Dagmar. For first time in her life she began to feel less fortunate than her sister.

An underlying, though unspoken, factor which added to the tension building within the family was the fact that the other family members considered Alex to be not quite good enough. They felt he lacked social status, was unsatisfactory for Dagmar, and an embarrassment to the family in general. Dagmar, quite naturally, was indignant at this display of arrogance and was very defensive about her choice of partner. It did not help that Anna was married to a dynamic go-getter who had played a strong role in building up the family business and was a good provider. All Dagmar could claim in defense of Alex was that he was a very good father who had a lot of patience with his baby son and took almost all the weight of parenthood off his partner's shoulders.

## MEETING THE CHALLENGE

Equipped with the details of this colorful back story, I began to take stock of my task. Dagmar had emerged as a rather narcissistic character with a strong sense of entitlement born out of the fact that she had always been her parents' favorite child. Now for the first time in her life she was the one who had to ask for favors, and her sister had the upper hand.

Dagmar appeared to be very envious of her older sister, who had a strong, supportive husband who had helped her build up their father's business. Anna was visibly more successful than Dagmar, who found it very hard to have to go to Anna and humbly beg to be let into the company. Having many years ago turned her back on the family business, Dagmar was now forced by desperate circumstances to perform a *volte face*. Not that she was in any way ashamed to do so; she considered it no more than her entitlement as a family member to be allowed into the firm and she deeply resented Anna's reticence.

Anna, meanwhile, harbored a sense of injustice that had stayed with her since early childhood when all the "goodies" were reserved for her younger sister. She also suffered from feelings of inferiority and of never having been good enough for her family. Despite this, she had proven herself to be competent and through hard work and dedication had shown that she could be very successful in the family business, an environment in which she had always been the least favored. Now her little sister wanted to intrude into her world and Anna was struggling to deal with the resurgence of many painful childhood anxieties that she thought had been buried forever.

Not only was Dagmar now impinging on Anna's business and family life but her stepmother was also applying pressure to make her yield to Dagmar's advances. It was like a re-enactment of her childhood, with the interests of the favorite daughter again being promoted over her own. Anna's status as a pivotal member of the family and head of the family business—something that she had achieved against the odds through a lot of hard work and dedication—was under threat, and she was not prepared to give up the position for which she had fought so hard.

Although she tried hard not to show it, I am quite certain that the unprecedented spectacle of seeing her younger sister come cap-in-hand to ask for a job with the family firm afforded Anna a certain amount of satisfaction. Nevertheless, there's no doubt that Anna wanted to keep her younger sister at a distance for fear that she would somehow upset her career and family life.

Viktoria also found herself in an uncomfortable position. On the one hand she had profited significantly from the way Anna and Karl had expanded and developed her deceased husband's business. But on the other, she was clearly unhappy seeing that her stepdaughter was not only more successful in her career than her own daughter but also happier in her private life.

## THE COACHING DILEMMA

My coaching assignment was extremely tricky because of the complex family dynamics that lay behind everything and that influenced the behavior of the main protagonists in a very emotional way. In a typical coaching situation, it is often possible to alleviate some of the personality issues by distancing clients from troublesome colleagues and allowing the situation to find its own equilibrium. Here, this was out of the question.

How could I hope to resolve this tangled web of conflicts and rivalries in a few coaching sessions, when to do so would probably require years of psychotherapy for the main protagonists? In any case, how could anyone find a solution that would satisfy each of the individuals without addressing the strong irrational forces that seemed to guide their actions? And where did my loyalties lie? With Dagmar, who had approached me and toward whom I had become slightly ambivalent as events had unfolded? Or with Anna, whose company paid my bills and who had succeeded in eliciting my sympathy and understanding? Was I engaged in "mission impossible?"

## COACHING IN A FAMILY CONUNDRUM: COMMENTARY 1

*Gudrun Becker*
### 1. Analysis

The starting situation already implies some difficulties/hindrances for coaching. As presented, the motivation of the coachee to participate in leadership training and coaching is due to the pressure generated by the sister, representing the family. It seems that the coachee is not particularly interested in the coaching but accepts it as precondition to getting a job in the family business.

The case focuses on family dynamics without emphasizing the coaching objectives of the coaching and the coachee's concerns. Obviously the relationship between the sisters has been a burden since childhood. The "unfair" strategy of the coachee in using her influential mother and confronting her sister (CEO) as well as the brother-in-law with her intention to join the family business worsens the sensitive family situation.

In this context, the coach's use of psychotherapeutic terms to describe the different characteristics of family members (e.g., Viktoria is "obsessive-compulsive," Dagmar "narcissistic") struck me strongly. In any case it's good to know about the family background, which of course has some influence on the coaching process.

The coach seems to perceive her role as "problem solver." The professional understanding of the role of a coach is to partner with clients in a thought-provoking and creative process that inspires them to maximize their personal and professional potential instead of searching for solutions. As for loyalty, the coach should be impartial or neutral toward all parties involved throughout the process.

The personality of the coachee is briefly characterized by the coach as professionally successful, busy but lonesome, career-oriented, impulsive (she quit her job from one day to the next), moving from financial independence to an insecure situation. The coach uses the metaphor of a bulldozer to represent her. The picture of the coachee is multifaceted and sometimes inconsistent. The coachee gives the impression that she is very calculating and plans her steps in advance. However, sometimes she seems to be softer and more vulnerable.

After reading the case, the following hypotheses came to my mind:

- The coachee tries to copy the life plan of her sister without taking into consideration her own ideas about her "dreams," or future perspectives.
- She would like to join the family business because *at the moment* this seems the simplest solution to her current situation.
- She sees her sister's life as a "role model" because, in contrast to her own life, the sister seems to be really happy with her (family) life and successful in business.

## 2. Recommendations

It would make sense to reconsider the whole coaching process because it appears some clarification is necessary. Obviously there is a strong tendency for the coach to become much too involved in the family business.

(i) (Re-)contracting—considering the client–coach–coachee triangle. It would be necessary to meet all parties involved in order to find a common agreement about the coaching objectives, terms and conditions, and to clarify the roles and responsibilities within the whole process.

(ii) The coachee's concerns.

- Clarify the coachee's intentions, wishes, and ideas.
- Verify the coachee's motivation: She didn't come to coaching voluntarily; she was pushed by her family. Inspire the coachee about this coaching opportunity. Encourage and elaborate different future scenarios with the coachee. What does the coachee really want to achieve in the next few years? (For example, one option could be to work full-time again, while the father takes care of the baby.) Where does she see herself in two or three years' time? What about work–life balance?
- Question the coachee's intention in joining the family business. What are her reasons for joining? What are the advantages, disadvantages and risks? What are the challenges and the added-value?

### 3. Reflections on the role of the coach

- The coach asks herself how she can find a solution that will satisfy everyone. From my point of view, she is not responsible for the whole family. Maybe it could be helpful for her to reflect about her role as coach and rethink her concept of self-responsibility and self-guidance.
- The coach is facing a conflict of loyalty between client and customer. She is obviously biased, because she has more sympathy and understanding for her client's situation. As I mentioned earlier, a coach should be impartial. Therefore, it could be useful for the coach to check her own self-steering mechanism and compare it with similar coaching situations she has known.

### 4. Assess the balance between coaching and psychotherapy

- Discuss the possibilities and limits of coaching and come to an agreement about the following steps with the parties concerned. The coach should be transparent in her proceedings although the coaching content remains confidential between coach and coachee.
- Psychotherapy only comes into the picture if family members express their willingness to resolve the long-lasting family conflict. In this case, the family as a whole needs to be open to conflict resolution. It is possible to find ways for the whole family or for individual members.

### COACHING IN A FAMILY CONUNDRUM: COMMENTARY 2

*Peter Boback*
I think this case goes beyond a one-on-one coaching situation. The coach embarked on a family business consulting process with all its vicissitudes and

complexities. While I find it quite challenging to figure out what exactly is going on, the consultant's most tricky task might be to choose the appropriate intervention focus that will not only be helpful for one or other of the players but does justice to the entire (family business) system.

When I read the case, the following questions came to my mind:

1. What is the problem? Better, which problem should the coach choose to focus on? Who among the players (I see three major protagonists: The younger sister, the older sister, and the mother) has what problem?
2. Who is the "client"?
3. What are the terms of the contract and whom has the coach/consultant contracted with?
4. What are the possible working hypotheses?
5. Along which lines should the coach or "family consultant" plan the interventions? (This may be the most difficult thing to decide.)

The "client" (the younger sister) has been obliged by her family to attend an executive development program as a kind of prerequisite to joining the family business after her two-year maternity leave. Attending this program seems to be a compromise between the major players in the family business to appease a conflict created by the *fait accompli* announcement of the "client's" decision (supported by the mother) to join the family business, which has been run responsibly by the older sister and her husband since the father's (company owner's and founder's) death.

From the perspective of the three major players, the "problem" seems to be that:

- The "client" (favored daughter and younger sister), after having studied and worked abroad for a couple of years, gives birth to a boy. Given the circumstances of this new lifestyle decision, she ends up in financial difficulties and "decides" to go "back home" and join the family company. Though her mother is in coalition with her and supports this move, her older sister is resistant.
- The older sister experiences the "decision" of her younger sibling to join the family business as intrusion. Years back, when her younger sister decided to leave the dull family business in order to study and work abroad in fast moving, exciting, high-tech companies, she and her husband took over the family business after the father's death and developed it successfully.
- The mother seems to take it on herself to look out for the interests of her younger (favorite) daughter. She may be pleased to have an opportunity to bring her daughter back home, closer to herself, by integrating her into the family business. She will also be able to take care of and educate her grandson.

Systemic family therapy talks about "index clients." Being the "index client" in a system (family, organization, etc.) means that behaviors shown by a selected person are perceived as problematic to the extent that the individual is considered to need a "treatment" (therapy, executive development program, coaching, etc.) and is pushed by the relevant system to comply with it. My question is: Could other players in this family dynamic be considered as alternative "clients" (people in need of support, consulting, and/or therapy)? For example, the mother? (See my working hypotheses below.)

In the coaching contract there are at least three parties involved: The "client" (younger sister), the older sister, and the mother. Who is asking for the coaching? Who is paying for it? Who is expecting what results from the coaching (this is a question for the anticipated executive- development-program output as well)? According to the case narrative, consultancy by a professional coach has been defined as a prerequisite by the family; the "client" had to agree to it before a final decision could be made about her joining the family firm. What working hypotheses can we make?

1. Is there a good business reason for integrating the younger sister into the family firm? Is there an appropriate role for her? Given her particular skills set and experience gained abroad, is she the right choice for the family business? And what about her motivation? Does she really want to join the "dull" family business? If the question is to help her financially, aren't there other ways to support her? Why not buy her out?

2. What would have happened to the mother if the younger daughter had decided not to come back? While her daughter may be in financial need, the mother seems to be in psychological need. The fact that the younger sister is in financial difficulties and plans to come home and join the family business could be considered as a gift she offers to her mother. The mother might be happy to see her "lost daughter" come back home and provide her with a meaningful task: Help her favorite child and her grandson out of a desperate situation. In exchange, she might be freed from a situation of loneliness and isolation with her stepdaughter and son-in-law.

3. The younger sister lost (or "sacrificed") her autonomy—financial and professional—in the moment she decided to have a child and to live in a partnership with her boyfriend. Is it possible that the fact that the two sisters both have a son brings the (real and symbolic) question to the table: Who is the legitimate successor to the family firm?

While the working hypothesis (1) touches on questions of motivation and contracting accessible by rational discussion, hypotheses (2) and (3) presume possible "hidden" contracts, loyalties, and conflicts.

Interventions should comply with the "do no harm" rule and start with rationally accessible topics. The coach could:

- Help clarify the motivation of the younger sister to join the family firm. Is working for the family business really what she wants? Does she think she can add value? If the major reason for wanting to join the family business is money, aren't there other ways to help her?

- If the answer to this is "yes," work with the parties involved on a reasonable contract for the younger sister's integration in the firm. What's the role that makes most sense for the firm? What are the required skills and competencies for this distinct role? What are the engagement rules for her and the other parties involved (older sister, brother-in-law, mother, etc.)?
- If there is evidence that the younger daughter's decision to come back home is more an act of loyalty to her mother than a business decision, the "sacrifice of autonomy" needs to be reframed in an appreciative manner.
- The case narrative evokes the impression of other "classic" family dramas, like Cinderella and the biblical story of the prodigal son (in this case, daughter). Can these cultural stories be of help when it comes to making the family system understand, feel, and appreciate what they are dealing with in regard to the coachee's request to join the family business?

I found this case very interesting. It engages the reader's intellect and emotion. The tricky question is to choose the right level of intervention and to peel the onion from outside in.


## POST-CASE NOTE

*Katharina Balazs*

Dagmar and I had agreed on eight coaching sessions over a period of four months. The pressure was on both of us because by the end of that period she needed to have secured a regular income. After just a couple of sessions I realized that the roots of the problem went very deep and by the end of the third month I was beginning to show some serious stress symptoms myself. I was convinced that I would not be able to help Dagmar find a solution.

Luckily, the solution found us. It was around this time that Alex's fledgling medical supplies business finally started to get its first serious clients; but they were not in Austria, where they all lived, but in Poland, which happened to be the family's country of origin. The Polish economy at this time was doing very well and new enterprises of all kinds were springing up and flourishing. It quickly became clear that Alex was going to have to relocate to Poland in order to attend full-time to his growing business. And Dagmar, who knew Poland well, having been finance director for Eastern Europe in her previous job, loved the country and was quite prepared to relocate there with Alex and their son.

Nevertheless, she was still intent on joining the family firm—indeed, until Alex's business was properly established, they would have to supplement his modest income. Then during one of our coaching sessions a solution began to emerge and we developed the idea of launching a Polish subsidiary of the family business. It was the perfect answer: The security industry—especially private home security—had great potential in Poland and there was very little in the way of domestic suppliers. Dagmar took the idea to Anna and Karl, both of whom instantly saw its attraction. After some consideration on both sides it was agreed: Dagmar would set up a Polish branch of the family business and run it herself.

The last I heard was that Dagmar was doing very well building up the business in Poland and that the Austrian parent company was continuing to prosper under the joint leadership of Anna and Karl. So it seems that in the end everyone had their cake and ate it too: Dagmar works for the family business but in a role that allows her to make her own decisions; Anna still has control of the Austrian company and is free from any disruptive day-to-day rivalry with her ambitious younger sister. The only person who is less than happy is Viktoria, whose favorite grandson now lives too far away for her to see him regularly. But maybe that's a small price to pay for a happy family—and a successful business.

# 14

# CAN YOU COACH AROUND A DEAD END?

## MARCIA REYNOLDS

*Case summary*

Marcia Reynolds deals with a high-potential female executive who is eager to work hard on earning a promotion opportunity, and wants the coach's help in identifying the developmental areas on which she needs to concentrate. However, the coach soon finds out from the coachee's bosses that the coaching is being used just to keep the coachee happy: She is not viewed internally as promotion material. Unfortunately, the management is not willing to discuss the coachee's career chances with her in an open manner. The coach questions whether she should continue working with someone whose final goal is unattainable.

*Context*: The case takes place in a large biotech company in the United States.

## BACKGROUND

One of the trickiest assignments I have ever had to undertake came after I was engaged by a leading biotech company to help with a leadership development program for female managers. Designed to prepare the company's best women for senior management roles, the program involved mentoring, training, performance assessments, and nine months of coaching provided by third-party specialists selected by the company.

I was assigned to coach Sunita who at the time was working in the sales division as the account manager for one of her employer's largest clients. Sunita was a fully qualified MD and had worked as a medical director running a large clinic before taking her first position with the biotech company. She was eager for promotion and despite having two children and her aging parents to care for at home, she felt she had the ability and energy to take on a more demanding leadership position. And since she was still in her 30s, it was not unrealistic of her to expect to see some significant career development in years to come.

## MY APPROACH

I started the coaching process by reviewing the results of a recent performance assessment with Sunita over the phone, following up with a meeting at her office to determine our initial coaching goals. During the course of this meeting, Sunita told me she was aware that some people thought she was too aggressive toward others. Her view was simply that she was passionate about her work and that her enthusiasm was sometimes misinterpreted by her colleagues. Sunita also suspected that cultural differences might have affected people's perception of her—she was of Asian origin, although now a naturalized US citizen.

We also examined some typical behavioral characteristics of high-achieving women in order to consider Sunita's strengths and weaknesses in context. This helped me to identify some issues that Sunita should address, such as her need always to be right, her reluctance to delegate tasks that she felt others could not do as well as she could, and her tendency to take critical feedback too personally. Pretty soon I had identified our initial coaching goals.

The first was to improve Sunita's self-awareness and help her control her emotional response to colleagues. I wanted us to explore the disparity between her self-perception and the feedback she was getting from other people and to use this to enhance both her verbal and non-verbal styles of communication. This, I hoped, would help Sunita become more effective and influential in her dealings with colleagues at all levels. I also wanted to help Sunita develop methods of dealing with and resolving conflicting ideas and decisions. I wanted her to practice reading and interpreting the behavior of others, especially those with different motivations and styles from hers. This would help Sunita to promote her ideas persuasively without over-selling them and appearing pushy. Third, I wanted to help Sunita to develop her own style of leadership so that others would begin to see her not only as the brilliant physician, researcher, and marketer that she manifestly was, but also as a model leader.

Early on in the assignment I conducted a thorough assessment of Sunita's current position by interviewing her immediate manager, his manager (the vice-president of the division) and two of her direct subordinates. What I discovered left me in no doubt that Sunita faced some major—perhaps insurmountable—obstacles in her path to promotion. Sunita's immediate boss told me, off the record, that he put her on the development program simply to keep her happy. What he really wanted was for me to talk her into being satisfied with her current situation. Senior management did not see her running a business unit. They felt she could never rise above a medical director position.

Sunita's boss was convinced that she did not possess adequate leadership abilities because she was incapable of delegating important tasks. She didn't trust other people with critical information about her client and kept her client relationships to herself, to the extent that she would not allow anyone else to get close to the client. The divisional vice-president also felt that Sunita lacked leadership skills. With so many other people competing for the top positions, he said, she just wasn't good enough for promotion. I asked him to specify what it was that Sunita needed to develop in order to become promotable some day and he said he would get back to me. He never did.

Both Sunita's boss and the divisional VP were quite happy for me to feed these criticisms back to Sunita. But when I asked if they had conveyed any of this to her themselves, or were planning to, they both said they didn't feel comfortable giving her direct feedback. They complained she always took it badly, getting defensive and refusing to accept their views. At this point I began to feel that Sunita was not the only one who needed to develop better leadership skills. The response from Sunita's direct reports was dramatically different: They raved about her. They felt she was not only a good team player but they also learned a lot from her.

## THE CHALLENGE

After I completed the interviews, it was clear that while I could coach Sunita to improve her emotional intelligence and communication skills, there was nothing I could do to improve her chances of promotion. Her path toward a leadership role was non-existent. Nevertheless, I had been hired by the company to coach her and she was an important employee—so what was I to do? Should I try to steer Sunita away from the promotion she aspired to and tell her to make the most of her current position? That didn't seem a realistic option for an ambitious high-achiever like Sunita. Alternatively, was I expected to talk straight to her, outline her limited options, and risk talking her into leaving the organization? I knew my professional duty was to help guide Sunita on her career path. The tricky part for me was to make us both feel comfortable with the coaching process and ensure that it was based on trust, honesty, and real, achievable goals.

All this was happening in the aftermath of a global recession when the opportunities for promotion into new leadership roles were far fewer than when the women's development program was launched in the mid-2000s. Indeed, the company was planning at least two rounds of job cuts that year. Many of the women taking part in the scheme knew they would not be promoted after going through the program, yet they were happy to carry on because they knew that they would be better positioned once business picked up again. This had the effect of creating a large pool of well-qualified people waiting to compete for any senior management positions that might subsequently arise. And as Sunita had less sales and marketing experience than most of her colleagues, she was automatically at a disadvantage, even though she was confident that she could rise to the challenge.

Sunita needed more business experience and was willing to make a lateral move and work on a product launch team (a typical path for those on the management track) to obtain it. But she still lacked the skills to sell herself. I suggested right at the beginning of our coaching relationship that she ask her boss to spell out what it would take for her to become a candidate for promotion. If she could work with him to develop a list of goals, at least we would have a path to follow that could keep her motivated.

Sadly, Sunita's boss was unable (or unwilling) to give her any specific targets beyond suggesting that she reduce her "aggressiveness" and somehow make her leadership qualities "more visible" to upper management. His vagueness simply compounded her frustration. Even her mentor—a vice-president in another division—failed to give her any helpful ideas for moving forward; his best advice was to lay low until the economy improved.

Without any meaningful support from her superiors, Sunita seemed trapped in a dead end. As her coach, I began to ask myself some searching questions. First of all, should I continue to coach her knowing that our ultimate goal was unattainable? Second, if, under these circumstances, Sunita decided she couldn't stay at the company, would it be ethical for me to continue coaching her? After all, the company would then be paying me to help Sunita take her skills, knowledge—and possibly a key account—somewhere else. I also had to consider if it was possible for Sunita to gain anything by staying in her current position. Despite everything, she might still benefit by developing herself with the help of my coaching and enhance her performance in her current role. And what about her managers? Was it right for them to use me to deliver news they felt unable to impart themselves? Certainly, she needed to know the truth and I could perhaps help her come to terms with it. For me, all these conflicting considerations boiled down to one fundamental question: Who was my client—the company that hired me or the person I was coaching?

## CAN YOU COACH AROUND A DEAD END? COMMENTARY

*Beate Heller*

This tricky case addresses a topic that many coaches carry deep in their breast. Where do your loyalties lie? Are you loyal to your coachee or to the company that is paying you? The spectres of loyalty and objectivity should be dealt with from the very beginning with the commissioning client.

I very often find myself in such a situation and tell my client that in every case, my responsibility, loyalty, and prerogatives are the coachees', not the company's. I also make it clear that I will not share any information with them about my client but that from time to time, if themes develop where they as a superior could intervene to the benefit of the workforce, I will inform them. So far, this has always been respected. If it isn't, the situation becomes untenable, because to coach someone means to share his or her inner world, hopes, fears, fantasies, and aspirations for a period of time. As coaches, we assume a fairly powerful position that must never be abused. It is vitally important that, if one finds oneself in an ambivalent situation, rigorous and detailed notes are kept. The client should be informed that this is happening, but it is also a form of self-protection for you, the coach.

If you come upon a situation that is potentially ambivalent, it is your job to convince the client gently that they need to take it further. Otherwise you might find yourself sitting on a time bomb.

What became clear to me after a while is that for every protagonist there is an antagonist. And the antagonist may very well end up becoming the person sitting in front of you. What both often have in common is that they complain about this or that but have failed to take responsibility for their present situation.

Marcia poses several questions.

1. Should I continue to coach the client knowing that the ultimate goal was not attainable?

Yes. As a coach you become a partner for a journey for a certain while. It often happens that the destination changes underway as the client changes, which is a good sign. And what are the coachee's real goals after all? To get the promotion or to enhance self-awareness? Sometimes the functional goal (promotion) and the behavioral goal become more and more divergent with the coaching process. With growing self-reflection clients may question their initial (superficial) career goals, once they start digging into their inner world. I think it is a coach's task to guide the client through the jungle that Marcia describes so well in this case.

2. Was it ethical for me to continue the relationship? Who was my client—the company that hired me or the person I was coaching?

If the client were to leave the company and take her skills and knowledge somewhere else because the coaching had opened her eyes, why would it be unethical to continue the relationship with her? A company harboring a superior who will not tell her the truth about her impossible promotion conscientiously takes the risk that she will leave (or might even expect her to leave) and behaves much more unethically than the coach who helps her to see the truth.

3. Would it be possible for Sunita to find value in staying with the company and maintain a comfortable lifestyle?

This is difficult to answer as the client herself should know best what is good for her.

From this case, I would find it hard to imagine the coachee staying in the company just to maintain a comfortable lifestyle. This would mean neglecting her eagerness and ambition and enjoyment of life. A lot depends on what is understood by a comfortable lifestyle: This could easily frustrate and bore her as much as a workplace where her development is not honestly supported.

4. Was it right for Sunita's managers to use me to tell her the truth?

No: It was a sign of management incompetence and disrespect. The managers themselves need coaching to take better responsibility for their people by telling them what they really think. Unfortunately, the abuse of coaching is a sign of weak leadership. Generally such managers don't care too much about their subordinates and don't develop strong bonds with them, which makes it easy for them to let others communicate what they should be saying. If the coaching helps coachees see what's going on behind the scenes, and help them take consequences, the coaching has been successful.

## POST-CASE NOTE

*Marcia Reynolds*

I believe that in order to maintain trust, the person I am coaching must always take priority over the company that is paying me. If the employer wants me to do something that is not in the best interest of the client, I will cancel the contract. In this instance I felt that I was capable of coaching Sunita on both her emotional intelligence and on making decisions that were the best for her future, and so I continued with the assignment.

However, I was careful never to personalize the relationship and to avoid having to answer the question of what I would do if I were in her position. Sunita was very hurt by the way senior management saw her and very confused about her future options. Yet I had to be careful not to lead her in one direction or another. The decision of whether to stay or leave the company had to be hers.

After the first month of coaching, Sunita agreed to give it her best shot for six months, after which time we would reevaluate her position. During those six months we worked on her behavior in meetings, on how to deal with difficult colleagues, on how she could get her team more involved in solving client problems, and how she could obtain more recognition for her projects from upper management. I explored the likelihood of her being reconciled to remaining in her current position—but it was quite clear from the outset that this would never satisfy her aspirations.

After six months of coaching, Sunita talked to her boss about her future. Despite the progress she had made, he remained implacable. As far as he was concerned, she was no more likely to be promoted than she had been when he placed her on the development program. I wasn't at all surprised when Sunita chose to resign. But when she announced her decision I asked her frankly if she really felt she had given it her best shot. Her response was immediate and emphatic: "Absolutely, yes."

That was the affirmation I needed. I felt she was making her decision logically and not from an emotional response to the situation. I did not coach her to find another job. However, I did coach her to think through each step as she notified people and made plans for her exit. As fortune would have it, the company announced another round of job cuts and Sunita was able to take a severance package that afforded her enough time to find a new job.

I enjoyed coaching Sunita even though I felt the people she reported to lacked integrity and leadership skills. I believe that, had they been honest and direct with her from the beginning, she might have stayed longer in her position to develop her skills further. I could cope with our relationship because Sunita was willing to do what she could to be seen as a leader even if her chances of promotion were slim.

However, I had difficulty coping with what I felt was her abandonment by the senior management team. I didn't like that they had "outsourced" difficult decisions to me. Sunita had embarked upon what she had been led to believe was a leadership development path but which turned out to be an intentional dead end. In one of the world's largest biotech companies even the HR department failed to provide any support in helping Sunita map out her career path.

I believe the company lost an exceptional employee but there was nothing I could do to alter the situation. It is hard to keep your client's hopes up when doors keep slamming in her face. In the end, I felt Sunita made the decision that was best for her. And even though I am sure that the company, which had paid me to coach Sunita, lost out in the end, I was confident that I had not failed in my duty to them. The decision to engineer Sunita's departure was entirely theirs and I was proud that I had remained neutral.

# 15

# THE NEEDS OF THE GROUP VS. THE NEEDY COACHEE

## *THOMAS HELLWIG*

*Case summary*

In Thomas Hellwig's case, one of the participants in a group coaching engagement brings loaded personal emotional baggage to the coaching session. The other participants are surprised by the level of personal disclosure and emotional engagement of their colleague. The coach is concerned with the effect the behavior of the participant can have on other members of the coaching group. He also raises the challenges of transference and possible counter-transference in this coaching exercise.

*Context*: The case takes place in an Executive MBA (EMBA) program run by a French-based, international business school that offers its participants group coaching opportunities.

## BACKGROUND

The duration of the coaching element in the Executive MBA (EMBA) program is about 10 months, with four coaching sessions in that time period. The interventions include a group coaching session some three months after the start of the program, when participants consider their 360-degree feedback surveys and are debriefed by the coach in the group session. Participants then have at least two follow-up phone calls with the coach before the group reconvenes two months before finishing the program, for another day of group and one-to-one coaching sessions.

This particular group was a diverse mixture of occupations and nationalities. As the executive coach contracted to work with the group, I was responsible for coaching and carrying out both the group and one-to-one interventions, under the supervision of the professor directing this part of the program.

## THE CHALLENGE

The sole Frenchman in the group, Pierre, was a 29-year-old marketing executive who admitted to having struggled with problems in his professional and personal life and had failed to complete his first degree. His parents had divorced during his adolescence and it was to this that he attributed most of his emotional problems, even to the extent of having had suicidal thoughts following his parents' separation and the departure of his father. Pierre's mother had high social expectations that he believed had instilled in him a fear of failure (a fear he admitted plagued him even on the executive program). As a young man Pierre had undergone psychoanalysis to help him overcome the problems he had in dealing with his emotional, social, and sexual relationships. After a while Pierre, thinking he had overcome his psychological problems, stopped seeing his analyst, only to discover later that the underlying causes still remained.

All this was outlined to me and the rest of the group at the very beginning of the first session, when Pierre announced that he was very self-aware and expected everyone to be very open with him. Strangely, though, Pierre then kept quiet for most of the rest of the day, contributing little to the discussion of other people's presentations and choosing to give his presentation last of all.

The EMBA group coaching session always starts off with the "ice-breaker" exercise of each participant drawing a self-portrait illustrating how they see themselves; this is followed by a discussion of their 360-degree feedback survey. When Pierre's turn came to deliver his presentation, he produced his self-portrait and explained the imagery he had used: A broken-down house symbolized his head, a gun represented his work and his heart was shown as a castle—indicating that it was both a fortress and a place of conflict, he explained.

During this session, Pierre broke down several times when discussing his parents, his early childhood, and his own marriage (which, he explained, was already on the rocks). He also became very upset when discussing his job and in particular his relationship with his immediate boss whom Pierre considered was not up to the job.

## MY APPROACH

This sort of thing doesn't happen very often on the EMBA and the rest of Pierre's group was visibly shocked by this unexpected emotional outburst. They were nevertheless sympathetic toward Pierre and, with their support and encouragement, he struggled courageously to complete his presentation—all the while reminding us how self-aware he was and how he was the only one within the group who had dropped his guard and "gone naked."

The extent of Pierre's nervous excitement was obvious not just from his frequent emotional outbursts but from his physical behavior. He smoked heavily and, when he couldn't smoke, constantly bit his nails and gnawed obsessively on plastic spoons. At the end of the group session I took Pierre to one side and had a conversation with him to assure myself that he was capable of continuing with the coaching process. We also discussed some ideas for a personal action plan, which Pierre agreed would need to be in place for our first follow-up call.

The aim of the first telephone follow-up call is principally to fine-tune the individual action plan. However, Pierre's session had to be extended to two calls because he wanted not only to review his action plan but also start some sort of therapy interaction with me. He knew that, as well as being his coach, I was a medical doctor with a degree in psychotherapy (as well as an MBA) and he felt I could help him deal with some of his emotional issues.

On the final coaching day Pierre came across as much more relaxed and determined in both the group and one-to-one sessions. He declared that he had benefited a lot from the EMBA program, learned a lot about leadership development, and had improved hugely in terms of his self-confidence. He also announced that his relationship with his wife had improved and their marriage was back on a sound footing. Nevertheless, I noticed that Pierre's chain-smoking, nail-biting, and spoon-chewing continued unchecked.

## THE COACHING DILEMMA

As a coach, it was my duty to manage Pierre and prevent his histrionics impacting on the needs of the group as a whole. I was keen to prevent him taking center stage and did not want the other group members to feel uncomfortable or to be inhibited by Pierre's lurid descriptions of his relationships and sexual problems. My task was to define the boundaries of the coaching relationship and advise him to seek alternative professional help for his underlying psychological problems. Personally, I also had to manage the transference of his feelings toward me as his coach.

Even before our first group coaching session I was expecting some difficulty with Pierre, having previously read through his 360-degree feedback form and his personal appraisal. What I hadn't anticipated was the emotional outpouring that confronted us at that first group session. Thinking on my feet, my first reaction was to give him space and let him tell his story; but I was careful to avoid encouraging him to expose more of his complex psychology than was absolutely necessary, as I feared derailment of the session if the other participants were present.

Instead, I tried gently to reinforce the notion that Pierre's main objective was to complete the EMBA program successfully and thus boost his self-confidence in all aspects of his personal and professional life. In our one-to-one sessions I discouraged Pierre from setting over-ambitious behavioral goals for his action plan, suggesting that he focus on realistic and practical issues such as engaging more effectively with his team, communicating with his boss, and tackling his nervous habits such as nail-biting and heavy smoking.

To preempt Pierre's transference toward me and avoid any risk of my becoming emotionally entangled with him, I took care to discriminate rigorously between issues appropriate to the coaching process and personal issues more appropriate to other forms of counseling and psychotherapy. In fact on several occasions I advised Pierre to seek professional psychological help from other sources, but my suggestions fell on deaf ears.

## MEETING THE CHALLENGE

In hindsight, I felt that I was able to deal with Pierre in a professional way, helping him stay on course and complete his EMBA program. He gained a lot of self-confidence (according to his self-assessment) and his relationship problems apparently improved. Although I was unable to persuade Pierre to seek counseling with another specialist, I felt that I successfully avoided the dangers of counter-transference and remained emotionally detached. I was helped to a large extent here by the program director and the professor supervising the coaching element. Furthermore, the group as a whole did not suffer from Pierre's emotional outbursts; all participants completed the program to their satisfaction and without alienating Pierre within the group setting.

## . . . AND FAILING TO MEET THE CHALLENGE

Despite helping Pierre complete his EMBA successfully, I failed to persuade him to adopt more realistic targets for his personal action plan. Despite reporting a boost to his self-confidence, Pierre never addressed his behavioral action targets—the nail-biting, smoking, and spoon-chewing—and he continued to pursue these vices energetically right through to the end of the program. In fact, Pierre chose not to include nearly all of the targets for improvement that I had initially identified in his action plan. Consequently he didn't work on them and made no progress. Hence, as a coach I felt that I had failed—although with hindsight, I wonder whether, given Pierre's volatile psychological state and the nature of the coaching intervention, I was being too ambitious.

Should I have offered Pierre some further help in the form of individual coaching either within the EMBA contract or under a private arrangement? Was there ever truly a risk of transference and counter-transference and did I handle the situation well?

## THE NEEDS OF THE GROUP VS. THE NEEDY COACHEE: COMMENTARY

*Antonio Galvan Luna*
During coaching interventions, it is very common for clients to see the coach as someone reliable to whom they can address many issues and problems in areas other than simply business. The current business environment teaches us to treat

work and personal life as different matters, and that they shouldn't interfere with each other; but in my opinion they are not totally separate. On the contrary, they are intricately mixed together and the right balance between the two can determine success. For this reason, I think that it is understandable that Pierre went "fully naked" in the coaching session and that he opened himself to that degree with the coach. This has happened to me on a couple of occasions, even in academic environments. For example, I teach an entrepreneurship course at a Spanish university, where every professor is assigned as a mentor to a group of five to 10 students. I have been surprised when clients start telling me about their personal issues, out of the blue—and even more when I start getting the feeling that they really want to hear my opinion. I believe that Pierre should definitely get professional advice, as overcoming his problems will greatly determine his success as a manager and an individual.

The difficult thing for the coach in this case is that Pierre sees the group sessions as an opportunity to solve his personal problems, and not as a professional development opportunity. In a recent article,[1] Steven Berglas, a business coach on the faculty of Harvard Medical School's Department of Psychiatry, identified several points that coaches should always remember, three of which are particularly relevant to this case:

- Coaches aren't paid to make people feel good.
- Coaches respect boundaries between the professional and personal realms.
- Coaches are not life-directors.

Perhaps it would be good for the coach to talk honestly to Pierre during a personal session about his opinion of what Pierre needs and what is happening to him. Of course this would have to be done carefully, so as not to worsen matters for Pierre, but not retaining the coach's objectivity. I think that failure to do so would greatly harm the coach's performance with the rest of the group, and especially with Pierre.


## POST-CASE NOTE

*Thomas Hellwig*

The ESMT coaching colloquium provided me with further insights through the peer review of my case. A couple of colleagues pointed out the one fact I seemed to have overlooked: That despite the care I had taken to balance Pierre's needs with those of the rest of the group, I had ended up investing far more effort in coaching him than I had in coaching any of the others. Had I looked more dispassionately at the evidence emerging during our 10 months of coaching on the EMBA, I might have noticed a pattern to Pierre's behavior that only became apparent with hindsight: He manipulates relationships up to the point where people have had enough and seek to distance themselves from him.

So, as one person at the Colloquium correctly observed, Pierre had managed in the end to manipulate me so that I would ignore the boundaries of our coaching relationship. Another colleague asked whether I had felt "excited and proud," having sorted out such a difficult case. Maybe I did. There is no doubt that interesting or challenging cases can be seductive for a coach who might be tempted to invest more time and effort in a certain relationship than in others.

## NOTE

1. S. Berglas (2009). *Six Tips on Hiring a Business Coach*, http://www.forbes.com/2009/12/04/hiring-business-coach-entrepreneurs-management-berglas.html, April 12, 2011. Accessed on October 3, 2011.

# 16

## COACHING IN A FOURSOME

### *SHARON CHIRBAN*

*Case summary*

Sharon Chirban presents a case where a business owner contacts a coach to help her with personal growth and development. The coachee is particularly attracted by the coach's experience of working with athletes, as she is very athletic herself and sets a high value on physical achievement. Although the initial contract was about business, as trust between coach and coachee develops, the latter confides in the former about intimate aspects of her emotional and sexual life. The coach has to deal with the issue of boundary-setting or risk becoming involved in a complex mélange of business, relationships, sexuality, and emotions.

*Context*: The case takes place in the United States.

## BACKGROUND

Michelle is, by anybody's standards, a formidable woman. She runs a small business that she launched on her own a few years ago—but it won't be small for much longer. It is growing rapidly thanks to her creativity, enthusiasm, and savvy business mind. She's an ambitious forward-thinker and has plans for franchising her business, which, if successful, will see it take off in a very big way.

Like many small businesses, Michelle has benefited from working with a non-profit association staffed by volunteers and dedicated to educating entrepreneurs and helping them start, grow, and succeed in business. Although she is supremely confident and knows her own mind, Michelle is not too proud to seek the help and advice of an expert when she feels she lacks knowledge or experience in a particular area.

And that's what led Michelle to contact me. She was looking for a consultant to help her with her personal growth and development as a business owner and somewhere along the line my name came up. I do a lot of work with top athletes and this must have struck a chord with Michelle who is no mean athlete herself. Indeed, she feels that her physical and intellectual performances are inextricably linked; she reckoned that what works for an Olympic athlete would probably work for her, too. One of the areas I focus on with athletes is helping them deal with emotional problems that can obstruct their optimal performance. This was what Michelle was looking for; she wanted more control over her emotions and was especially keen to address her anger management both in and out of the office.

Michelle's is an intense personality with a very masculine streak of aggression. When she wants to unwind, she invariably engages in some sort of extreme physical activity. Her kind of sport is not the kind normally associated with women, and very few men do all the things she does. She plays rugby, she does several martial arts, she fences, and she lifts weights for up to three hours at a time. She's an impressive figure standing over six feet tall, blonde with angular features, very fit, and frequently dressed in gender-neutral clothing. One of Michelle's favorite pastimes is motorcycling. Last year, to test her nerve, she rode the Tail of the Dragon at Deals Gap, North Carolina. This is a stretch of two-lane highway with a reputation for being America's most challenging motorcycle route, with 318 bends in 11 miles. Every year the road claims the lives of a handful of unlucky motorcyclists whose skills or nerve fail them at a critical point.

This is the sort of challenge Michelle relishes. She seeks the adrenaline rush that comes from pushing herself to the limits of her fear threshold. But although she loves danger, she is not reckless; she describes herself as a "prepared risk-taker" who is always in control. After riding the Tail of the Dragon, she felt tremendous elation—but having done it, she felt no need to do it a second time.

## MY ROLE AS COACH

Although Michelle engaged my services as a coach, she was aware that I also run a clinical psychology–psychotherapy practice and wanted to know a little more about this. She herself had been in therapy earlier in her life and the experience had not been a particularly good one. The therapist had been a woman who, as Michelle put it, "had poor boundaries"—she had tried to establish a personal bond instead of maintaining a professional relationship. Michelle had found this intrusive and very unsettling. She confessed to me that she had difficulty trusting women, though it remained unclear as to whether that predated her encounter with this therapist or was a consequence of it. Suffice to say, I was on the alert for potential conflict following this revelation.

As far as her family life was concerned, Michelle seemed to have no problems that could be impacting on her professional life. She had been happily married for 18 years and had two daughters, aged 16 and 12. Her husband, although not directly involved in her business, spent a lot of time with her and was intimately involved with her business decision-making.

Our coaching sessions all took place in my office, mainly because of the limited privacy available in Michelle's own business environment. Given her interest in my clinical training, we established a relationship that was essentially fluid and permitted some crossover between the coaching and clinical consultancies. This has proved to be an effective arrangement and remains ongoing today.

A central theme of my work with Michelle acknowledges as her "alpha tendencies." About six months into coaching, she drew up a list of the issues we had discussed that neatly summarized her defining traits:

"1. Trust issues
 2. Vulnerability issues (tied to trust)
 3. Pro-active
 4. Protective instinct for others (sometimes overly protective)
 5. Action oriented (DOING something brings comfort)
 6. Edge oriented
 7. Wired for fight instead of flight
 8. Growth oriented
 9. Impatient
10. Averse to rigid systems
11. Extreme sense of personal responsibility
12. Loyal
13. Difficult history with female relationship (tied to vulnerability)
14. Disciplined
15. Struggles with unintentional intimidation."

We spent several months working exclusively on Michelle's "quick to blow" style and trying to build some space between her feeling and her actions. We made good progress, and pretty soon Michelle began to feel she had more control over her emotions than previously. Now she wanted to explore other issues related to business relationships. This involved less coaching and more therapy as we began to explore Michelle's background and upbringing. She revealed that she and her four siblings were all adopted as babies and none of them was biologically related. Her relationship with her mother had been fiery and at times violent, as her mother was both physically and verbally abusive.

Over several sessions, I began to identify key factors influencing Michelle's guardedness with women and her relationship with men, whose company she craved. Michelle's parents divorced when she was 16 and this proved a milestone in her emotional development. She effectively severed all contact with her mother and found the relationship with her father becoming stronger. After a childhood spent at war with her mother, Michelle's home life finally started to settle down.

About eight months into our coaching sessions, Michelle sent me an e-mail updating me on a number of emotional issues she had been struggling with, including recent news that her father had suffered a stroke. In it, she said:

Just so that my life doesn't seem all gloom and doom . . . I have been getting an exceptional amount of support from both Tom [her husband] and John [her operations manager] . . . [who] has been running interception for me regarding 90% of all business/employee issues. Our company is growing its membership base despite the economy [October 2008]. And, outside of some sleep issues, my health is good.

I also figured out a significant aspect of the "tightness" in my chest. It came after my meeting with you. Do you recall the dream I told you about before the end of the meeting? On the drive home, I was confused by why I felt very angry at myself for telling you about that dream. So I went through the process again in my mind and when I got to the part about telling you about this mother-figure embracing me . . . and the way it felt . . . that was when the tightness jumped.

So, here I have a dream that causes the "squirmy" feeling. It's not far from the dream I had some time ago about you providing comfort to me . . . and how difficult it was to tell you that part. Only this dream was harder because I ENJOYED being comforted by this woman. (Some serious squirming here.)


## THE CHALLENGE

After about 18 months of working together, Michelle told me that there was a subject she wanted to discuss with me but which she felt very uneasy about broaching. She wasn't sure that it was "safe." We'd covered self-issues as they pertained to her personal life and to work, and she was doing well in the coaching relationship. Even her fear of exposing herself to female empathy, support, and warmth—the blurring of boundaries that gave her the "squirmy" feeling—was under control. She could talk about the discomfort and tolerate it.

But she was very nervous about introducing this new issue. First, she questioned me again about my approach and sought assurances that I was not judgmental. She wanted to know how I would handle situations that I may not be able to relate to personally and of which I might disapprove. I replied—to Michelle's evident relief—that, as a professional, I had to be non-judgmental and that I would never allow my own prejudices to influence my conduct toward my client.

Despite this careful preparation, when Michelle finally did introduce this sensitive new subject, it came as a bombshell. She explained that she had been having an affair with John, her operations manager, for the previous 10 years. This of course changed everything and I immediately wondered if this would unravel the work I had done with Michelle. Then she told me that her husband, Tom, knew all about the affair and had known for several years. In fact he was quite relaxed about it. As a couple, they had agreed that Michelle was quite capable of having a strong emotional and sexual attachment to both men.

This revelation took us into completely new territory. This was no longer a straightforward business coaching relationship; I was now counseling Michelle on the most intimate aspects of her emotional life. Nevertheless, she still wanted me to help her move the situation on and asked several things of the coaching sessions in the months following this disclosure.

Michelle wasn't emotionally confused about this *ménage-à-trois* but she realized it was potentially disruptive from a social and professional viewpoint, principally as a result of other people's prejudices. She just wanted me to help her find the best way of putting it on a steady footing so that she could adopt a fully open marital arrangement. As far as I was concerned, there was nothing to prevent me serving as a sounding board for her on the various issues surrounding this decision. Michelle was, after all, a taker of calculated risks and she simply wanted to set the boundaries for an open marriage with diligent, mindful preparation. She thought through some ground rules and presented them to Tom; she wanted him to have the benefit of the same freedom that she had with her colleague and lover John. There were a few basic ground rules all agreed to:

1. Every partner needed to be in a fully open relationship—or single and fully informed of the other relationships.
2. Michelle and Tom's children were to be protected from knowing about this new arrangement until they were mature enough to be told, or started asking questions.
3. In order to protect the children and safeguard the reputation of the business, partners outside the marriage could not be members of their immediate community.

Besides being unconventional, the situation was complicated further by the fact that Michelle was trying to find a full-time job in her company for John, who currently operated as a freelance consultant. His passion was for the creative aspect of Michelle's business—indeed, the two had met while working together at another company operating in the same industry—and he didn't like the workaday tasks of an operations manager.

Michelle shared John's frustrations and told me that she felt that his creative talents would be of unique benefit to her company. This may well have been true, but I wondered on several occasions to what extent Michelle was trying to rationalize her desire to please John, ease his dissatisfaction with his work, and create a closer bond with him. Michelle brought Tom along to a few of these coaching sessions in order to discuss and refine the ground rules. At other times, John came in with her to meet me, talk about their business relationship and the transition they hoped to make so he could join her staff full-time.

So far, so good, except for the one glaring oversight that remained unmentioned for months. John was married with two very young children, and his wife, Cindy, knew nothing about his affair with Michelle. Thus at the very start the most fundamental ground rule had been violated. For a long time Michelle tried to avoid addressing this issue. Her business was doing well, she felt in control and both Tom and John were giving her the love and support she needed. In one of our coaching sessions she told me how, after the quarterly review meeting in the office, she, John, and Tom had gone back to her house to celebrate their latest business success.

After a few drinks and much mutual congratulation, Tom encouraged John to take Michelle upstairs and celebrate in an altogether more libidinous way, which they duly did. John subsequently left the bedroom, leaving the door open for Tom to join Michelle in bed. The uncomfortable question of Cindy's interests didn't seem to be an inhibiting factor to the behavior of this *ménage-à-trois* and with one golden rule irrevocably broken, the entire situation was on a precipice. The coaching relationship was now on the line.

## THE COACHING DILEMMA

Although ostensibly Michelle's business coach, I now felt that I was being inveigled into this complex threesome as some sort of facilitator. My role was to help them negotiate their different marital, sexual, business, and social interactions. As Michelle related the graphic account of her night with Tom and John, all I could think about was Cindy. I felt that she had been violated and the fact that all three had acted collectively seemed to compound that violation.

I felt that I had to confront Michelle with her own broken rule and make her account for her inconsistency. It was the most difficult session we had had. Michelle was on the defensive—and her favored form of defense is preemptive attack. Meanwhile, I was aware that I was pushing my neutrality to its limit and I needed to avoid being dragged into the maelstrom. I needed to stay on the outside and was therefore prepared to put our professional relationship on the line and begin withdrawing from the assignment if Michelle couldn't accept my boundaries.

## COACHING IN A FOURSOME: COMMENTARY

*Sabine Dembkowski*
The key themes that struck me when I read this case were "boundaries" and "contracting."

In our practice we focus on business coaching and state this very clearly in our kick-off sessions. Yes, we do explore private issues as far as they relate to work issues. I understand that due to the strong clinical component of this coach's background, coaching conversations incorporated the personal history of the client, private matters, and love life. For me, this would have been a case where I would have separated out the business and personal at the outset and referred the client to explore the relationship aspects with a professional with a clinical qualification. However, I recognize that in this particular case, it could be possible to hold both types of relationship with the client.

I wondered what exactly had been explored and discussed when building the foundation for the coaching program, and what was agreed in the kick-off session—in essence, what themes and issues were part of the contracting? What exactly was the aim of the coaching program? What aspects of her personality did Michelle aim to develop?

It seems that many issues were discussed and over time matters became more and more private, exploring intimate issues. I wondered if at any stage the coach and the client had reflected on the direction the sessions were taking, and whether they explored the actual starting point of their professional coaching relationship.

Early on in the relationship it appears to be clear that the client had issues with establishing trust relationships with women. I wondered how the coach dealt with this in the course of this specific coaching relationship.

What really struck me was that the lack of boundaries the client had displayed, in blurring her business and private life over time, was replicated in the coaching relationship. I wondered if this was reflected upon when the coaching conversation started to develop in this direction. I also wondered if it is the role of a coach to develop plots for dealing with a threesome. On reflection, would the coach have drawn the line earlier and refocused the discussions on the initial topics of business growth?

For me, this case highlights the importance of investing in the contracting phase of a coaching program and regular pulse checks where coach and client come back to the initial contractual issues.

## POST-CASE NOTE

*Sharon Chirban*

It was tough, but we worked it out. Michelle could not deny her failure to observe her own ground rules and accepted that she had to rethink her desires and set new objectives in her personal life. She and John no longer have a sexual relationship; with my help, she worked through her feelings of loss and helped John come to terms with the need to get their relationship on a more sustainable footing. Although no longer lovers, they remain close friends and enjoy a balanced business relationship.

During this difficult process, I have had to draw another line. Michelle has continually tried to put forward the notion that I am the only person John can talk to either about the changes in their relationship or in his unhappy marital situation. Although Michelle's company pays me to coach its staff, including John, I have steadfastly refused to provide that level of coaching to him. I have instead offered on numerous occasions to find a good therapist to help him process his feelings of loss and ambivalence in his marriage, an offer that he has yet to accept.

Michelle is a charismatic, appreciative, and very demanding client. She holds me in high esteem—more than I deserve—and makes it very tempting for me to try and be everything to everyone. But during the process of coaching Michelle, I have worked out how far I'm prepared to go in analyzing the complex social, emotional, and professional environment with which she has surrounded herself. I can clearly see where I must draw the line so that my work can be creative, productive, and helpful.

Michelle's abortive attempt to enlist me in constructing a workable open marriage was doomed to failure. After agreeing to the original ground rules (rule one of which was instantly broken by the collective failure to consider Cindy's interests), Tom broke rule two by starting an affair with a woman from the couple's own social circle. His lover then divulged details of the affair to another friend, who expressed horror at the news and declared a fierce disapproval of open marriages.

In a state of panic, Michelle called me with a desperate request to meet up in order to plan how she should break the news to her two daughters, just in case word got out. This was territory into which I definitely did not want to stray, so again I made another referral, suggesting an expert in tricky adolescent parenting situations. Wearing my therapy hat, I could have provided some help in solving this problem but I had now set my parameters and Michelle's family life was no longer on my agenda.

## Lessons learned

I guess this coaching experience has been a little bit like riding the Tail of the Dragon: Very challenging, fraught with risk, littered with unexpected twists and turns, but ultimately exhilarating. It has also taught me many valuable lessons, such as when to ride and when to get off the bike.

As I worked on my presentation for the ESMT Colloquium, I became acutely aware of this particular client's notion that I could be "everything to everyone." Such a client appeals to the coach's narcissism; to be so highly valued can be alluring. So it is important to keep checking your boundaries when a client comes to the coaching process with such complex and colorful life issues.

Furthermore, not all coaches are equipped to deal with "messy" cases like this one that do not easily fit within the lines. I generally cope well in such circumstances and in this case I was willing to renegotiate the goals of our coaching relationship as the client proceeded to introduce new and very challenging items to the coaching agenda. When I eventually drew the line, it was not because the case was becoming overly complicated or I was concerned about "mission-creep"; I drew the line because I saw value inconsistencies that I was not prepared to overlook because of the harmful ramifications for another person.

# 17

# REFUSAL TO BE COACHED

## *ANNA URNOVA*

*Case summary*

Anna Urnova runs a group coaching session with several challenging participants. One of the managers, who is significantly older than the coach and the other participants, is initially cooperative and signals that she has learned something. However, after the end of the group coaching session and on the eve of individual meetings between coaches and coachees, the participant refuses to participate and talks negatively about the whole coaching experience.

*Context*: The intervention takes place in Russia.

## BACKGROUND

It is not unusual for a coach to feel intimidated by a particular client. Perhaps the client is hostile and reluctant to be coached. And sometimes the client is a strong, dominant character who likes to be in control at all times. Whatever the reason, the coach can be made to feel uncomfortable in the client's company; in these circumstances everything depends on how the coach responds, as I found out recently when asked to provide coaching as part of a leadership development program for a big corporate client in Russia.

The client organization was a large Russian company undergoing a period of rapid change. A recent merger was being finalized, key appointments were still being announced following a major management shake-up earlier in the year, and of course, like all large corporations, the company was facing the fallout from the global financial crisis. I was familiar with the company and its circumstances, having already carried out some successful one-to-one coaching assignments for some of its executives.

## MY ROLE AS COACH

I was one of a team of executive coaches hired to provide half a day of group coaching followed by one-to-one coaching sessions the following day. The aim of the group session was to help the participants practice their leadership skills in a group setting, while individual sessions were intended to assist individual clients in understanding their personal assessment data and integrating them into their personal development plans. A few days before the event I was provided with the names of the clients allocated to me, together with their full biographical details and assessment data, so that I could prepare for the individual coaching sessions. Although I had worked with the organization before, this was the first time I had been asked to carry out group coaching and I couldn't help feeling a bit apprehensive.

## THE CHALLENGE

When preparing for the individual coaching sessions, one particular individual, Natalia, worried me. Having read her biographical information, I suspected that my session with her would be difficult. Natalia was almost my mother's age; she had a son my age. I couldn't help wondering whether she would accept that I was sufficiently experienced and competent to coach her. Something else troubled me: Why had the organization sent her on a leadership course? As a senior executive with more than 20 years' management experience, she appeared to be in a different league from her colleagues on the course. Furthermore, she was only two years from the usual retirement age. What were she and her employer expecting to get out of this exercise?

Natalia's feedback reports were overall quite positive with the highest scores given by her boss and the lowest by her direct subordinates. She appeared to be good at delivering results, leading people, and managing relations, but not so good at managing conflict. Her lowest scores were for flexibility, emotional stability, and her ability to handle ambiguity. Natalia and her boss both thought she had potential for future career development whereas those who worked directly under her seemed to think she had reached her career ceiling and would not cope with promotion.

Her psychometric data showed an extrovert character with clear preferences for making decisions based on consensus and personal values rather than rules and logic. Natalia admitted to needing to feel in control and considered her main strengths to be honesty, helpfulness, willingness to take responsibility, and an ability to get on well with people. At the same time she wished to be more emotionally stable, more spontaneous, and to improve her work–life balance. The people she most had difficulty dealing with were, in her own words, "unprofessional managers who stick their noses into other people's business."

On the basis of this information I decided that in Natalia's individual coaching session I would focus on her strengths, in order to build her confidence, before exploring ways in which she could use these qualities to address issues such as her tendency to overwork and become emotionally stressed.

Right from the beginning of the group coaching session I realized I had been allocated a particularly "tricky" group of individuals. There were four of them, three women and one man. The man was so quiet and detached that he seemed almost asleep; however, the three women (of whom Natalia was, of course, one) were not merely animated but actively confrontational. They questioned me at every turn—even challenging me when, in my introduction, I said that every participant would be acting out an eight minutes' role-play in front of the group. One of the women interrupted to complain that this was not what they had been promised by the trainers and produced her program binder to prove her point. Her indignation persisted even when it transpired that the agenda clearly stated that a coaching role-play would last "from six to 10 minutes."

Things did not improve very much after that. There was constant sniggering and rolling of eyes, the three women talked over me, engaged in parallel conversations, and even answered mobile phones in defiance of agreed rules. Surprisingly, of the three women, Natalia (whom I had expected to be the most challenging) was the most positive and at times was even supportive of me. She clearly carried some authority with the other two, who constantly deferred to her instead of to me. Nevertheless I appreciated her support and thanked her openly.

However, discipline within the group remained a challenge throughout the session. Rest breaks and coffee breaks dragged on far too long and it was a constant struggle for me to get everybody back on task. When I tried to exert some authority, the three women seemed to think I was being bossy and seemed to resent my attempts to assert my role as coach.

## MY APPROACH

Natalia was the first to perform her eight minutes of role-play. She did well and received a lot of positive feedback not only from me, but also from the rest of the group. I don't recall giving her any critical feedback at that point but I do remember noting with some surprise that she was not very comfortable even with positive feedback. She appeared to want to preempt others' comments by offering her own critique or brushing their comments aside; it sounded as if she was inviting praise and resisting it at the same time.

Her next opportunity to perform for the group involved Natalia playing the role of one of her own staff; the idea was to make each coachee act out a situation they had encountered in real life. In this instance, Natalia was playing the part of a young single mother whose work was suffering as a result of her stressful home life. The part of Natalia's manager was played by one of the two younger women.

To me, the exercise seemed successful. The younger woman managed to force Natalia into opening up by leaving long pauses between questions—Natalia took the cue and spoke up in order to fill the silence. Afterwards, Natalia admitted that the approach of her opposite number had been productive and very different from the approach she herself took as a line manager in a real work situation.

At the end of the session I asked the group for their feedback and was pleased when they all said the session had been useful. Natalia herself said that of the many leadership development courses she had attended, this was the first in which she actually learned something new, namely the power of asking open questions and pausing to listen. So despite the somewhat turbulent nature of the session, I felt quite satisfied that I had helped my group and that they had all got some value from it.

## MY DILEMMA

After the group coaching session I was approached by a member of the company's HR department who wanted to warn me, ahead of the following day's individual coaching sessions, that Natalia had demonstrated a very negative attitude toward the leadership development course. This was a major concern because Natalia had power in the organization and exerted a lot of influence through the corporate grapevine. The HR executive asked me to make every effort to show Natalia the value of coaching and address her negativity. I replied that I had found Natalia more cooperative during the group session than some of the other participants and that I was not unduly concerned about her attitude.

However just minutes later, as I waited to speak to Natalia about the following day's session, one of the other coaches told me that he had just witnessed Natalia having a furious row with the program supervisor. I waited in vain for Natalia while other coaches earnestly enquired what was going on. Eventually the program supervisor came and told me that Natalia was refusing to have an individual coaching session with me tomorrow. It appeared that she found my manner distant, cold, and arrogant and did not feel there was sufficient rapport between us. However, she had been persuaded to sleep on it and would let the company know in the morning whether she was prepared to cooperate or not.

That evening I pored over Natalia's feedback documents and assessment data trying to convince myself that there had simply been some misunderstanding and that tomorrow's session would go ahead as scheduled. But early next morning the company called to say that Natalia had not changed her mind and the company would therefore not be requiring my services after all.

## REFUSAL TO BE COACHED: COMMENTARY 1

*Gudrun Becker*
A number of questions came to my mind after reading this case:

- Why had Natalia, the coachee with whom Anna had a problem, been chosen for the leadership development program? Was there a hidden agenda for including Natalia in the course?
- Why did the coach not make the apparently disruptive behavior of the group a subject of discussion?

- What has triggered the coachee's strong reactions to the process?
- Is the coachee herself a better coach?
- Would Anna, the coach, be willing to be coached by Natalia, the coachee in this scenario?

Considering these questions, I developed the following hypotheses.

There may be a different understanding of coaching between the organization that contracted for this project and the coach. The working plan for the coaching session and the time schedule appear to be strictly predetermined, without any room for maneuver for the coach. There may be confusion about Anna's role: Was she expected to be a moderator or facilitator, and not explicitly a coach in this scenario?

The work hypothesis of the coach appears to be contradictory: On the one hand the coachee is described as an experienced, successful, and confident executive. Natalia's behavior during the group coaching session reinforces this image. On the other hand, according to the planned intervention of the coach, Natalia needed support to strengthen her self-confidence.

The behavior of the group members in the coaching session expresses their reluctance toward the leadership development intervention, which could be a sign of resistance toward organizational change. The participants may have felt powerless within the organization and have used the coach to vent their frustrations.

The issue of seniority was an important value for the group involved in this coaching intervention, and it could have been the basis for the acceptance and approval of professional expertise.

The participation of Natalia, an older and more experienced manager, in the leadership training and this particular intervention may have created resistance among the younger executives. Not having discussed the issue openly, the coach found herself to be used as a scapegoat in this situation.

The coach lost authority in front of the group because she didn't discuss the difficult working situation with the participants.

The lack of acceptance of the coach by the coachee was reinforced by the positive feedback offered by Natalia to Anna at the end of the group session. The coachee may have felt a confirmation that she was good in the role of a coach herself. For her, there was neither a critical reflection of her performance nor a perspective for new learning opportunities. Anna's self-doubt about success in the forthcoming individual coaching session may have been reflected in the reassuring reaction of Natalia to the course publicly given to Anna.

With these hypotheses in mind, I thought about what could have been done differently. I think that it was necessary to discuss the group's resistance to coaching from the very beginning of the coaching situation. The position of the coach could have been strengthened by doing so. It could have also helped to gain clarity on the background of the group's behavior and contribute to the development of a constructive working atmosphere. By putting up with the group's disturbances, the coach probably undermined her overall position as someone who could help the group in general and Natalia in particular.

## REFUSAL TO BE COACHED: COMMENTARY 2

*Silke Matthies*

My first impression when I read Anna's case was that her situation was very complex and muddled. There may be several starting points for considering how to handle the situation differently. I will start from a global perspective, looking at the roles of the corporate client and the coaching organization, as well as at the setting for the group and the coaching process. After that I will look at possible issues of program content, the team, and the individuals involved.

### Corporate client

The corporate client faces dramatic changes due to the financial crisis and pending organizational change. These circumstances definitely have an impact on the corporate and leadership culture. How does the communication concept of providing feedback and a coaching leadership style fit into the corporate culture? Change is often accompanied by uncertainty and anxiety about the future. The expected organizational changes mentioned in the case involve a management shake-up that may have consequences for the individuals involved.

As far as the leadership development program in which Anna was involved is concerned, it is not unrealistic to think that participants might not see the benefit on working on their coaching skills. They might also feel under too much pressure to perform role-playing. The anticipated change, the lack of perceived benefit of the training, and pressure to participate in anxiety-stimulating activities (role-play) might trigger strong emotions, which then contribute to resistance. The latter is demonstrated by the participants' behavior during the coaching session. Was the program inappropriate in the circumstances the company was in?

### The coaching organization

The corporate client is apparently very important for the coaching organization. There was probably high pressure to perform particularly well in this assignment. What was the purpose of including coaching in the leadership development program? Did the coaching organization decide to offer coaching to the corporate client because they are comfortable with the methodology, or because they have access to coaches? This is not discussed in this case—but it may be critical

REFUSAL TO BE COACHED

to look at how the program and its coaching component were introduced to the participants and linked to their organizational reality.

Also, I wonder what kind of information about the participants' likely attitude toward the program the coaching organization provided its facilitators and coaches with. For example, information about the prior participants' experience with leadership coaching, acceptance of coaching as a developmental approach by the client company, and previous leadership development interventions could have helped Anna prepare to address potential issues in the introduction to the group session. From my own experience, it is essential do so, in order to create the trust necessary for group interaction. In this case nothing is mentioned about the overall introduction to the program in general and the group coaching session in particular, although both might be critically important for the success of the coaching relationship.

## The setting

The coaching organization has consistent coaching standards and clear expectations. I wonder, however, how flexible those expectations are. What would the contractor think about deviations from the coaching methodology to deal with the issues of team dynamics and disturbances? The time schedule—a half-day for the group session with four participants—seems to be rather tight, with little room to deal with group dynamics effectively. Additional questions arise about the readiness of the participants to work with the methods selected by the coaching organization.

It might be helpful for Anna to reflect on her personal guidelines for facilitation and coaching. What are her criteria for refusing an assignment? What is her relationship with the coaching organization like? Can she address potential issues frankly? What kind of information and what kind of support does she need from the contractor before she dives into an assignment? Based on the information in the case, I am left with an impression that Anna was abandoned while dealing with a challenging situation; the coaching organization was either unaware that she needed help, or was not willing to offer it.

## The theme

The content of this intervention was coaching and leadership. It's important to know what attitude participants have toward the given topics of an intervention in order to balance their needs. For example, is it possible that the role-play focused on issues that seemed irrelevant to the anticipated organizational changes and the financial crisis? The potential misfit between the real needs of participants and the program offering could have been one reason for resistance.

## Group dynamics

For a group to be able to work together, a contract for cooperation is necessary in order to perform successfully. It is helpful when people get to know each other, clarify expectations, and explain what is important for each of the participants to be able to cooperate with others in a trustful and respectful manner. The forming process takes some time, usually 30–60 minutes. Was this covered at the beginning of the intervention? Another important factor to work effectively in a group setting is to pick people up where they stand—in other words, to refer to their current situation and, if necessary, to address their skepticism toward the content and the process, when introducing the session. I think forming and link to the current situation were missing here, and both would have been essential for dealing constructively with participants' resistance. At the very least, in this situation Anna could have switched to a meta-perspective and discussed what was going on in the group as the dynamic was unfolding. Why did the participants ask so many questions, giggle, and talk among themselves? What do participants need in order to start work on the task at hand? If expectations and rules of engagement had been clarified right in the beginning, Anna could have referred back to them. The insights from this meta-conversation would have been helpful to determine how to go on with the session more effectively, and also to provide a general feedback to the contractor for the preparation of future programs.

## The coach

There was a lot of pressure on Anna: The project was important for the contractor, she was running a group session for this organization for the first time, and she had quite a senior coachee. How could she have dealt with the pressure better? Did she have a chance to reduce it? One option might have been be to ask the coaching organization for an easier group to facilitate. Perhaps it would have been helpful to think about crucial group situations and figure out a strategy to deal with them upfront. Another way to handle the situation might have been to discuss her concerns regarding the seniority of her coachee with the coaching organization. Why did they select Anna as a coach for Natalia? The answers to these questions might have been a resource for Anna and a good introduction for the coaching: Anna might have begun "Perhaps you wonder, why I am your coach. The organization has chosen me because . . . ." It might have been an option to refuse Natalia as a coachee and to propose a more senior coach instead. If seniority remained an issue during coaching, it would be hard to focus on the process, because the coach would remain busy dealing with her own feelings and anxieties. I could imagine that this refusal would be seen as an indicator of self-awareness and professionalism, rather than a weakness.

## The coachee

Natalia acted as a *de facto* co-facilitator during the group session, was very cooperative, and provided a lot of valuable input. She clearly needed to be in charge and to exercise control. I assume that playing the role of a co-facilitator gave her the feeling of having control. I can imagine that in this situation a subtle power struggle started about who controlled the situation. Being supportive and productive during the workshop was probably a position in which Natalia felt comfortable, exercising control and influence over a situation where some other participants were distracted. Receiving feedback on her performance in the role-play might have put her in a position where she was no longer in control, and this might have stressed her. Taking the role of a coachee (subordinate), as she partially acknowledged later, was new learning for her. She might have realized how her direct reports felt when she acted as their boss in real life. She may have also realized that her subordinates had more power and control than she had previously thought. It could be that this difficult learning and the unwillingness to be in an uncomfortable coachee position led to cancellation of the coaching session the next day, which allowed her to be in control again. Moreover, the coaching organization's team was now ready to do everything possible to please her. This is, of course, only one of several possible explanations of what could be going on at that moment.

Individual coaching might be challenging for Natalia. Assuming she agreed to participate, it would be very important to give her opportunities to decide how to continue with the process and to create a safe place for her, where she would have some control over the course of action. I would address Anna's surprise at hearing that Natalia was thinking about canceling the appointment. I would explore the differences in perception of the previous day, possible reasons for thinking about cancellation, and aim to change her mind. I would then explore what a valuable outcome for Natalia would be and what she needs to work on in order to achieve that. Referring back to the real situation, I think talking to Natalia about her decision not to participate in the individual coaching session would be interesting. I would not attempt to convince her to be coached, stressing that coaching is voluntary, and that I accept her decision. Nevertheless, understanding why Natalia did not want to continue would be interesting.

For future coaching assignments, Anna might think about the kind of coachees with whom she can work effectively, and where limits such as age, personal issues, or cultural differences might harm the process. It would also be useful to have a more systemic outlook to such an assignment and take the context into consideration.

## POST-CASE NOTE

*Anna Urnova*
The events described in this case took place in the space of just a few hours. But it took me six months fully to come to terms with what had happened.

I kept asking myself the same question that had occurred to me when I first read through Natalia's biographical summary: Was I the right coach for this woman? But I was missing the point. I should have asked myself whether I was expected to help the client or to prove that I was a good coach. My initial concern actually stemmed from my own insecurity and the doubts I had over my ability to appear competent and in control. Consequently my eagerness to prove I was a competent coach had made me appear stern and excessively business-like. Hence, from the start there was very little or no rapport between me and my coachees.

Another contributing factor was my failure to define my key client. I was focused on delivering the task for which I was briefed by the corporate client; when faced with strong resistance and negativity from the group, I saw this as an obstacle that had to be overcome in order to deliver results. What I should have done was focus on maximizing the learning opportunities for the group instead of concentrating on ticking the boxes on the agenda outline provided by the corporate client. In other words, I was focused on *doing things right* rather than *doing the right things*.

In the wake of this unsuccessful experience I faced another challenge: Coping with my own personal and professional reaction to events. The most difficult thing for me to deal with was the fact that Natalia's refusal to be coached happened publicly, in front of my coaching colleagues and the other coachees. Furthermore, I was informed of her refusal by a third party rather than by Natalia herself. My first reaction was shock and denial. But when I heard the following morning that Natalia was definitely not taking part, the reality of rejection started to dawn on me. I felt so angry that I could think of nothing else. I was angry with Natalia, angry with the coaching group, angry with the program supervisor for giving me the most recalcitrant group, and angry even with my fellow coaches who hadn't drawn the short straw. Eventually, anger turned to embarrassment. I looked at the situation through the eyes of the corporate client and other coaches and suddenly saw Natalia's rejection of me as a terrible and irreparable failure. I became discouraged, and less keen to take on new coaching assignments.

It would have been very difficult for me to move on without the support I received in the form of regular supervision and the peer group review at the ESMT coaching colloquium in Berlin. Here I was surprised and relieved to hear mostly supportive comments and questions that helped me look at the situation from a different point of view. I found I could separate myself from the events and look at the situation from outside. Moreover, I could hear what other coaches actually thought of my performance. I was able to forget my preoccupation with professional competence and accept that a coach is just a normal, fallible human being with problems to solve and challenges to meet. Hearing other coaches describe their own difficult cases helped me to understand that tricky coaching is a normal part of coaching work.

# 18

# WHEN YOUR CLIENT FEELS LIKE A SCAPEGOAT

## SABINE DEMBKOWSKI

*Case summary*

Sabine Dembkowski is hired to work with the coachee on his career choice (specialist banking or general management role) and on responses to the recent financial crisis. Drastic measures have been taken to save the coachee's part of the business from the negative impact of the crisis, and the client is at a loss on how to respond to a new set of stakeholders who are not trained to understand the language or world of banking. The coach is expected to act as a sparring partner for the coachee. The coach has a strong reaction to the financial crisis, due to her personal values and views on what is right or wrong in how the banking sector should operate.

*Context*: The case takes place in the United Kingdom.

## BACKGROUND

My client "John" is a very senior manager in a bank specializing in property and public sector finance. The bank is one of the top 20 banks in the United Kingdom and the sister organization of a FTSE100 financial institution. John is highly intelligent. He studied in two European countries, has an MBA from a leading business school, and underwent formal training as a banker. During his early years with the bank he worked in London, New York, Frankfurt, and Luxemburg. John gained experience across a wide range of the bank's functions, including a stint in the investment banking department. John was fortunate in having the support of good mentors who helped him gain early promotion to management roles. He has proven to himself, and the bank, that he can be equally successful in a specialist banking or a management role. So, in short, a highly successful, accelerated career—but now John is facing several dilemmas and this is the basis for our coaching relationship.

The first of John's dilemmas focuses on the type of role (specialist banking or management) he should pursue. He likes certain aspects of each role and these attributes are on a par with each other. Throughout his career he was never

100 per cent certain if he should specialize or take up management challenges in the bank. In his own words it "somehow happened" that he was put into management roles and finally arrived in a top management position in 2006. John is therefore currently focused on management but is by no means certain that this is the right path for him.

John's other dilemmas stem from the current financial crisis. At the time he took his current role his unit was on a steady course. Although it was not the most profitable side of the bank, it was, due to its specific exposure to property and public sector finance, a solid business. However, in 2007 troubles (over and above normal business hiccups) started to emerge and severe losses were uncovered. As the financial crisis deepened, the bank, as well as its parent organization, came under media scrutiny. In fact, the losses of the bank were so severe that it was one of the first high-profile financial institutions that had to take up a government guarantee and the UK government holds now a significant stake in the organization.

Thus the bank, and John as one of its top managers, finds itself exposed to a new group of stakeholders—government and civil servants. He feels uneasy, as these stakeholders are part of a very different culture and make decisions that feel "alien" (his word) to a banker. He has also realized over the last few months that these stakeholders not only come from a different culture, but also make decisions on grounds that are hard for him to understand, that is, the decision might be popular with the public but, in terms of the facts, simply be wrong. The new stakeholders also have a very mixed understanding (some very limited) of banking processes and the way instruments and investment vehicles are designed and work. The vocabulary of this stakeholder group is very different and in meetings basic banking terms and processes have to be clarified so that issues can be discussed.

John finds this all very frustrating and sometimes feels he is talking to a class in banking 101. In addition, the constant need to explain and justify actions means that progress is very slow and there are new, additional layers in the decision-making progress. On a rational level John, of course, understands the need for these new checks and balances but emotionally the situation just adds to his questioning of his current role.

The government underwriting of, and stake in, the bank puts an additional pressure on John in that he now faces constant media attention. He feels uncomfortable as solutions have to be worked out about how to handle the situation and, at this stage, it is not clear exactly how this can be done. Yet the media have demands that need to be satisfied. John therefore feels "pushed by the system" to speak without really saying anything, which is not at all his style and he hates it.

John's bank suffered severe losses, as did the parent organization. His bank is used as what he calls the "internal bad bank." As a result, any losses, papers, or memos that can be vaguely attributed to it are pushed in its direction so that the FTSE100 parent organization can demonstrate that it has a relatively "clean sheet." John feels that his organization is the scapegoat for the main parent's failings—a view reinforced by the main board's direction to John to assist in the preparation of the bank for sale and/or IPO within the next five years. John is uneasy in his role, as he sees it, of "dressing up an ugly bride."

## MY ROLE AS COACH

In the midst of all the upheaval in the financial world, John decided to engage me as his coach to act as a neutral sounding board and sparring-partner. He felt that he had to make a decision about the direction of his career. Did he want to be a "state banker," a "real banker," a "top manager of a bank," or a "new kind of top manager of a bank?"

John recognized that without some outside assistance he was never going to devote time to reflecting about what was best for him. In addition, once he had made a decision about which role to pursue, he wanted to work on developing himself as a brand and clearly position himself in his own organization and the wider banking community in the United Kingdom. Given the context and pressures of his role and the need for careful stakeholder management, he also wanted me to help him to reflect, see, and manage the demands of the various stakeholder groups.

At the beginning of the program in March 2009 we agreed to see each other for a session every two to three weeks. The frequency of the meetings would be reviewed after three sessions. At each session we had a full program, as the news about the severity of the losses unfolded and various stakeholder groups started to defend their position. My role therefore was also to help John focus on his agenda while acknowledging the environment in which he was working.

## THE CHALLENGE

There are various factors that made this case difficult to handle—in fact, it was more difficult than any other I have had in my career to date. This was a high-profile client who was unwillingly in the center of attention of the bank, the government and, last but not least, the media. The prevailing climate of panic during the financial crisis put enormous pressure on John, and on me by association, to find real solutions to his and the bank's problems. Of course my focus was on John's agenda rather than the bank's and I wanted to help him ensure that he was not a personal scapegoat either for his employer or in the eyes of the media. Media attention might be welcome at other times to help build reputation but John was receiving more than he wanted; yet at the same time he wanted me to help him sustain and develop his reputation in the world of finance in the United Kingdom.

I also found it hard to distance myself from the crisis and not fall into the trap of exposing my own views about what is, according to my personal value system, right and wrong, and how the whole system is supposed to move ahead. The next factor was the large gap between the know-how and interests of the various stakeholder groups. In a way this bank found itself in a position where it was a "public-private" partnership, a first in that form and time. Thus, the culture and new norms were developing in front of our eyes as we progressed with the coaching program. So I could not rely on my previous experience within other organizations, such as professional service firms, where it is quite clear what is expected of clients who want to become a partner or position themselves within a group of partners.

The specific situation of the banking and financial crisis and the various stakeholder groups provided a contextual complexity that went way beyond any other cases I have experienced. The closest was someone who was part of a matrix organization in a global operation. In each of my sessions with John, it was a challenge for me really to concentrate and separate the wheat from the chaff so that I could best support him in his decision-making process and plans for the future.

## DEALING WITH THE CHALLENGE

For me the biggest challenge in this case was to focus on the client and his needs despite the context of a global financial crisis. I had to find a way to control my own emotions to be, under the specific circumstances, the best sparring-partner I could. I decided to stick to proven processes, tools, and techniques, and to adopt a strict regime that allowed me to leave my own thoughts and concerns at the door when I started each coaching session so that I was not overwhelmed by the potential importance of the work we were doing and the decisions I was supporting my client in taking.

## WHEN YOUR CLIENT FEELS LIKE A SCAPEGOAT: COMMENTARY

*Peter Boback*

I think the good news here is that John has a coach to help him navigate through the normal madness of the contemporary banking world. Just the fact that he has regular meetings with a sparring-partner creates the necessary safe and reflective space that is crucial for survival and for developing new ideas and options. Reading the case I understand, and even feel, the pressure experienced by coachee and coach. Part of Sabine's professional performance and contribution as the coach consists in acknowledging the reality of this high pressure, to stay near and emotionally present, to endure and to contain.

In coaching managers and executives I try to sort out what in the narratives and challenges I hear might be a "situation to be in"—and what a "problem to be solved." My experience with coaching people in what I call "postmodern organizations"—fast moving and often erratically and unpredictably changing—is that most of the challenges that create problems are "situations to be in," or exposure to demands the coachee feels little influence and control over. These situations are more frequent than "problems to be solved."

I found the following meta-concepts useful to structure and orientate my thinking while coaching in such an organizational environment. The postmodern organization is characterized by a threefold lack for the people working there: Lack of direction (despite rather "pompous" vision, mission, and strategy statements coming from the top, a concrete translation into meaningful individual objectives is often missing); lack of connection (how to connect trustfully with people if teams and managers are reorganized every six months); and lack of protection (unstable organizations cannot serve as boundaries and protective containers any longer).

My impression is that some or even most of these characteristics apply to the organization John is working in. The guiding principles for the coaching interventions should be to help the client work on remedies for these insufficiencies in the organizational environment. For me they are threefold:

- Taking care of yourself. The coach can help John to take care of himself, namely, to identify risks in the environment and to develop strategies to prevent John from being damaged and to manage the risks around him. John needs to learn to live in an organizational environment that has lost its containment function.
- Figuring out what John really wants professionally. This is an ongoing and important topic. For example, John and his coach could check the options of possible career moves within and outside the bank. Issues such as building your own brand, reputation management, and analysis of options could be topics for coaching work. Working on those issues might give some kind of protection against what might happen and what is beyond John's control.
- Clarifying responsibility. What is the concept of responsibility held by the bank, senior management team, or the board? What is John's concept of responsibility? What is his role and what responsibilities are associated with it? What are the questions he has to answer? Which should he escalate to appropriate places and (higher) managerial levels? Is it possible to clarify his responsibilities? If not, how can he make sure that he does not become the victim of scapegoating? After clarifying the concept of responsibility, John could then develop an internal and external communication strategy based on this role and responsibility concept.

Additionally, John might consider the tasks he is confronted with—and says he hates—as good learning areas. Could he reframe these uncomfortable tasks as opportunities to enlarge his own behavioral repertoire? For example, what about exploring giving banking 101 classes to civil servants, learning to deal with the media attention, and exploring how to answer expectations from people coming from different cultures (e.g., politicians)?

## POST-CASE NOTE

*Sabine Dembkowski*

I made a purposeful decision to increase my supervision and take more time out for myself than I would under normal circumstances so that I did not become absorbed by the crisis and its specific, potentially draining, and negative energy. Specifically, I increased my exercise regime and devoted more time to relaxation. I also tried to ensure that John was the only client I saw on a particular day so that I could be totally focused.

What also helped me was sound preparation for each session. I read through my notes from the previous session and any inter-session emails. I also kept track of context by reading about John's bank and the financial situation in general—this was important so that John did not have to spend too much time on bringing me up to speed and I could focus on him. In the sessions I stuck to a systematic approach and a variety of tried and tested processes, tools and techniques. Most notably these were:

- The Achieve Coaching Model®—this provides the basis for a sound and proven coaching process.[1]
- Foundation building—adapted from solution focused brief therapy (SFBT) and the tools and methods of its developer, Steve de Shazer. These helped to provide a sound basis for our working relationship and established a point we could return to when things became tricky in the coaching conversations.
- Stakeholder mapping—this helped me to establish the "territory" and stay on the top of the names, relationships, interests, and specific motivations of various people and groups of stakeholders.
- Branding methodology—this is an adaptation of a branding methodology I learned while a consultant with Monitor Group and used with clients such as Coca-Cola and ING Bank. The basis processes worked well in assignments with high-profile managers who were eager to develop a position for themselves and in essence "brand" themselves.

## WHAT I FOUND DIFFICULT TO COPE WITH

This was principally the information I received in the sessions that highlighted the severity of the gap between what was "sold to the public" and what was actually happening. Clearly, I have seen a lot in my time as a strategy consultant and executive coach but this case topped it all. The situation really challenged me to keep the sessions on track and John moving forward.

## NOTE

1. The Achieve Coaching Model® emerged from an international best-practice study of executive coaching. We found that experienced executive coaches go beyond the

confines of the GROW model to achieve measurable and sustainable results with their clients. The model details a systematic, seven-step coaching process that makes the whole executive coaching process more transparent for:

- Organizations that wish to implement a systematic process to achieve measurable and sustainable outcomes, and a greater ROI from their spending on executive coaching.
- Executive coaches who want to enhance their own coaching practice.
- Executives thinking about embarking on a coaching program who want to know what to expect.

# 19

# OVERCOMING FEAR AND VULNERABILITY

## *SANDY STADELMANN*

*Case summary*

In Sandy Stadelmann's case, a young and energetic high-potential female employee needs support to prepare for conducting a performance review with an older and more experienced subordinate. Effectiveness in handling this interview is seen as an important condition for establishing the coachee as an effective leader in her department. Coach and coachee have very limited time to develop the self-efficacy and skills needed.

*Context*: The case takes place in Europe.

## BACKGROUND

Claudia, a dynamic executive in her late 20s, worked in customer service for a well-known international sports equipment producer. She joined the company with no previous experience in the industry, having worked overseas for several years as a travel guide. Nevertheless, after less than a year with the company, she was selected for promotion as one of three newly appointed team leaders. Now Claudia, who was known for her friendly manner and hands-on, problem-solving approach, was leading her former colleagues. With her appointment the department, which is responsible for receiving and processing all product returns and customer queries, had been extensively reorganized. Whereas individual team members previously undertook specific tasks, they now all had equal responsibility for the full range of activities within the department.

Harald, a member of the team in his mid-50s, was a member of the works council and an old hand at the company. After more than 20 years with the company there was little he did not know about handling product returns and customer complaints. Indeed, Harald himself was once head of the customer services department, although the circumstances surrounding his apparent demotion were long forgotten. Along with all his colleagues, Harald had seen some significant changes in his job as a result of the recent reorganization. He had to learn how to use a new IT system; he regularly had to take customer calls; and he no longer had sole responsibility for the trainees in the department, a task he had enjoyed and had been good at. Harald resisted these changes from the outset and refused to integrate himself into the new structure. Previously friendly and patient with both customers and trainees, his behavior was now gruff and abrasive. He refused to contribute to team meetings, his body language was hostile and obstructive, and he undermined Claudia's authority with mocking and deprecatory comments, usually within earshot of other members of the team.

All Claudia's attempts to improve team morale and achieve a fair distribution of workload failed. Training sessions in telephone etiquette and IT were a waste of time, as was the workshop on task distribution and the face-to-face conversation that took place between Claudia, Harald, and the head of the department.

## MY ROLE AS COACH

When I accepted this assignment, mid-year performance interviews were pending and the head of department was pushing for them to be carried out as soon as possible. Claudia was feeling very uncomfortable about the prospect of a discussion with Harald, whose performance and overall contribution to the team was unsatisfactory but, as an older, more experienced male employee, knew he could intimidate and browbeat Claudia in a face-to-face interview.

My role was to help Claudia prepare for what would undoubtedly be a challenging interview. The aim was to equip her with the tools she needed to make her point and conduct the discussion in a controlled and poised manner. But there was not a lot of time available—the coaching session was to be completed as soon as possible and was not to last longer than five hours. It was therefore agreed that Claudia and I should have a preliminary discussion after which we would decide if and how we should proceed.

I found Claudia very polite and articulate. But the bright and cheerful manner with which she greeted me soon gave way to one of gloom and despondency when she began to describe her problem with Harald. In a voice strained with anxiety, she described how she felt in danger of becoming Harald's victim. She clearly didn't have the management skills needed to deal with difficult and obstructive people but she knew very well that she had to find a way to handle Harald. She needed to restore the efficiency and team spirit of her department and for that she needed Harald to accept her as team leader. Claudia believed that she could not do this without professional support, so we agreed on the goal of enabling her to conduct the discussion in a confident manner.

## THE CHALLENGE

I quickly identified several issues that Claudia needed to address. The first was her emotional response to the problem: She felt she was no match for Harald, who was knowledgeable and a skilled negotiator. The challenge here was to overcome her fear and vulnerability and make her feel active and self-confident.

Claudia also lacked the basic communication and behavioral skills needed to conduct difficult and confrontational encounters with her staff. Although a capable leader in many respects, Claudia had a tendency to fall into stereotypical submissive roles—for example, as a woman in respect to men, as a young person in respect to older people, and as an inexperienced manager in respect to more experienced colleagues. She did not permit herself to criticize her counterpart in these circumstances, nor even lay down any ground rules, although this was one of the things she was expected to do in her new role. My task (again, in a short space of time) was to help Claudia feel more confidence and control in these interpersonal relationships.

In many ways, Claudia's behavior was typical of many women in similar positions. She was very self-critical and felt a pressing need to fix the problem. At the same time she was inhibited by any manifestation of discord or confrontation. It didn't help that the purpose of her interview with Harald was not clearly defined. The official purpose was to review the attainment of agreed performance targets and plan Harald's targets for the coming year. But not surprisingly, Claudia was expecting the discussion to focus on Harald's criticisms and dissatisfaction. Under these circumstances, the interview would fail to achieve its required goals. The challenge here was to enable Claudia to retain control of the discussion and not become sidetracked. This was not going to be easy. An aggressive or dictatorial approach was not the answer. To reach an understanding with Harald and get him on side would require Claudia to remain calm and positive at all times.

## DEALING WITH THE CHALLENGE

My main worry with this assignment was whether, given the time constraints and the complexity of the situation, I would be able to provide Claudia with the tools she needed to carry this interview out successfully. Several previous attempts to break the deadlock in Claudia's department had failed; coaching was just the latest attempt. I wasn't even sure that coaching was the answer. Two other options occurred to me: Mediation between Claudia and Harald to air their differences and reach a workable solution; and courageous conversations to deal with Harald's resistance to the way things were currently organized.

I bounced these ideas off two of my colleagues with no success—we each preferred a different approach. However, since I had been asked to coach Claudia, I decided to explore various coaching methods to see which might work. Observing that Claudia needed to develop a stronger, more stable, position in order to cope with the more confident Harald, I began to focus on two possible techniques.

One was to address Claudia's *internal conflict* using Schulz von Thun's "inner team" method, which helps the coachee identify and understand conflicting thoughts and develop a solution-oriented view of the situation. The other was to address the *external conflict* raised by the relationship using the "meta-mirror" technique. This focuses the responsibility for change in a relationship on the client rather than on the other individual in the relationship the client wants to improve. I use Schulz von Thun's method often and it has proved successful in similar circumstances to Claudia's. Accordingly, after some careful thought, I accepted the assignment on the basis that I would employ this technique.

## MY APPROACH

I arranged to have three sessions with Claudia. At the first session I noted that Claudia's leadership style was supportive and understanding, and I made three specific observations.

First, Claudia's style of conversation made it easy for the other person to deflect her questions and statements and turn them back onto her. If she did not immediately receive answers to her questions, or if the other person responded with their own question, she invariably ended up providing the answer herself. I suggested she address this tendency in two ways: She should endure awkward breaks in the conversation and demand answers to her questions.

My second observation related to the way Claudia presented herself through posture and tone of voice. I decided to conduct an experiment using a modification of Keith Johnstone's improvisational theater technique. I asked Claudia to adopt the sort of body language she thought could be interpreted as displaying a complete lack of confidence. We then looked at this posture and started to reverse the negative elements until we found a solution that projected the very opposite in a way that felt authentic and comfortable for Claudia. I asked her to practice using this positive body language automatically.

Third, I noticed that Claudia's strong emotional responses interfered with her ability to think clearly and calmly. I decided to untangle the emotional level and the fact level and to address them separately in the next two sessions.

When we met for our second session, Claudia had worked on the tasks and exercises I had set her and felt she was making progress. I then explained Schulz von Thun's "inner team" theory and encouraged her to identify the internal voices and their messages/intentions. Using this technique, we were able to identify a nearly forgotten but helpful voice and to "rearrange her inner team." The results were impressive: Claudia's entire attitude altered visibly as she began to perceive herself as increasingly empowered.

Claudia came to the third and final session in a fundamentally stronger frame of mind and was clearly ready to work on strategies and goals for her discussion with Harald. She described her previous strategy, which consisted mainly of making polite requests to Harald that he was able to ignore or circumvent. There was no leadership here. To help Claudia change this situation, we looked at it from Harald's perspective and worked on developing an approach that would allow Claudia to articulate her wishes and demands in a friendly way but without giving Harald an easy get-out. We then focused on specific goals, first defining a minimum baseline target below which Claudia would not go. Then we concentrated on her main aim of improving the team situation as a whole by looking for positive benefits she could offer Harald that would benefit the team as well. I followed this with a teaching session on the structure of constructive feedback in which I emphasized the importance of managing Harald's expectations by clarifying the topic for discussion, and their respective positions, at the beginning of the interview.

By the end of the coaching Claudia had learned how to formulate clear first-person statements and assert her authority without slipping into dictatorial or confrontational behavior.

## OVERCOMING FEAR AND VULNERABILITY: COMMENTARY

*Svetlana Khapova*

This case concerns the conflictual relationship between a young female, cooperative leader and an older, experienced, and boycotting male team member. Although the case is about two people, it is written in a way that invites coaching for Claudia—the leader. The case discusses her leadership style, feminine manner of managing, etc. Interestingly, all case challenges also concern Claudia, rather than Harald. In my opinion, however, it is Harald's story that needs attention.

The case suggests that Harald had previously been friendly on the phone with clients, but no longer. He has been demoted from the position currently occupied by Claudia several years before. The reasons for demotion are unknown. He had a more responsible job before, and obviously has a lot of experience. Why not approach his expertise in a useful and respectful way? Why not give him a new responsibility?

The case clearly shows that Harald is a powerful man. He is not simply a man to whom it is difficult to talk, but he is also the person who determines moods in the team. Could we view him as an informal leader in the team? Otherwise, why would the team even notice his reactions? Could Claudia try to get him on her side?

Harald is actually only in his mid-50s. While many people would suggest that he is too old, and not interested in learning and development, the reality is that he still needs to work for at least 10 years, and may be even longer. Considering his career plateau, and even degradation, as the case suggests, as well as his loss of interest in work and team performance, there is definitely a need to ask important questions about his vision of his work and career. This could become the main theme of the mid-year performance conversation. Finally, the case seems to emphasize the gender issue in relation to leadership. In my opinion what needs to be addressed here is the issue of older employees at work, and their career and development prospects.

I would recommend that attention should shift from Claudia's problems to those of Harald, who would probably benefit most from coaching that would help him become reengaged in his work.

## POST-CASE NOTE

*Sandy Stadelmann*

Claudia conducted Harald's review discussion in a confident, controlled manner, entirely unperturbed by the apparent imbalances in their relationship. She reported that the discussion had been effective and constructive and that she had been able to bring out all the points she wanted to make without ever abandoning her leadership position. She had returned some lost status to Harald by giving him back his former responsibility for trainees. For his part, Harald had accepted Claudia's criticism of his disruptive behavior and agreed to make improvements. At the end of the session, he thanked Claudia for having been open and constructive and while the team dynamic in the following weeks was not perfect, it did improve markedly. Claudia is working on her role identity as a leader and will deepen her communication skills further.

I was pleased to see such a successful outcome to this assignment, but since then I have continued to wonder how else I might have approached these challenges. At the ESMT Colloquium we had a lively discussion in which my peers were able to identify several alternative ways of handling this delicate situation (although there still seemed to be no single "right" way of tackling it).

One interesting question was whether it should have been Harald who needed the coaching rather than Claudia. Another was whether or not Claudia would have been better served by a mentor rather than (or in addition to) a coach. This discussion was extremely useful to me in analyzing Claudia's case and it underlined how important it is to step back from an assignment when it gets tricky and check to see if there are alternative solutions you might not have seen at first.

# 20

# AN IMPOSSIBLE TRANSITION?

## AGATA HALCZEWSKA-FIGUET

*Case summary*

Agata Halczewska-Figuet's case recounts the experience of a coach who is asked to provide additional support to a participant whom the faculty teaching the program consider particularly vulnerable. The coach and participant engage in discussions related to the latter's career transition plans. Although the relationship has never been formalized, the coachee continuously contacts the coach, asking for advice.

*Context*: A coaching situation within an executive education program in an international business school.

## BACKGROUND

This coaching intervention took place in a European business school, as a session in an executive program. I had a dual role in this school: Executive director of an internal center, as well as an executive coach for some of the school's executive programs. In this case, I was contacted by the program director of one of the school's graduate executive programs. He had an unusual request: Would I be willing to provide occasional contact and support for a participant? According to the program director and the participant's coach, the man seemed emotionally unstable or possibly depressed. They felt that he needed extra institutional support, and as I was often on campus and easy to reach, they thought this would be a good solution. Participants in this particular program are on campus for a number of one-week modules over a 12-month period, and study for the program between the modules. The program director and the coach of the participant's coaching group in the program were relieved when I agreed to be available for conversations with the participant while he was on campus and in between modules if needed.

I met the participant, whom I'll call Andrew, during a business trip to Warsaw where he lived. Andrew was in his late 40s, Polish, married to a British wife, with three children. Andrew's disabled younger brother also lived with them. Andrew explained that his big challenge and the reason for coming to the executive program

183

was to be hired for a high-level executive job, ideally with expatriate conditions, with one of the international corporations present in Warsaw—he was in a job transition phase and was paying for the program himself. At that time, Andrew had been unemployed for a number of months, and was under considerable pressure to find the ideal job. He explained that he found himself unemployed after having worked for many years with his wife for a little-known charitable organization. Due to the changes in the leadership team, Andrew and his wife had been asked to leave the organization. Andrew's brother required special in-home care. Andrew told me that he could not afford to remain unemployed much longer.

I learned that Andrew was well educated, but the charity was the only organization for which he had ever worked. Despite spending his whole life in Warsaw, Andrew did not seem to have family or friends there; his nuclear family was quite isolated. Andrew's parents were actors. He mentioned that they often expressed regret that neither had ever been offered a starring role. Andrew seemed very happy to meet me, and talked easily in long and complex sentences. He expected me to help with finding him a new job as a corporate executive. At the same time, Andrew seemed to have only a very sketchy understanding of corporate organizations and functions.

Following this initial meeting, Andrew contacted me regularly when he was on campus for his program module. Every time, I spent up to two hours listening to his job search stories. It was difficult for Andrew to place his CV with headhunting firms as there was little variety or depth of experience in his career to that point. He had briefly been employed as project manager by a man Andrew described as a big "dealmaker" who expected Andrew to work very long hours. Andrew was unwilling to work this kind of schedule, and he eventually left the company.

After several sessions with me, Andrew mentioned that he was interested in exploring executive coaching as a possible career. He expected me to guide him in an exploration of various possibilities in this area, believing that he would be able to find work as a coach quickly. It soon became apparent that he was not ready to invest the time or money necessary to earn any qualification in this field, and his enthusiasm dissipated. Finally Andrew graduated from the executive program but wanted to continue the contact with me. I accepted e-mail exchanges but made myself unavailable for telephone conversations.

The contact ended when Andrew e-mailed me a long business plan for a consulting business he was planning to set up. He asked for my comments and perspective. I told him that I lacked expertise in this field and could not comment on the project. I did not respond to his next two e-mails, and we had no further contact after that.

## THE CHALLENGE

There was ambiguity in the role that I initially accepted. In my understanding, I was helping the program director and the group coach to keep an eye on a participant who seemed fragile. My role was never really explained to the participant, so he expected me to be his personal career and placement advisor, giving him, on behalf of the school, strong guidelines on how to get from his leadership position in the organization where he had formerly worked, to an undefined, top-level corporate function.

I had doubts that Andrew would ever be hired for a top executive position, given the limits of his past professional experience. However, I found myself caught in this role because of my larger administrative role as Executive Director. I felt responsible for doing my bit to ensure the overall success of the program. I also sensed a deeper misunderstanding between Andrew and myself about my role. In our discussions, I found that it was not easy to engage Andrew on a self-reflective path: He seemed reluctant to discuss his own competency, or analyze his past professional experience, which seemed incongruous, given his wish to find a top executive position. I had the impression that what he wanted was technical advice on how to manage a career transition from non-profit to for-profit sectors. Also, Andrew never opened up to me about his thoughts, reflections, and doubts. This made him sound over-confident and unrealistic. I did not feel I was in a position to tackle the impression he made, as I did not have any coaching contract with him.

I was very uncomfortable with the situation. I felt it was impossible to create an authentic working relationship, and I eventually felt that Andrew's insistence on immediate solutions was preventing us from making better use of our time. I couldn't resist thinking that at the end we both were left with a feeling that our collaboration had been unfruitful.

## AN IMPOSSIBLE TRANSITION? COMMENTARY

*Annette Voss*

The case is about coaching taking place in a business school: One of the program directors, experienced in executive coaching, agreed to informally coach a participant in an executive program. The contact fizzled out after several sessions and additional e-mail exchanges. From the coach's perspective, the coaching did not lead to any acceptable results.

First of all, it would be interesting to learn more about the coach's motivation: Did she want to help colleagues who were in a tricky situation? Did she take a real interest in the concerns of her client? What exactly did *she* want to achieve by coaching her client? If she could start a similar process again, how would she define her role today?

Reading between the lines, I get the impression that the client asks for career advice and encouragement, but the coach refuses to work on those issues for a number of reasons. Beyond the fact that a detailed contract is missing, did they discuss and agree on any outcome to be achieved at the end of their collaboration?

I feel that the coach's tight time schedule may have prevented her becoming involved in longer coaching processes. But, in spite of that, the detailed description of her client's characteristics and his professional and private background indicate that she provided a lot of listening. I am not sure if the same applies to clarification and reflection. Obviously, she did not offer too much feedback ("I did not feel I was in a position to tackle the impression he made, as I did not have any coaching contract with him."), although she had noticed lots of tricky aspects. Could this be one reason for her impression that the intervention had been unfruitful?

This case raises a number of questions:

1. Should executive directors who are not directly responsible for a coaching module step out of their administrative role to provide additional coaching, or does this create potential problems? How can this be handled effectively?

   I am an occasional program director and am sometimes faced by this question. If time allows, I usually offer a coaching session of one hour (maximum) to talk about an important, specific goal the participant wants to achieve (more or less following the GROW sequence.) Otherwise, I prefer to recommend other, qualified coaches to ensure a professional, efficient coaching process without tough time limits (since I have too little time to handle more than one longer coaching process at once).

2. The importance of establishing a relationship and agreements before taking on a coaching assignment is often overlooked. How could this situation have been handled better?

   Establishing a trust-based relationship takes a lot of time. Agata is described as an experienced coach and a committed member of the school's management team. I am sure that if she had been able to take more time, she and her client would have made use of this process.

3. On a more fundamental level, how should responsible providers of executive coaching and leadership development handle participants who show psychological fragility? Does this case highlight the need to have a psychologist or supervisor on call specifically to handle cases that fall outside the area of expertise of administrators and executive coaches?

   In my experience quite a few participants show some kind of emotional fragility during a program. Quite often, peer or group coaching, or even a short one-on-one coaching session, seem to help them deal with it. If a specific behavior indicates deeper problems or the need for a therapy, the schedule may not allow a serious coaching practice on-campus, even for an on-call expert. Could it be of more value for the participant to advise a professional coaching process (or therapy) off-campus and, if required, recommend experts who are experienced in the particular area to be worked on?

## POST-CASE NOTE

*Agata Halczewska-Figuet*
The three key issues that this case raises are

1. Organizational role boundaries: Lack of clarity between organizational roles—in this case, the administrative and the coaching roles—can create ambiguity and confusion.
2. Coaching domain: Lack of agreement about the coaching domain—in this case, between exploring leadership competencies or job placement counseling—can result in inefficient communication between coach and coachee.
3. Coaching timeline agreement: Lack of understanding about how often the coach and coachee would meet, and when the coaching relationship would be terminated, left both individuals feeling that the intervention was ineffective.

From the point of view of my colleagues, the fact that I was an "inside-outsider" as well as a seasoned coach made me the ideal person to watch over this participant. However, from my perspective, the assignment was more delicate. As the Executive Director of a center that often provided coaching modules to this particular program, I felt partially responsible for the overall success of the program, and therefore, I did not feel I could refuse my colleagues' request, even though I was not engaged as a coach in this program. This situation created a discontinuity in organizational role boundaries.

Confusion was also created in the coaching relationship because neither Andrew nor I knew what the agreement between us was, or rather, we each had a different idea of the agreement. Andrew took full advantage of what he believed to be access to a personal executive coach who was also an experienced HR professional. I, on the other hand, was increasingly aware that my time commitment wasn't creating any specific value for Andrew. Adding to my reluctance to continue the working relationship with Andrew was the fact that our meetings often occurred in the evening, taking time away from my family.

In addition to the lack of a therapeutic relationship, a coaching agreement, and shared outcome expectations, there were no clear time limits, either for the number of sessions or the time period over which the sessions would take place. Not surprisingly, after the program was over, I had to kindly, but firmly, put an end to Andrew's continuing requests for business plan analyses and job placement guidance.

# 21

# THE RESISTANT CLIENT

## *GUDRUN BECKER*

*Case summary*
Gudrun Becker is working with the director of an African agricultural consultancy program run by an international agency and sponsored by two separate European partners. The director's decision to appoint expatriate officers instead of national field experts to head regional offices has been very unpopular. The coach uncovers cultural and gender tensions and resistance to address problems with relationships at all levels. While the intervention appears to be successful initially, the director's recidivist behavior undermines the progress made.

*Context*: The case takes place within a West African country.

## BACKGROUND

It is not unusual for coaches to accept an assignment only to discover they have bitten off more than they can chew. Often, this is because the initial client contact has not fully understood the problem that needs to be addressed and has failed to provide a comprehensive brief. Sometimes, the complexity of the problem is such that the original basis of the intervention proves inadequate. This happened to me when I accepted an assignment to coach executives working on an agricultural consultancy program in Africa. My client had failed to notice that he was himself part of the problem. This is quite a common situation and most executive coaches have encountered it. In this case, one of the client's shortcomings was his failure to take his leadership responsibilities.

The program was being run by an international team in partnership with a local organization based in the country's capital. My client was the program director, an expatriate appointed by the main international partner. He managed a team of two other expatriate experts and six national experts based at the program's headquarters in the capital, all of whom were employed directly by the international agency. He was also responsible for three regional offices supporting the program's field activities. Each of these regional offices was led by an expatriate technical manager from another international agency and supported by an expert local advisor employed by the main international partner. The three technical managers were expatriate women; the three advisors were local men.

The regional offices were all experiencing difficult internal working relationships that stemmed mainly from the fact that the international technical managers were employed by one international agency and their local advisors by another. This clash of agencies had already caused problems on the program and intensified greatly when the program director nominated the three female managers as executive leaders of the regional offices.

## MY ROLE AS COACH

I was appointed directly by the program director to provide coaching for all the executives on the program team for an initial period of nine months. This involved coaching individuals at all management levels at the program's head office to strengthen their leadership skills and improve overall management efficiency. At the same time, I was asked to implement a coaching program for the regional teams to help them find solutions to their internal difficulties. The aim of the coaching was to analyze the actual work situation in the regional teams and identify appropriate steps to improve the work efficiency and job satisfaction of all concerned.

## THE CHALLENGE

The program director was a highly experienced executive who had worked on several complex multiagency projects during a career spanning almost 30 years. He was a conscientious worker and totally committed to the program so, not surprisingly, he had a busy schedule and was constantly under pressure from deadlines. Consequently, he expected his staff to take a proactive approach and to operate autonomously to a large degree. His informal "hands-off" style of leadership had mixed consequences. Some executives felt empowered and enjoyed the freedom to make their own decisions; others felt a lack of leadership and support. The overall effect was a loss of communication and disruption of the decision-making process.

The program director not only let his managers make their own decisions without consulting or seeking guidance from him, but also had a tendency to make unilateral decisions without consulting them. Some months previously, he had personally nominated the three female executives from the international partner organization as technical managers to run the regional offices. He then informed the entire team of the appointments in writing without any further explanation.

For the local advisors, all of whom were local men and employees of the leading development agency, this decision was incomprehensible and highly unsatisfactory. When I arrived, the atmosphere in the three regional offices was tense and communication between the technical managers and their expert local advisors was minimal. The technical managers did not feel respected in their roles while their advisors felt patronized and belittled. The managers seemed to have responded by becoming arrogant toward their advisors and showed a lack of professional respect for them.

All this took place within the context of an African country that retained its traditional culture of male dominance and strict social hierarchy. The appointment of three women as heads of the regional offices was difficult for the local advisors to accept. But this was only partly because their new managers were women; all three men had international experience. In addition, they were national experts in their field and were quite capable to perform the management functions themselves. For all of them this position would have represented a step forward in their career. The program director, in nominating these three women to run the regional offices, had displayed a woeful lack of cultural as well as professional awareness.

The clash of agencies and the friction between the female managers and their male advisors made coaching very problematic. The main difficulty from my point of view was my client's expectation (shared by the entire management team) that, as coach, I was there to solve their problems without the individuals involved having to question their own behavior or consider their responsibilities. They were all quite willing to discuss technical and organizational matters, but resisted any attempt on my part to address their professional relationships.

## MY APPROACH

Based on my discussions with the program director, I proposed a series of one-on-one interviews with all members of the executive team, followed by group coaching for each of the three regional office teams. This was to be followed by a kick-off workshop for all the executives where work would begin on implementing change in the organization. Finally, I would work with the management team on reorienting the program and agreeing follow-up interventions, such as on-going coaching sessions with the regional teams.

The one-on-one interviews provided me with information about the individual roles of the team members in the group, taught me about their concerns, and gave me some insight into the organizational structure and its working processes. This allowed me to build up a multilayered picture of the whole program. The interviewees were generally cooperative and eager to express their views and personal concerns. The positive outcome of these interviews facilitated progression to the group coaching sessions as well as further individual sessions.

The main aim of the team sessions was to find ways of easing the working relationships within the regional offices. These sessions combined standard coaching and training activities with some interactive exercises designed to improve communication, teambuilding, and interpersonal feedback.

## MY DILEMMA

After a while it became clear to me that the whole team was coming under pressure from steadily increasing workloads and that individual and team coaching were insufficient to tackle the emerging situation. I realized that a more holistic organizational development process, involving the entire team, was necessary.

Fortunately, the program director was willing to listen to my concerns and he agreed to extend my coaching to include an additional organizational development program for which he was prepared to employ a local consultant under contract to assist me.

With my role now redefined, I turned my attention to the program director and his heavy workload. I suggested that to help him spread the load we should establish a management team based at head office. This new team was duly appointed and I started work on helping them define their objectives and agree their respective roles and responsibilities.

Their principal role was to maintain the focus of the program, review strategic decisions, and create more space for creative thinking. At the same time we worked on creating a flatter organization and explored how this new leadership model would translate at regional level. This led to a heated and rather emotional discussion that ended inconclusively, although it was agreed that the issues would be revisited again with the support of the organizational development consultant.

## COPING AND NOT COPING

Overall, this assignment was successful and I was able to cope with several challenging situations. I eventually established trusting relationships within the whole program team and was successful in creating a sense of ownership of the process. My work to create more transparency in the division of duties and the definition of roles, functions, and working procedures was also successful. I was also able to help the client develop a detailed action plan for ongoing improvements over the following months.

However, there were aspects of this assignment that I was unable to cope with successfully. The first was the task of convincing the program director to change his behavior. Despite several discussions with him, I never succeeded in persuading him to take a critical look at his role as leader. He took professional advice neither from me nor from the national organizational development consultant, and after the end of my assignment simply returned to his old style of management. In fact one of the first things he did was to unilaterally transfer the three local advisors from the regional offices to the capital to take over different tasks, leaving the female technical managers in charge of the regional offices, running teams of interns and support staff. He also replicated the same contentious model by appointing another female expatriate from the other European organization to act as coordinator in another region—disregarding the problematic situation that this had already caused elsewhere.

Working on role clarification with the regional teams was possible only to a limited extent. When I attempted to address sensitive issues, like the existing conflict and the program director's nomination of the technical managers, the group refused to cooperate. Although the three female managers were asking for urgent coaching support, they were not willing to contribute to finding a solution. During the one-day workshop with the regional teams, and also in the peer group supervision with the regional managers, the women were very reluctant to discuss the actual conflict—to the extent that one of them actually walked out of the discussion. There was particularly strong opposition to questions about individual behavior patterns and attitudes. For me as coach, the attitude of these three female managers was very difficult to handle and it was almost impossible to make any progress as a group without losing some team members.

My problems were made worse by the fact that, after the initial one-on-one meetings, I was limited to intermittent group coaching sessions and had no opportunity to hold follow-up interviews with individual team members. The client's expectations of a coach in the international context are invariably high and very often—as in this case—the client has a tendency to overload the brief and expect the coach to tackle all the problems and issues at once. What I really needed in this case was the help of an assistant or co-coach to maintain the intervention and undertake various other subsidiary tasks.

Eventually a new conflict emerged between the management team, technical managers, and their expert advisors. I offered to assist in mediation of the conflict, but by then they had all returned to their regional offices and the opportunity to mediate was lost. While I had several individual telephone conversations with the people concerned, I was obliged to leave this situation unresolved with the hope that the local organizational development consultant would tackle it as soon as possible.

## THE RESISTANT CLIENT: COMMENTARY

*Silke Matthies*
There are several stakeholders in this case: The sponsors are the national Ministry of Food and Agriculture in an African country and two European organizations who run a join development program. The program works through a centralized team, staffed by one of the European organizations, and there are three decentralized teams in the field. Each of these field teams is led by a female, European technical advisor, who is in charge of the regional office. These regional heads have direct reports or colleagues who are male national experts with very good professional backgrounds. The female regional heads were appointed by the first European organization; the national experts were appointed by the second European organization.

The two European organizations seem to have quite different values and approaches to their mission that have already made past cooperation difficult. This situation worsened after the three female European representatives became regional coordinators and executives of the regional offices.

Gudrun's assignment was to coach department heads, regional coordinators, and the regional teams. She started with the regional coordinators and the decentralized teams in the field and quickly experienced a lot of resistance to change, especially changes aimed at improving the existing relationships.

My view is that coaching is not the best means to deal with the situation here. Although the setting is very different from the field in which I have experience, and I am not familiar with the national culture, it reminds me very much of transitional changes in the business sector. It seems to be an organizational development issue, which means that the value propositions of the European organizations and the national and European team members have to be clarified. A systemic approach is in order. Organizational development would define roles and responsibilities, as well as ways of interacting and cooperating between the different teams and units involved.

No information is given about potential budget and time constraints of this program. Nevertheless, I would like to sketch out what an alternative development process could look like.

In any of proposed settings mentioned, I would try to work in as solution-oriented and resource-activating a way as possible. I would avoid analyzing past problems and focus on positive examples where cooperation—especially in the regional teams—is going well. Since many decisions have been centralized and are top-down, I would start this process bottom-up, which means working in the regions. Here, I would run off-site workshops with the three regional teams, concentrating on the following questions: What is the purpose of the teams? What objectives are they pursuing? How do they want to reach these goals? What must roles and responsibilities look like to fulfill these goals? What is important to working together effectively? What kind of support do they need, and from whom?

I would then apply the same approach to the regional coordinators and later to the central department heads.

Finally, I would start to work on the interfaces between regional coordinators and regional teams, regional coordinators and the central team, and perhaps the central and regional teams.

I would share the results (objectives, clarified roles and responsibilities, shared values for cooperation, need for support) with the program manager, the heads of both European organizations and the responsible representative of the national ministry and compare them with their existing approaches and priorities. In this setting, a second facilitator might be a valuable resource. It might also be a good idea to have a representative of the regional coordinators, the department heads, and two representatives of the regional teams (one national, one European) present as well. These representatives could provide feedback to their colleagues afterwards.

After the results have been discussed and acknowledged by the sponsor and the program manager, team coaching might be valuable to support the implementation of the clarified roles and responsibilities as well as the agreed rules of cooperation. On the regional team level, it might be helpful to work once again with all three teams together. This "bundle" approach might provide a more relaxed atmosphere in which to address existing issues.

My fear would be that continuing with simple coaching (be it on a one-on-one basis or as groups) might end up forcing the coach to play "mailwoman," delivering unpleasant messages to the different teams and stakeholders.

## POST-CASE NOTE

*Gudrun Becker*

Although I tried from the very beginning to clarify my role and the client's expectations, the program director nevertheless attempted to transfer some of his executive duties to me. This is a common problem in coaching and an easy trap to fall into—I resisted this and the program director was not pleased. All my efforts to get him to reflect on his executive responsibilities were unsuccessful. When my initial engagement came to an end he decided not to renew my contract, explaining that he wanted to continue working with the local consultant because of his presence on the ground. I suspect that, under pressure and in the belief that I was going to solve his problems for him, he must have decided that I had failed to live up to his expectations. Although I could see his point, it was not easy for me to let go, especially at a time when the conflict in the regional offices appeared to be worsening. I would have at least expected to remain involved in the process. Later I discovered that the program manager chose not to renew the organizational development consultant's contract as well.

Feeling that I had failed in this assignment, I sought professional supervision to help me reflect on my coaching practice and take a critical look at my ability to navigate as coach and consultant.

The ESMT Coaching Colloquium provided a good platform on which to exchange ideas with other international coaches who had experienced similar situations. The peer-group supervision in particular provided an excellent opportunity to learn from other coaches. The discussions helped me to see my professional action from a different point of view and opened new perspectives on future coaching cases. Ultimately, though, discussions with other coaches at the Colloquium reinforced my belief that careful contracting at the beginning of an assignment—and if necessary renegotiation of the coach's terms of engagement—is essential for a successful coaching intervention.

# 22

# COACH, CONTAIN THYSELF

## *ERIK VAN DE LOO*

*Case summary*

In Erik van de Loo's case a manager faces mutiny among his staff as the result of office relocation and asks the coach to help him deal with the situation. The coach, working with a colleague, faces aggressive resistance from participants in a group coaching session, who start scapegoating the coaching team. The coaches need to find a way out of a hostile situation while maintaining control. The case is followed by self-reflection questions that give the reader the opportunity to provide his or her own commentary on the coach's story.

*Context*: A coaching intervention for staff in a local office of a medium-sized company in Benelux.

## BACKGROUND

Antonio had a mutiny on his hands. His team of 14 specialized and highly skilled professionals was up in arms about their recent relocation to new office accommodation. Morale had plummeted and productivity was beginning to suffer. Although hitherto popular with his staff, Antonio now faced open revolt; worse still, every effort he made to mollify his team seemed only to fan the flames of discontent. Having run out of ideas, Antonio decided he needed a professional coach to help bring his staff on side and restore peace.

About a year before I got the call from Antonio, he and his team had learned that they were to move out of the smart, stylish offices in a handsome old townhouse that had been their home for the best part of 20 years, and relocate to a modern glass-and-steel, open-plan office building at the company headquarters. The team was particularly upset that each of them would no longer have a private office; they felt this represented a loss of status amounting to a *de facto* demotion.

The team entered a downward spiral of anger and frustration and engaged in endless discussions with Antonio without any improvement in the situation. Antonio had initially tried to reassure his team, telling them that, unwelcome though the move undoubtedly was, he would take care to ensure that there would also be benefits. But the team wasn't buying it—there could be no up side to this betrayal. Antonio hoped that, when it eventually happened, the move would prove less traumatic than his team had feared. Instead, they complained that their new situation was even worse than they had expected. Nothing Antonio did could restore their confidence and the grievances became louder and more hysterical.

The team complained that they could not work in this hostile new environment: They spoke of "intolerable" noise levels; of being dazzled by the sun's glare reflected from the glass-clad tower block next door; of "strangers" wandering through their personal space en route from one department to another; of the lack of privacy and suitable meeting rooms. They hated the new office and were ashamed to have to work there.

Absenteeism increased; productivity fell. People said that they had lost their motivation to work and that they no longer trusted Antonio. His two star performers openly threatened to resign unless they could move back to their old office. By the time I and my fellow coach arrived on the scene, Antonio was refusing to discuss the issue any more as doing so seemed simply to stir up more anger.

## MY APPROACH

I was appointed, together with an assistant, to analyze the problem and provide a consultancy service and executive coaching for the team. We began by holding meetings with Antonio, his boss, and three members of the team individually, after which we decided to organize a session with the whole team together. Five minutes before the meeting was due to start, all 14 members filed into the room and sat silently waiting to begin. The atmosphere was extremely oppressive, like the heaviness that precedes a thunderstorm. Both I and my co-presenter fell silent, too, with the unintended consequence that the tension in the room increased further. I suddenly felt very nervous and, with a rising sense of panic, found that I could barely think coherently. To calm myself down I focused my attention on the clock and decided to wait for the last two minutes before formally opening the meeting exactly at the appointed time. This, I thought, would send the message (if only to myself) that I was still in control. I therefore opened proceedings exactly on time, introducing myself and my colleague and reiterating the intended purpose of the meeting—to find a workable solution to the conflict over new office environment—as previously discussed with some members of the group individually.

After an initial silence, the group suddenly exploded with an outburst of angry accusations. Four or five team members started shouting all at once, accusing us of stupidity, ignorance, and collusion with Antonio and attacking what they saw as our unprofessional lack of impartiality. As far as they were concerned, we were only there to try and make them accept something that was manifestly unacceptable. I was deeply shocked and even rather frightened: Two members of the group had risen to their feet, shouting and gesticulating aggressively; all their frustration and anger was suddenly unleashed on me. They seemed completely to ignore my colleague, who (together with Antonio) simply sat in total silence. I looked at my colleague in a vain appeal for help—but he didn't respond at all. I was on my own in front of an angry mob. So I too adopted the silent strategy and stopped responding to their accusations in the hope that the storm would blow itself out. I became an observer rather than a participant and regained my ability to think logically: They weren't really angry with me; I was just an outlet for their frustrations. As the outburst gradually lost momentum, I began to look beyond the four or five most vocal individuals and noticed that the majority of the team appeared much less agitated, though not necessarily less hostile. The one exception was a young woman who looked remarkably relaxed and who seemed to radiate positive energy toward me. I therefore addressed myself directly to her and asked how she felt about the situation. She explained that she had just returned to the team from maternity leave and that while she certainly preferred the old office environment, there was nothing they could do about it and the challenge now was to make the best of the new situation. At this, two other members of the team rounded angrily on her and demanded to know how she could dare to be so disloyal and disrespectful of her colleagues as to attack them from within and undermine their case. Thoroughly chastised and humiliated, she closed her mouth and did not utter a single word throughout the rest of the meeting.

## THE CHALLENGE

At this point I suggested we take a break for coffee and let some of the heat dissipate a little. My colleague and I left the room and found a quiet spot where we could gather our thoughts and plan how next to proceed. We began to analyze the sequence of events that had brought the team to this destructive state of affairs. We both wondered what kind of anxieties had made them focus their anger on us. If they were that upset, why had they not called a strike and made some concerted display of rejecting the new working conditions? Why did they seem willing to attack us, the consultants, and even each other, rather than Antonio? We hastily drew the conclusion that there were probably three principal sources of stress and frustration preventing them from acting upon their anger.

The first was the team's relationship with their leader, Antonio. He was a kind, gentle man who had worked amicably with most of the team for several years and who clearly had great difficulty in dealing with this sudden breakdown in trust between them. He had made promises that he couldn't keep and thus had become the focus of blame and a primary source of frustration for the group. Strangely, though, the group appeared protective of Antonio and although sorely disappointed in him, could not bring themselves to unleash the full force of their frustration upon him. However, I had an explanation for this paradox. I knew from my initial interview with him that Antonio had had a difficult childhood and that from a very young age he had had to fend for himself and his two younger siblings. Even now, many years later, he was haunted by the belief that he had failed his brother and sister and I suspect that he now felt the same sense of failure and impotence toward the 14 members of his team. Although they knew nothing of his traumatic childhood, the team could not fail to appreciate Antonio's sincerity and his genuine efforts to mitigate their situation.

The second source of stress was the perceived threat to the team's autonomy within the organization and the possibility that the team might not even survive intact. Antonio's boss had delivered an ultimatum to the effect that if the problem was not resolved amicably by a certain deadline, he would personally step in and sort it out. Antonio and his team knew what this meant. During the restructuring exercise that had resulted in the team's relocation to the new office it had been suggested that, because their specialist work was not part of the core activity of the organization, they should become an independent body outside the group. Fearing that they could not survive on their own, the team fought to remain part of the group. Their wish was granted, but at a price: They had to move into head office. Now, although very dissatisfied with their new position, the team risked being cast out of the organization entirely and this was preventing them from taking a more militant stance.

The third factor holding them back, we hypothesized, was conflict within the team itself. In addition to Antonio, the official leader, the team included two very powerful personalities—a married couple—who had been part of the team since its formation several years previously. This couple dominated the group and seemed to dictate what could and could not be said; it was they who had effectively silenced the young woman when she dared to voice her own opinion. Dissenting voices were not tolerated and any challenge to their self-appointed authority risked destabilizing the team.

Having identified the three factors that seemed to us to be responsible for the deadlock, my colleague and I decided to reconvene the meeting and find out if the group would be willing to discuss them with us.

## DEALING WITH THE CHALLENGE

After a break of 15 minutes we returned to the meeting and asked the team if any of them could suggest what it was that prevented them from finding a workable solution to their grievances. I was relieved to see that instead of reacting angrily as they had earlier that morning, the team now seemed willing to engage in a fruitful and constructive discussion. They spoke freely of their relationship with Antonio, their loss of trust, and their paradoxical desire to protect him; they also discussed their fear of being exiled from the organization and the price they were being made to pay for remaining on board. But, as we had expected, the issue of conflict and tension within the team itself was not addressed, nor did we try to introduce it to the discussion.

As a coach, I was surprised by how threatened and intimidated I had felt at the beginning of the session. The team members were angry and I was a handy scapegoat for them. Even though they had no argument with me or my colleague, their aggression was nonetheless quite shocking. For a while I felt impotent and out of my depth, overwhelmed by fear and incapable of thinking clearly. However, I dealt with the situation in three stages:

- Survive the onslaught: I needed to survive this critical, very tricky situation of being attacked ourselves.
- Get back in control: I needed to regain my basic capacity to think analytically and take control of this explosive situation. I had to make the transition from scapegoat to observer and then reestablish my status as coach.
- Put out the fire: The third stage was physically to leave the group. By suggesting we break for coffee while tempers were still running high, I effectively defused the tension so that when we met again 15 minutes later, we had all had time to calm down. I used those 15 minutes to reflect on what had happened and make sense of it with my colleague. Putting some physical distance between us and the coachees also allowed us to return with renewed authority and make a fresh start.

Coaches and consultants need to be able to contain themselves when faced with the strong and sometimes destructive force of a group of people. It is important not to see painful and tricky moments such as we experienced as mistakes or accidents. In fact, the key to understanding a group's problems is often to be found during the most emotional and hostile exchanges. But when that happens, it is essential that the coach remains in control at all times and maintains sufficient distance from the group. The coach should never be on the defensive; success in such a situation is about surviving the attack and making sense of the chaos.

## REFLECTION POINTS

Imagine that you have been asked to prepare a commentary for this case. Taking a systemic approach, what do you believe are the influential elements at play? How would you interpret the actions of individuals, dyads, and the group as a whole? Are there specific questions you would ask Erik about his intervention and the decisions he made? Erik worked with a partner, giving him the valuable option of discussing and interpreting events with a colleague as they unfolded— have you ever worked with a partner in a coaching context? How would you have felt if you were the coach in this case, and how would you deal with your own emotions?

# 23

# GENERATIONAL DRAMAS IN A FAMILY FIRM

## *ELISABET ENGELLAU*

*Case summary*

Elisabet Engellau, working with a colleague, is invited to deal with a family's conflict over control of the family business and succession. The case is followed by self-reflection questions that give the reader the opportunity to provide his or her own commentary on the coach's story.

*Context*: A coaching intervention for the senior executives of a $100 million family business in France.

## BACKGROUND

A colleague contacted me concerning possible counseling for the managing director of a $100 million family business. The reason for the request was a conflict between the owners, father and son, around control and leadership of the company and succession. They each owned around 50 per cent of the business, separated into two semi-independent legal entities. However, the two companies were linked through complex production, marketing, sales, and distribution systems. For the past year, the son had been working from home (not at head office), as conflicts between him and his father over the management of the business had forced him to take some distance.

A few days later I met with the son, who presented two letters from his father. The first was personal, accusing the son, his wife, and his children of excluding him from their family activities and vacations. In the second letter, which focused on the business side of their relationship, the father proposed splitting the business into two completely independent units. The content of the two letters was the catalyst that prompted the son to contact me, looking for professional help on how to handle this delicate personal and complex professional situation. He wanted to find an acceptable solution that would not result in "destroying" either his father or the company.

The company can be described as a market leader with products in a highly regulated industry. Ever since the grandparents founded the company in 1932,

200

it has grown continuously. Today, the company has manufacturing facilities located in four different countries around the world and their clients can be found in 150 countries.

The father, in his mid-70s, is president and owner of half the company. He took over the original company with his mother after his own father's death in 1958. He has no formal education. Recently widowed under traumatic circumstances, the father has displayed depressive symptoms and expressed a sense of loneliness. He denies, however, that he is depressed. His wife—described by their son as infantile and dependant—had undergone long-term treatment for severe depression. The son was their only child.

Two years before the death of his wife, the father's mother had died. She had lived with her son and his wife and was a daily presence in the company until her death. According to the son, father and grandmother were very close. The father has few if any friends and few social contacts. Most of his activities outside the business have to do with his passion as a stamp collector.

The father is described by his son as quite authoritarian with old-fashioned views on child rearing, which has led to conflict with the son's wife. His leadership style is autocratic, detail-oriented, and very operational, with little focus on long-term strategy. The father's business is responsible for manufacturing in France and India, and sales and distribution in parts of Europe and the rest of the world, excluding North America. The company is not doing well, which the father blames on the general economic situation. The production facilities are waiting to be modernized and expanded and financial infusion from banks is needed for this purpose.

The son, 50, is CEO and sole owner of the international group. This business is responsible for production, distribution, and sales in the USA and Canada plus distribution and sales in the United Kingdom, Benelux, and Germany. The company is run by professional managers, with the son at the helm. It has grown dramatically since its inception 15 years ago. The father has no role or ownership in this business.

The son was essentially raised by a nanny and was very close to his grandmother. He is an engineer by training and also has an MBA. Before joining his father's company he worked as a consultant for a few years. His wife is a professional in her own right. They have five children; the eldest son is studying for an MBA. They are a close family. As the only child, and with the recent death of his mother, the son feels responsible for his father. The family lunch every Sunday continues as a tradition as it has done over the past 30 years and the father expects to spend vacations with the son and his family.

The managing director is now 83 years old. He was employed by the father, in the early 1960s, with the mandate to expand the business internationally. He has done so very successfully. He has no ownership in the company. Currently, he is the father's right-hand man, in charge of worldwide sales and distribution for the father's business. He has no role in the son's company. He has expressed a wish to retire on many occasions, something the father rejects outright.

The son has made unsuccessful efforts to set a deadline and an agreed process for the retirement of the managing director.

## THE CHALLENGE

I realized, from the information given in my first encounter with the son, that this assignment was going to be an extremely tricky one. I agreed with him that I would take it on, on condition that I could involve a colleague who is specialized in family business governance, to which he agreed. It is my experience that working as a dyad is an extremely good way to conduct reality testing about the psychodynamics of a situation.

Since that first meeting we have met with the son on several occasions to prepare or follow up on more formalized meetings with the three directors (father, son, and MD). We started by interviewing all three individually, and then met with father and son on one occasion before scheduling more formal meetings with all three once a month. We have so far had three "board meetings," which we have summed up in detailed reports signed off by all parties.

Major themes in these meetings have been:

- The conditions for the son's return to head office.
- The definition of roles and responsibilities in the business.
- The retirement of the 83-year-old MD.
- The current financial situation in the two companies.
- The formation of an executive team in the son's company.

So far we have achieved a certain level of trust with the three directors by being very careful to bring everybody's point of view to the table. The son is now back in the head office and so far no signs of open conflict have arisen between the three. My feeling is that we have managed the different emotional outbursts and feelings of mistrust well. However, we have still a long way to go to put some of the discussion points into action.

In our coaching partnership, we realize that the two of us play quite different roles. One of us takes care of the more manifest issues, while the other (myself) focuses on more latent issues. We believe that this dyadic mode of intervention has proved highly effective. My colleague runs the more procedural parts of the meeting, including rules (the normal "hygienic" factors for meetings) to make the meetings effective. I deal with what might be described as the "undiscussables." I put the uncomfortable questions.

A considerable amount of time has been spent on designing the best way to integrate the two businesses. We make very sure that all parties get equal airtime, which did not happen previously. While we are discussing these manifest issues, and when the timing is right, I bring out some of the more latent ones. For example, one of the elephants in the room has been the rivalry between father and son—an Oedipal situation that we are trying to work through. This situation is exacerbated by the father's great need for recognition. We also have to deal with other unresolved issues, such as the roles that the deceased mother and grandmother continue to play in the fantasy life of surviving family members. We believe that the relationship between father and son has considerably improved by discussing these issues in a gentle way. We realize that more work needs to be done so that both parties can work through past hurts.

Taking all these psychodynamic issues into consideration, we have now reached the stage where we can talk meaningfully about succession. We are currently addressing the following goals:

1. To negotiate the MD's retirement and make sure it is effected.
2. To continue to manage the delicate relationship between father and son (both personal and professional), and find a meaningful role for the father inside or outside of the company.
3. To have an agreement on the transfer of power to the son, who could then take full responsibility for the whole organization and its future.

Although succession is one of the major (if not *the* major) themes in any family business, in many ways, every family conflict is unique. We are still trying to muddle through this complex situation.

## REFLECTION POINTS

Imagine that you have been asked to work with this family. How would you prepare for the assignment—would you seek a partner to join you? If so, think about how you and your partner would work together. How would you divide roles and responsibilities? As we have seen in several cases in this book, family business coaching interventions often raise specific challenges. How would working in a family business situation make your coaching approach different from that of working in a publicly listed company? Would you feel capable of bringing family as well as business issues to light? How would your own family history, professional experience, age, and values play a role in building your relationships with the parties involved in the case?

# 24

# THE CRANKY COACH, OR THE CONTRACTOR REGRETS

## *KATE McCOURT*

*Case summary*

Kate McCourt's case and the reflective questions that follow present an opportunity to explore the relationship between the coaches working within a teaching program and the program staff who hire them. The reader is invited to think about the various stakeholders involved in the coaching process.

*Context*: This case takes place in a European business school that uses coaching as part of its educational offerings.

## BACKGROUND

Marco was an imposing figure, standing more than six feet tall in an elegant suit and scanning the room with ice-cold, piercing blue eyes. I suddenly had the feeling things weren't going to be good enough for him—and I was right. I offered to show him to his seminar room where the group coaching was going to take place while the three other coaches, who had also arrived a bit early, tagged along, shaking my hand with a confident smile and disappearing with a "Thank you" into their respective rooms. Almost immediately, Marco re-emerged from his room with a list of requests and concerns for me to sort out—which was disconcerting, as I was the contractor and Marco was the supplier. The boot was on the wrong foot and for a few seconds I just stood there wondering if there had been some misunderstanding.

I was running an open enrolment leadership development seminar, now in its fifth cycle, at ESMT. The program's main faculty and I were confident that we had the seminar designed just right—we had received outstanding feedback from participants and companies from previous cycles. This was a popular course, designed as a learning laboratory where participants could engage in exercises that would provide insights into their leadership behavior and identify areas for further development, and coaches were generally eager to work with us on the program.

A core component of the program is a 360-degree feedback exercise completed by participants and their observers in advance of the program and debriefed in a full-day group coaching exercise on the third of four days. This is still something of a novelty in the field of executive coaching, so we tend to work with coaches who are familiar with both the method and our target group of international mid-level to senior executives from large corporations. The feedback exercise is a highlight of our program, and an invaluable day for our participants, who use the wisdom and experience of the group of five or six participants, guided by an executive coach, to explore their feedback results over the course of a full day.

To ensure the success of this component we try not only to prepare participants in advance but also to engage coaches with the appropriate experience and background to match participant group needs as closely as possible. Our high selection standards also mean our choice is limited and so we are constantly searching for suitable candidates with whom to expand our network of executive coaches. In this case, Marco had come highly recommended to us by other seasoned coaches and colleagues.

## INTRODUCING THE COACH

Marco was born of Italian and German parents, grew up in Germany, and was trained and worked as an emergency room nurse, before joining a top pharmaceutical company in Switzerland. Through his company he also earned a degree in clinical psychology in France and, finally, his MBA in the United Kingdom. Before becoming an executive coach, Marco held positions first in sales and then in a senior management position in marketing in the healthcare industry. He has a formidable intellect, speaks four languages including excellent English, an impressive academic background, and impeccable references. Add to that his knowledge of the group coaching method and Marco seemed to be a perfect match for our program.

We initially offered Marco a contract for one cycle, with the option of further engagement—an option I felt sure we were bound to exercise as he seemed to fit our requirements so well. As far as I was concerned, Marco had had a fairytale career so far and I was expecting the best of the best. I imagined him to be a corporate high-flyer, a real go-getter, but with the compassion and people skills I associate with the nursing profession. I wondered what drives a person to acquire all those degrees and forge ahead in the cut-and-thrust world of corporate sales, only to leave the high-pressure business environment to return to a "soft" profession like coaching.

## THE CHALLENGE

Approximately one week before the event, coaches receive their list of participants, along with short personal profiles submitted by each one and the corresponding

360-degree feedback reports. At least, that is the idea. Not infrequently, some participants fail to fill in their personal profile and some observers fail to complete the feedback questionnaire. Also, we often have participants who, instead of our feedback survey, provide us with recent results from an alternative feedback instrument from their company. They are naturally reluctant to have to repeat the exercise after such a short period of time. These things are unavoidable and can complicate things for the coach, but we try to spread the burden by balancing the coaching groups so that no single group has multiple participants with missing or marginal information.

The type and style of feedback and self-assessment can also vary significantly from one participant to another. Many participants, for example those working within global high-tech companies headquartered in Germany, tend to receive strong feedback. Others from different business backgrounds less so. The fact that most participants are in the process of progressing toward a more senior position often creates a gap between their own self-assessment and the assessment of their superiors and direct reports. Again, knowing this, we make the coaching groups as diverse as possible, as we know from experience that participants gain from the insights of others with different backgrounds and different types of feedback from themselves

Roughly a week before the program took place, I sent out all the available self-assessment and feedback information to each of the coaches. Around half the groups had a participant without a personal profile and all of the groups had a participant with either an alternative 360-degree feedback report or one with too few observers to yield meaningful results. I pointed out these shortcomings in my covering note to the coaches and explained that I expected to see them 45 minutes before we began in the morning for a quick briefing. This was the point at which the e-mails started to roll in from Marco.

His first message suggested that I had clearly forgotten to include all the profiles and reports and asked me to forward the missing information. I replied immediately, informing him once more that when the one missing profile and one missing report became available to me I would send them straight to him or—if that were not possible—I would have them sent over to his hotel the evening before the coaching day. Rather worryingly, Marco seemed to ignore my assurances and proceeded to write on three further occasions to remind me to send him the missing information straight away. I responded to the first of these and ignored the next two—there seemed to be no point in repeating myself.

## MEETING THE CHALLENGE

When, on the day before the coaching event, I received all the missing information I had these documents delivered to the hotel where the coaches would be staying. The following day I arrived at our main entrance at 7:50 am and went straight to the seminar room so that I could check everything was set up for the day. Then I headed off to the coaches' briefing on the first floor. Marco and a few others had arrived early so I decided to show them their respective seminar rooms before we returned for our briefing with the other coaches.

It was then that Marco presented me with his list of concerns. He was not happy about the location, the lighting, the room size, and the number of colored marker pens (only 40 for five people). I assured him that this setup had worked well on all the previous occasions we had run the program and that there would be further clarification during the briefing. By now I was thoroughly irritated by Marco but I remained calm; I told myself that it was just nerves and that he would soon settle down after the briefing.

The purpose of the briefing is to run through the setup for the day and let the coaches know anything in particular that they should be aware of. Marco interrupted twice to ask questions about payment and when the booking for the next seminar would take place. Although these are valid concerns for every coach, they were not appropriate topics for discussion at this kind of meeting. I therefore told Marco that we would clarify these issues some other time and that I would not discuss them now. By now I was struggling to contain my exasperation and must have been visibly annoyed.

Despite the somewhat stressful start, the coaching day ran smoothly. The participants seemed happy and even Marco ended the day in a good mood, saying his goodbyes with a smile and a wave. "So he's basically a good guy after all," I told myself; I had been right and it was just a case of nerves. That the participants enjoyed their group coaching was reflected in their comments in the course evaluation, where each coach is rated on the overall quality of their session. We provide all the coaches with their evaluations to ensure transparency and learning support. Although all the coaches had performed well, I couldn't help a somewhat childish feeling of satisfaction when I noticed that Marco's evaluation ratings were below the group average.

## DEALING WITH THE CHALLENGE

From the outside a business school might seem like an easy-going and friendly place, yet when you delve into its inner workings you notice that it is a breeding ground for professional rivalry, where bombastic, overgrown egos constantly seek to score points against their peers. It's a great place to explore human behavior. Within business schools, people compete not just with other schools for the lead on research, teaching outcomes, and reputation but, as in any organization, there is competition internally for recognition on a number of fronts, including professionalism—something on which I pride myself.

In fact, this struggle to be professional and to be acknowledged as such is my principal motivation and the main contribution I feel that I can make to our organization. My interactions with Marco had raised some difficult questions in my mind: I wondered not only if he had been acting unprofessionally, but if I also had acted in a way that was perceived by him, and by others, as unprofessional. Marco had questioned my authority and this slight deficit in his performance had restored my confidence—I had been right.

Having sent out the evaluation results, I received a long e-mail from Marco enumerating the many reasons why my failure to provide him with all the information in advance had left him unable to perform as well as the others. He also told me that he had discovered that another coach had received a higher fee and that he would like to have the same fee for the next engagement. He also provided me with his own feedback list, outlining the ways in which he felt we should adapt our setup to be more similar to coaching events in which he had participated in.

After this I had really had it with Marco. Before receiving his e-mail I thought he had done well enough and was ready to invite him to coach for us again. But now I felt like giving him a piece of my mind and then dropping him like a hot brick.

## WHAT HAPPENED NEXT?

After cooling down, reviewing and debriefing the program with the full program team, and discussing the performance of all the coaches, I decided to give Marco another shot. All the energy and effort he was putting in certainly showed that he cared. Above all, he had performed well, participants had liked him, and his profile fitted well with our selection criteria. I wrote to him saying all this and also describing once again what we expect from our coaches, that is, being able to deal with our target group and the fact that not everyone will provide us with information on time. We need executive coaches who bring a lot to the table and who thrive in ambiguous situations. I also informed him that we could consider raising his fee if he performed well on two further occasions. At this point Marco eased off and confirmed for a date nine months later. To reinforce my point, I refrained from booking his services again until reviewing his performance at the second cycle and then booking him for another far-off date.

In the end, Marco got the point and has now coached with our organization on numerous occasions. He continually performs well and has become one of the smiling confident faces that I enjoy engaging for seminars. Certainly I could have refrained from using Marco's services again, but I felt that his profile fit very well, he had exceptional references, and he did seem to have the best interests of all stakeholders in mind. In other situations I might have acted differently (and in fact have done so without regrets), but I am glad that this time things worked out differently.

Looking back, I think I could sense that Marco is a very pleasant person, once you get to know him—and this turned out to be the case. I have to admit that I found it challenging to build rapport with Marco at first, most probably because I saw something of myself in him—namely wanting to be recognized for a high level of professionalism and drive. This of course might explain why I was so adamant about keeping him on board, because I appreciated his efforts and could relate to what I perceived as relentlessness, even if this did not suit me. When we have very strong negative reactions concerning the behavior of another person, it may tell us something about ourselves. Nobody is a stranger to counter-transference reactions. Questioning whether the contracted coach was reflective enough on his own behavior led me to reflect more about myself, whether I always leave the impression I set out to make, and how this needs to be continually adapted according to occasion. I realize that I am not always successful and that I too have been given a second chance by someone who appreciated what I was trying to achieve.

## REFLECTION POINTS

This case is quite different from the others, in that it puts you in the shoes of a person who works regularly with coaches. If you were the program director in this case, how would you deal with Marco? Does Marco have a point in saying that the relationship between a coach and program manager affects the outcomes for coachees? As a program director, how do you assess your relationships with the coaches you contract with? Do you have a good system for helping new coaches feel comfortable? Do you revisit first impressions, and try to develop potentially excellent coaches?

As a coach, do you have ways to deal with your pre-program jitters, or other sources of stress? How do you interact with the people who buy your coaching services on behalf of an organization? Be honest, do you recognize any of Marco's traits in yourself?

# 25

# THE SUPERVISED COACH: DEALING WITH FEEDBACK

## MURRAY PALEVSKY

*Case summary*

The first part of this case deals with Murray Palevsky's challenge over an element of group-coaching protocol, the follow-up conference call, and the decision of one group member not to participate. The second part describes the coach's feelings and attitude toward the coachee and the feedback the coach received while participating in the 1st ESMT Coaching Colloquium in December 2009. The coach shares the feedback from this conference and reflects on how his coaching style was improved by the process. The case highlights what was initially "tricky coaching" and what was tricky in terms of gaining insight into one's performance.

### BACKGROUND

The case I am about to describe involved a group-coaching exercise that was part of an executive program (AMP) for senior leaders, at a top business school. The coaching element of the AMP is well known: It normally comprises five participants, plus the coach, and takes place over a day and a half. The first day is spent in group coaching and the following half-day consists of one-on-one sessions.

After the completion of the AMP, there are three follow-up conference calls, the first of which is facilitated by the coach. Subsequent calls may or may not involve the coach, depending on the wishes of the participants. The coaching activity itself begins with each participant drawing and presenting a self-portrait. This is followed by analysis provided by the application of the GELI 360-degree feedback process (see Note 1, Chapter 5), supported by reference to personal feedback information, plus biographical data supplied via the participant's original program application.

As usual, I started this particular session by asking my group to prepare their self-portraits. This literally involves drawing a sketch or diagram rather than words—it forces the participant to be imaginative, using sketches to illustrate a number of abstract and specific factors—"head," "heart," "future," "work," "leisure," and so on. It has proven to be an effective way of setting the stage for subsequent activities and I was pleased to see that the group seemed to grasp the idea with a good deal of enthusiasm.

Each participant then took it in turns to present their portrait to the group, inviting discussion and sharing insights together. The first presentation provoked a good response from the group—the day was getting off to a good start. The second presentation was even better. It is always interesting to see how different people respond to being asked to draw their portrait: Some are a bit sheepish, others are extremely proud of their work, and some are ambivalent about it. Nevertheless, in my experience it rarely fails to create a strong bond of group cohesion.

## A NON-COMPLIANT PARTICIPANT

It was only when the third person began to talk about his self-portrait that I started to feel I might have a problem. There was no sense of tension in the presentation; the comments were bland and uninteresting. We weren't getting anywhere. I looked at the self-portrait and noticed that, despite the explicit instruction not to write anything but use drawings and sketches only, this portrait was covered in text. My instructions had been quite clear, so was this man being willfully uncooperative? Or was he just really uncomfortable about drawing?

I decided not to say anything at this stage but to wait and see how things developed. As I watched him explaining his portrait, I began to notice that he behaved very differently compared to his colleagues. Unlike the others, who were clearly enjoying the session, this participant seemed very uncomfortable when asked to talk about himself, his work, and his home life. Although he was following the basic format, he wasn't giving anything away. He spoke in very general terms, avoiding specifics, and offering very little in the way of opinion about anything.

The only insight (if it can be called that) was that he described himself as "quiet" and "private." He was certainly both of those: In the supporting biographical feedback information, his direct reports described him as "remote" and his wife said he was "uncommunicative." His entire demeanor bore this out: He was erecting a barrier between us. As his coach I wanted to challenge him and make him disclose more about himself, but how could I do that without making him retreat even further from the group?

As I listened to his presentation, I really began to wonder about this guy. What was he about? Why was he talking so much about the big picture and avoiding anything specific about himself? All references to himself seemed highly edited and over-simplified—at times it sounded as if he were quoting passages from the autobiography of an elder statesman. This was supposed to be a coaching session, not a salon conversation.

I found this a very difficult situation to understand; I sensed both resistance and compliance at the same time and became convinced that this person was just playing along with me and, ultimately, just wasting our time.

## IDENTIFYING THE PROBLEM

Participant number three—let's call him Paul—was beginning to emerge as a very complex character. The feedback from his GELI analysis appeared to show dazzling scores in "visioning" and "designing and aligning" (which deal, respectively, with strategic leadership and goal-setting), while his scores in the "life balance" and "rewarding and feedback" dimensions were practically the lowest possible.

Reading through his answers to the individual questions in the GELI analysis unearthed some intriguing insights. Participants are asked to read a series of statements and then score the degree to which they believe these statements apply to them on a scale from 1 to 7. Paul scored below average in all questions relating to his ability to delegate tasks, interact with people at all levels, and provide support and feedback to those who reported to him.

In response to the statements: "I am physically active," "I engage in non-work related activities," and "I find ways to simplify complex situations for my employees," Paul scored the lowest overall within the group. He was also the only member of the group to score 1 for the statement: "I have at least one close friend with whom I can talk about very personal issues." This, I felt, was a crucial indication of Paul's underlying personality. Overall, the picture of Paul that emerged was one of an aloof workaholic who was extremely bright, worked more or less autonomously, and gave his direct reports very little responsibility.

Interestingly, the written comments from Paul's managers and senior colleagues didn't hint at any problem with personal interactions at all:

> Paul has a formidable intellect and exceptional work ethics. He is a man of real integrity!

> Paul has a positive influence wherever he goes. People love him. He will be the star of the AMP!

> Paul is extremely strategic in his outlook, he always looks at the bigger picture.

On the other hand, comments from those who worked under Paul showed a different character entirely:

> Paul needs to take life less seriously. He needs to laugh more. He needs to have more fun.

> He doesn't spend enough time at home with his wife. He needs to pay attention to his fitness level. He should learn to say "no" at times.

> Paul should learn to delegate with the requisite responsibility and accept that not all things need to be done his way. He should listen more and accept the opinions of others.

So Paul was highly respected by senior management both for his intelligence and his ethics but was seen as overbearing and uncommunicative by his direct reports. While I had no problem discussing all the positive feedback with Paul, and felt sure he would have no problem with that either, when it came to the issues that needed addressing I knew I would meet with resistance.

Paul sent out clear unspoken messages of what was on the table for discussion and what was not. He was diligent in focusing attention on a picture of himself as an ideas man and repeatedly harked back to his lifelong dedication to social activism and philosophy. It was all very positive. Only much later did I realize that all the while he was quietly rebelling against participation in the group. This was because Paul stayed focused and gave good feedback to the other group participants. Looking back it was almost as if he decided there was one set of rules for him and different rules for the other group members. For him, it was a one-way street and his personal life was not up for discussion.

## THE CHALLENGE

When the subject of work–life balance came up, Paul gave the strong impression that this was not something he needed to strive for. In fact, his silence on the topic told me that he was completely aware of his lack of work–life balance but that it did not bother him. It may well have bothered others—most notably his wife—but that seemed a secondary consideration for Paul. He did not try to argue his position in response to feedback from the group; he simply resisted discussing it or agreeing to do anything about it.

I now had a clear mental picture of Paul: He was hugely appreciated by his superiors for his productivity and tireless dedication to his job but was an isolated peripatetic manager who didn't listen to his direct reports or interact with his co-workers. He had practically no personal life and had difficulty expressing personal feelings, while his complete lack of engagement in any physical activity gave the impression of someone almost disconnected from his body.

But although I could see *how* Paul operated, I still had no idea *why* he behaved in this way. I couldn't see behind the barrier he had erected between us, and the absence of any playfulness or imagination in his self-portrait (demonstrated by his use of words instead of images), coupled with his doggedly logical mode of thinking, left me at an impasse. Why was he keeping me, and the other members of his group, at a distance?

## DEALING WITH THE CHALLENGE

Of course, I didn't have to address Paul's underlying personality issues; I could continue the coaching session without confronting him and maintain a harmonious rapport with the group. But I wanted to challenge him. And I decided to do so the following day, during the one-on-one coaching session when I could draw on some of the material from his personal feedback pages.

One of the first items I raised with Paul were the responses of his wife on the feedback questionnaire, in which she described him coming home from the office very late at night and rarely engaging her in conversation. What was Paul's take on this? He replied simply that by the time he got home from the office he was so tired that he didn't have any energy left for talking. With as much delicacy as I could muster, I enquired if it was true that he didn't actually speak much with his wife at all. Paul nodded agreement. So, I continued, did he want to discuss this in more detail? Unsurprisingly, he preferred not to.

Obviously, this was a delicate and very personal matter. But Paul did not appear to take offence at my asking the question. He replied with total honesty and in a matter-of-fact way but at the same time would not engage in an emotional discussion. He didn't refute or deny anything—the facts were all correct—but there was a complete lack of desire to engage in any attempt to unravel any of the issues I raised or even to view them from his standpoint as a problem. Paul wasn't interested in trying to change his behavior.

Despite Paul's refusal to delve into his communication problem, I felt it was nonetheless my job to highlight this and draw it to his attention and to the attention of the whole group. Perhaps they could then embark on further discussion about this on their own.

Because of Paul's unwillingness to talk about his communication problems with me in private I decided not to pursue this line of questioning. Instead we spent most of our time in the one-on-one session talking aimlessly about his career advancement plans (with occasional attempts by me to suggest ways in which he might create more of a team atmosphere and listen more to the people who worked for him). Frustrating though this was, I ended on a positive note by giving Paul assurances that, given the respect he commanded from his superiors, he was certain of a bright future.

After one-and-a-half days of coaching, the group left to enjoy their summer vacation. We convened again at the beginning of September, when I gave them some guidance for the follow-up conference call later that month. The idea was to hear how they were getting on with the personal action plans they had drawn up during the AMP sessions, and to encourage them to follow-up as a group.

The follow-up takes the form of a two-hour conference call a couple of months after the end of the program. I noticed that all the participants except for Paul confirmed their participation and when I emailed him to find out if he would join I received a message back from his assistant saying he was out of town and that she could not reach him to inquire about an alternative date and time. Hence I was not surprised when Paul failed to join in the follow-up conference call. He made no attempt to get in touch or participate in the subsequent follow-up calls and I heard no more from him.

## THE FOLLOW-UP CALL

Given that the follow-up call is an important tool in assuring the success of the group coaching and the interplay between personal reflection and the group interaction, you have to think about how you will ensure that it will happen. This is a real challenge when you're dealing with disengaged, ambivalent, or even hostile participants.

In this case I had made every effort to keep in contact with the participants between the end of the program and the follow-up call. Despite this, Paul ducked out. The remaining participants all joined in the conference call and found it very helpful but I still felt very disappointed by what I felt was my failure to keep Paul engaged. Rightly or wrongly, I felt that I had not pushed hard enough and that I had let him manipulate me. Maybe, had I been more assertive and challenged him more directly, Paul would have seen the coaching process through to its conclusion.

On the face of it, this is where the story ends. Most of the participants felt they had gained something from the coaching exercise. But for me it didn't really end there because I felt so frustrated by my failure to keep Paul on side and help him address his communication issues. The experience had raised so many questions; some were specific to this case (for example, why had Paul opted out of the phone call? If he couldn't make it, why did he not call and ask to reschedule the conference call? And why did he not communicate with anyone else in his group?) and some more wide-ranging. For example, what did this say about group coaching follow-up calls? What are the conditions required to have real group cohesion? Why was I upset by Paul's behavior, and what does that say about me as a coach?

## LESSONS LEARNED

I had a chance to answer these and other questions at the ESMT conference in Berlin in December 2009. The highlight of the conference for me was the break-out session in which we discussed each other's tricky cases. While it would not be entirely honest of me to say that I felt comfortable being examined by my peers, the intelligent observations they made were invaluable in helping me get to the bottom of my concerns and answer some of the questions that still lingered.

When I first tried to analyze Paul's case, my thoughts were focused on the issue of compliance and non-compliance—and certainly there is a strong element of that in the story. What were my counter-transference reactions? However, the observations of other coaches brought out something else that I had not noticed hitherto: I was taking this compliance issue far too personally. Of the six questions I wanted to discuss at the conference, only the last one dealt with *how I felt* about Paul.

I felt Paul wasn't allowing me to help him and that he was blocking the way toward my more complete success. I was angry with him for my own selfish reasons, the principal one being that he made me feel ineffectual. I was looking at this from the standpoint of someone who believed he had "the answers" but was not being allowed to get close enough to provide them.

In other words, what was bothering me was not that Paul was getting nothing from the coaching process but that I was being prevented from being effective. I was focusing on myself, not Paul. I felt that helping only part of the group was not enough; I needed to help everyone and Paul was preventing me from achieving this. What I had failed to appreciate was that Paul *didn't want to be helped*, at least not in the same way as the other participants. My mistake was not in failing to reach out to Paul, but of not giving him the space to consider his behavior without feeling that he needed to be helped.

The feedback I received from the other coaches at the conference helped me see that sometimes you have to let go and actually welcome the resistance of someone you're coaching. This was a valuable lesson not so much in coaching technique but in self-awareness. The coach should never let himself get between his clients and their goal. For both parties—coach and client alike—the process is about becoming aware of their own capabilities and what is appropriate or inappropriate behavior. To really learn about others, you first have to know yourself.

# CONCLUSION: IN PRAISE OF TRICKINESS

Many fairy tales and tribal stories highlight a mischievous character who, armed only with his native intelligence, is able to befuddle the wise, impoverish the wealthy, dethrone kings, and reward the poor and worthy. Sometimes, this trickster makes trouble for one and all, except those who realize that underlying all his tricks is a lesson to be learned. If you fool me once, shame on you. If you fool me twice, shame on me. The real winners in the tales are those who can make the elves, the magpies, the monkeys, or the djinns work for them.

The key message of this book is to show that there is no shame in finding oneself in a tricky coaching situation—all of us, even those who have been coaches for decades, have been there. The generous, open responses of the coaches in this book to our call to share their stories has proved yet again that the best way to avoid trickiness is to understand where it comes from. Fortunately, this is not such a complicated task. We have illustrated that the themes evoked when coaches talk about difficult situations are fairly common and widely shared. And in putting together this book, we reconfirmed our belief that a tricky coaching impasse can become an invaluable learning experience—even more so when shared with others.

We have let the voices of the coaches themselves reinforce in this book the value of writing case notes and meeting with colleagues to discuss tricky situations. The ESMT Tricky Coaching Colloquium has become an annual event, and we encourage readers to create similar contexts for confidential, collegial sharing and debriefing. We hear coaches saying that one of the disadvantages of the profession is that they are often rather isolated—as "internal-externals" working in organizations, or short-term partners for a series of executives—and we all find the opportunity to work as a community during the colloquia very enriching. Our experience is that we all benefit from coming together as a group of like-minded professionals, and pooling our understanding of trickiness—and the trust and openness that this kind of event creates will go a long way toward supporting the continuing development of coaching as a rigorous professional approach to executive and leadership development.

## TAMING THE TRICKSTER: A FEW LESSONS LEARNED

### Share the stories

The idea behind getting coaches to come together and explore tricky cases in leadership coaching came to us after reading dozens of books on coaching and noting their upbeat tone about the effectiveness of the coaching interventions.

We encountered reports from coaching organizations describing high returns on investment and slick accounts of coaching engagements that resulted in lasting success for all concerned. We also noticed a significant emphasis on techniques, tools, methods, systems—many of them proprietary or copyrighted—which seemed to promise that coaching is simply a matter of working through a guidebook or a checklist. To be fair, in a context in which a coach's livelihood is often dependent on obtaining the next contract, a certain amount of marketing of the coach and the profession is completely reasonable. Yet among the self-congratulatory reports, accounts of coaching interventions that were less than stellar, let alone tricky, were rare. This lack of cautionary tales not only hampers learning, but also creates the impression that all the "other" coaches out there are extremely successful. The truth is we are all facing the same "tricksters."

Another thing that caught our attention in the plethora of publications about coaching, as well as presentations at various coaching conferences, was the obscurity around what is really going on inside the coaching engagement. Granted, the discussions between coach and coachee remain confidential. However, without vicarious experiences of what is happening inside the coaching space created by others, it will be difficult to frame coaching as an activity that is on a par with established professional fields, such as counseling or therapy. The lack of published cases that coaches or would-be coaches can use to explore their own response to challenges and opportunities makes it difficult to create really meaningful learning experiences in coaching education and training. Human resources and learning and development professionals who hire coaches, but do not have coaching training themselves, may be in the dark when it comes to understanding the benefits and limitations of coaching as a leadership development intervention. Moreover, they may remain unaware of the various ways in which relationships between coach and coachee can develop, and so may be unprepared to be a supportive partner for both coach and coachee when their help or intervention is needed. The cases presented in this book offer the reader an opportunity to open the black box of leadership coaching and have a look at a process that is rarely unveiled. It offers descriptions of a variety of coaching situations, a mélange of issues that are important to coachees, and an assortment of approaches taken by the coach. We deliberately refrain from evaluating the sessions described in the book, because we believe that there are many possible solutions and alternatives.

## TOOLS: TO USE OR NOT TO USE?

The experience of going through the cases may leave the reader surprised at the vast variety of tools, techniques, methods, models, and instruments that coaches use in their work. From time to time the case authors and commentators refer to models and instruments that they have developed or adopted and use widely in their own practice. We think that this variety and, at times, competition between various coaching models, including those mentioned in the cases and commentaries in this volume, reflect the reality of the current state of the field of executive coaching. With an abundance of literature on various tools (including some of our own publications) already available, we chose not to address the applicability of specific tools to various coaching situations in this book.

We do want to point out that at times a coach may find that a particular tool he or she is comfortable with is not working. Rather than questioning what is going on, the coach starts looking for a different tool. In fact, the problem is still seen as a nail, but the hammer at hand is not effective. The coach, however, keeps experimenting with various types of hammers. Dependence on tools, albeit handled skillfully by the coach and expected by the client or organization, can play a trick on the coaching dynamics. If a coach relies too heavily on one approach, he or she may miss what is really going on in the professional or personal life of the coachee and relationships inside the coaching engagement. We are advocates of a non-dogmatic approach, and firm supporters of "whatever works," so long as coaches evaluate, reflect, and debrief the effectiveness of each method, and their own capacity to occasionally let go of the tried-and-true, and experiment with ambiguity, silence, and unstructured exploration.

## KNOW YOUR CLIENT, KNOW YOUR CLIENT'S BUSINESS, AND KNOW YOURSELF

The systemic, psychodynamic approach (described in the introduction to Part II) provides the coach with the broadest source of information and largest terrain for action. The brief received by the coach prior to the assignment may need to be reconsidered or renegotiated as the situation in which the coachee is embedded evolves or changes. Ignoring what is occupying the minds and hearts of the coachees, for example, as their organizations go through restructuring or as their families experience turmoil, is a mistake on the part of the coach.

Ironically, although we do advocate maximum clarity in the contract between coach and coachee (as well as other parties involved, such as the coachee's organization), we insist on the need to reevaluate the assumptions on which the contract is built multiple times throughout the coaching relationship. As the coachee and coach develop trust through their mutual engagement, the depth of the issue may increase, and the needs of the coachee may change or evolve from, for example, a superficial discussion on how to be more effective in conducting difficult conversations with subordinates to a much deeper one of what it means for a person to be a leader.

At times such developments lead to productive work on important and challenging issues. At other times, they can bring the relationship to the point where the coach can no longer be in a position to support the coachee in his or her growth and development. This may be the moment to end the relationship in a constructive manner and, for example, refer the coachee to another helping professional. The coach, however, may be reluctant to do so due to a variety of reasons: Rescuer syndrome, emotional entanglement, finances, concerns about professional reputation, or individual narcissism, to name a few. The trickiness of a coaching engagement may emerge due to the coach's inability to recognize his or her own limitations.

## TABOOS

You might have been surprised to see that a number of cases presented here involved a vivid sexual component that affected the work and life of the coachee, and had an influence on the process of coaching. Although no coach in this book was working on sexuality or related issues as a part of the initial coaching contract, some were confronted with having to deal with this complex, but unarguably important, phenomenon of human life and relationships. Moreover, some readers may be very attuned to the possible impact of erotic transference in the relationships between coachee and coach.

Dealing with the complexity of sexualization of organizational life, or other taboos such as death, substance abuse, or dysfunctional family relationships that might come up in a coaching intervention, is not for the faint of heart. Many studies are published on this topic in the field of psychotherapy, but the coaching profession is still in the very early stages of addressing taboos in coaching, and we know very little about how coaches handle ambiguous situations that, among other things, may evoke strong personal reactions. Personal feelings, values, and expectations about what is right in the organizational domain, tact, anxiety, and inquisitiveness may all get mixed in this situation. Issues of managing boundaries and, when necessary, disengagement become particularly acute, and the coach's own relationship with his or her sexuality may come to the fore in reflection or supervisory sessions.

## THE IMPORTANCE OF ROLE BOUNDARIES

The question of boundaries between coaching, consulting, and therapy is still open, and we encourage further discussion along these lines. The variety of prior paths and experiences that lead to coaching as a professional activity, at least at this relatively early stage of the development of the profession, complicate any attempts to set firm boundaries. We would add that permeability of boundaries, well-managed, can be a good thing. As the reader may have noticed from the cases presented here, coaches may come from consulting, management, or therapy. At times, a consulting engagement may be more effective with the use of coaching approaches. In other situations, what may begin as a therapeutic process may prove to be linked to the business decisions a coachee faces. In either of these cases, coaches may find their approach either restricted or enriched by their previous professional identity. They will undoubtedly benefit from their previous experiences; however, they may also need to give up part of their former identity and habits, when they start calling themselves a coach. This is not always easy. As we mentioned earlier, we are not purists when it comes to what is right or wrong in coaching; but we note that coaching often turns out to be just a trendy way of rebranding a consulting process, or an acceptable euphemism for a therapeutic intervention. At times we wonder if the coach is aware of the permeability of professional boundaries, and whether he or she reflects on the advantages and limitations inherent in such situations.

## HIRING COACHES: THE TRICKY QUESTIONS

Because we have now been studying coaching for years, we frequently receive requests from executives to help them set up a coaching program within their organization, incorporate coaching into a leadership development program, or establish criteria for their selection of coaches. It is not uncommon for participants in executive education programs in which they experience coaching modules to decide to continue with coaching, after having experimented with this method in a business-school setting, and to ask us for help in determining whether a particular coach is going to be right for them. We also have to decide which coaches to invite to join teams that work in the executive programs we direct. In all these situations, we have found it very helpful to ask candidate coaches a couple of questions about their tricky coaching experiences.

Their answers allow us to see the way that coaches treat difficult situations, how they deal with boundaries and limits, and how they work on protecting the interests of coachees. We find it helpful to ask coaches about learning points based on their tricky coaching experiences, as well as about advice they would give to someone else in a similar situation. We also discuss how the coaches look after themselves, including their professional growth and development: We talk about formal or informal supervision as part of maintaining their professionalism and mental health. Altogether, our experience of working with coaches suggests that we could find a way to provide learning opportunities for coaches and ourselves in a more structured, generalized manner.

Here we would like to add a plea for more flexible assessment methods for coaches and coaching interventions. In many executive programs, coaches are evaluated at the end of the day by coachees, often using a numerical scale. This system provides feedback to coaches and program directors, but we argue that it can do more harm than good. Calculating a score in this way can have an effect on the way some coaches work, making them feel under pressure to provide answers or force the coachee to make quick cosmetic changes, rather than dealing with the real issues at hand, which may open a can of worms that influences the rating. In our experience, it is very common for a coachee to leave a coaching session unsettled and discouraged—but more often than not, after reflection and experimentation, the coachee returns to say that the coaching turned out to be a very valuable experience. We would go so far as to say that some of the best coaches will, at times, have the worst ratings.

So how should coaching interventions be evaluated? First of all, the person or company hiring a coach or designing a program with coaching modules should ensure that the coach has reputable credentials and relevant experience. The intake interview should include questions about tricky situations the coach has experienced. The coach should be hired on a regular or long-term basis, so that he or she can learn, be observed, and possibly even benefit from seminars or other professional development opportunities provided by the school or business organization. Coaches, and program directors, should shadow one another and provide feedback. Coachees or participants could be interviewed at the end of a program to give their overall impression of the coaching experience. We believe that a longer-term, more developmental, view of coaches would reduce pressure on coaches to get top scores and allow for the more subtle, developmental approaches to coaching to flourish.

## CREATING A COMMUNITY

Many coaches still work without supervision, and many encounter similar coaching challenges; very often the coach inadvertently contributes to the trickiness of the coaching engagement. Learning to deal with a tricky coaching situation and with one's own role in its trickiness is an important step in a coach's growth and development as a professional.

This book is the result of our decision to approach the coaching community and invite coaches to share their tricky coaching experiences with others, commenting on each other's cases, and then engaging face-to-face in small, peer-group supervisions and consultations at the 1st ESMT Coaching Colloquium in Berlin in December 2009. The enthusiastic response we received from coaches signaled to us that the professional coaching community, particularly that part of it concerned with advancing the field, does indeed respond to this type of invitation to take time out and reflect.

We were particularly impressed when coaches spoke during their Colloquium presentations and in their contributions to this book about what the assignment and associated challenges meant for them, how they were personally affected by what was going on between them and their coachees, and how the situation challenged their view of themselves, their values, and feelings. For a reader familiar with the psychotherapeutic literature this shouldn't be surprising, as exploration of transference and counter-transference, for instance, in a therapy relationship is a given of supervision and case work. For someone who is more familiar with "airport" style coaching books, this may be a surprising revelation: The coach is a human being and may, just like coachees, also be subject to the influence of various rational and irrational forces; all the more reason to come together and test reality with trusted colleagues.

## REFLECTION IS PART OF THE JOB, NOT A VACATION

Quite a few coaches whom we invited to take part in the adventure of creating this book shied away from the opportunity. Some of them rationalized their decision by referring to lack of time due to an extremely busy schedule of coaching assignments in various parts of the world. Finding several days (or several hours a day for many days) to write up a case sounded like a difficult proposition. We were intrigued by the fact that people who preach the need for reflection when working with executives don't have the time (or courage) to follow their own recommendations. Others referred to the uniqueness of their coaching challenge and implied the risk of inadvertently hurting the client by revealing something about their tricky coaching situation that could be immediately recognized or that could point to a specific coachee. However, when working with the cases presented during the Coaching Colloquium, they often realized that their situation was not at all unique, and that other coaches and clients had dealt with something similar. Still other coaches told us that they were afraid that indicating challenges in their coaching work could potentially damage the image they were trying to project of a "Yes, I can!" coach who can handle any difficult situation with ease and success.

Respecting the decisions made by these coaches not to share their experiences with the wider coaching, HR, and executive community, we still found ourselves thinking about the signals those decisions give about the state of the coaching profession. Could it be that some coaches fall prey to the same pressures and rational and not-so-rational beliefs that make the modern executive coachee start running without taking time to reflect? Could it be that some coaches, like some coachees, perceive their issues and challenges to be idiosyncratic, not faced by anyone else, and, consequently, they shy away from learning from others and contributing to the learning of others? Could it be that some coaches, like many modern organizational high-flyers, expect to be invulnerable, constantly upbeat, and bulletproof in terms of success? If we accept that coaches are human, we can't deny these issues. As a result, the dynamics of the situation of the coachee may easily become intertwined with the dynamics of the coach's own needs, aspirations, fears, hopes, anxieties, personal histories, and other elements of the inner theater. The psychodynamic approach to coaching would argue that this is very likely to happen, and that both the coach and the coachee would be better off if they are aware of such a dynamic, and can address it during the coaching engagement.

## FOR ALL THE RIGHT REASONS

It is not for nothing that in the first part of this book we offer a checklist that can be worked through when entering a coaching relationship. Sometimes coaches don't think twice about accepting an assignment, and their reasons for doing so vary. At times it is the monetary side—what they will be paid. At other times, it is awe—the opportunity to work with an exciting organization or a person. The coach may get a kick from basking in the reflected glory[1] of engaging in a coaching relationship with a powerful organization or high-level executive. The arousal associated with the task may be so high, that the coach may fail to take the necessary due diligence in approaching the assignment. Whether it is the "greed factor" or the "awe factor" that prevails, the dangers of taking a wrong assignment are similar. In hindsight (or with sufficient distance—for example, by reading this book) one might at times wonder why the coach failed to do something that is obvious to an outside observer. The obviousness, however, can't be taken for granted when a person is under the influence of the excitement and attraction related to the coaching adventure that lies ahead.

## FAILURE IS RELATIVE

Coaches are often engaged in helping people who really do need help, and who struggle to change themselves or a situation. However, it can happen that despite all the hard work, there is no change in the perception of the executive by others in the organization. The leadership persona associated with a particular individual is co-created, composed not only of the behaviors and attitudes of the executive, but also of the image others have of him or her. At times, coaching efforts may be impressive and real changes made, but the organization still fails to see them. The image that the person has developed within an organization takes longer to change than the actual behavior of the individual concerned. It could be that the individual has lost credit in the organization, and may be better off somewhere else. In this case, the objective of the coaching may officially be perceived as unachieved. On the other hand, the coachee may go on to a successful start somewhere else. Likewise, an individual may be able to secure a promotion or a different image, but eventually be unhappy. If the coach helps the coachee succeed in the organizational rat race by supporting him or her in developing the "right" career behaviors, without taking into account the whole person, we may see an objectively successful coaching outcome with a not-so-successful person behind it.

## WELCOMING THE TRICKINESS

If after reading this book you decide to make a small experiment (as a coach, as an HR and learning and development professional, as an academic studying or teaching coaching, or as an executive who uses coaching or who explores how coaching could be helpful to the organization) to focus on trickiness as an opportunity for learning, we would consider our mission at least partially accomplished. If after reading this book someone decides that, although coaching might have seemed an attractive career option, he or she is not yet ready to deal with all the trickiness of it, we may have helped somebody avoid unnecessary challenges. If an HR professional now feels better equipped to talk about coaching with coaches and coachees, including situations where things don't go as expected, we have supported the productive use of coaching in organizations. However, if these or any other positive developments take place, as the contributors to and editors of this volume, we will not feel we can take the credit for ourselves. To paraphrase a well-known saying, we can only open the door; each person makes the choice whether to walk through it. If there is a positive outcome, all the work will have been done by the coaches—we will simply have created the conditions to make it possible.

## NOTE

1. R. B. Cialdini, R. J. Borden, A. Thorne, M. R. Walker, S. Freeman, and L. R. Sloan (1976). "Basking in Reflected Glory: Three (Football) Field Studies." *Journal of Personality and Social Psychology*, 34: 366–75.

# INDEX

Milton Keynes UK
Ingram Content Group UK Ltd.
UKHW020040251023
431267UK00004B/30